JOHN CLARE:
HIS LIFE AND POETRY

JOHN CLARE IN 1828

Bronze Bust by Henry Behnes Burlowe

JOHN CLARE:
HIS LIFE AND POETRY

by

JOHN and ANNE TIBBLE

WILLIAM HEINEMANN LTD
MELBOURNE LONDON TORONTO

FIRST PUBLISHED 1956

PUBLISHED BY
WILLIAM HEINEMANN LTD
99 GREAT RUSSELL STREET, LONDON, W.C.I
PRINTED IN GREAT BRITAIN BY THE PUBLISHERS AT
THE WINDMILL PRESS, KINGSWOOD, SURREY

To

THE LIVING POETS OF ENGLAND

IN spite of difference of soil and climate, of language and manners, of laws and customs; in spite of things silently gone out of mind, and things violently destroyed; the Poet binds together by passion and knowledge the vast empire of human society, as it is spread over the whole earth, and over all time.

WORDSWORTH.

CONTENTS

ILLUSTRATIONS

FOREWORD

OUR aim has been three-fold: first to put before the steadily growing numbers of Clare's readers his *Life* again, in the light of fresh knowledge, and here and there, we hope, maturer insight. Secondly, our aim has been to attempt to trace the development of Clare's poetry, in form and content. Since poets themselves are most often among their own most proper critics, Clare's aims, both when they were expressed and clear as daylight, and when they were struggling into consciousness, have been brought forward wherever possible. The third part of our aim may thus not be thought monstrous for mere prose persons: it has been no more than to endeavour to start what in Clare's case has been so long delayed, the fullest exploration of his poetry and his place among poets.

In spite of the appreciation of many outstanding present-day poets and critics, Clare is still much, and contradictorily, *sub-judice*. More than that, the best of his poetry is still not sufficiently known. Arthur Symons, in 1908, was the first to value him for the right things. Yet reviews of his poetry can still take astonishingly opposite standpoints since the pioneering of Edmund Blunden and Alan Porter in 1920: Clare is 'without deep emotion'. He is 'one of the most vibrantly strong' of poets. He has 'no form'. He has 'a most profound sense of form'. The time has come for an attempt to clear away at least some of the brushwood.

The indispensable *Poems Chiefly from Manuscript* of 1920 contains Mr. Blunden's sensitive and beautiful introduction. *Sketches in the Life of John Clare by Himself* was edited by Mr. Blunden, too, in 1931. Mr. Geoffrey Grigson's *Poems of John Clare's Madness* was published in 1948, and his Selection in 1950. Mr. James Reeves's Selection, with its poet's foreword, was offered in 1954. And Clare's *Letters* and his *Prose* both appeared in 1950. All that is essential for a considered estimate is at long last before Clare's public.

The text of his lyrics of the St. Andrew's Asylum period needs comment. There are three transcripts of these: the first and most important is that made by the house steward, W. F. Knight, before he left the asylum in 1850. The two volumes are in the Northampton Public Library. There is a second copy which differs in many details from Knight. This, too, is at Northampton. A third transcript, in part by the same hand as the second, is with the Clare manuscripts at Peterborough in the Museum. The variations in these sets of transcripts, often confusedly debatable as to authenticity, are not sufficient vitally to affect the judgment of Clare's poetry as a whole. Yet it would be good to have a decisive text of the prison poems, when the manuscripts come to light.

A few poems of the 1841 to 1850 period, printed here for the first time, are indicated in the text or in notes. Two or three minor corrections of our 1932 text have been made. These, in the places necessary, have been recorded. Nor have we found ourselves able to tell both the earlier and later parts of Clare's story without resort to his own vivid words as often as possible. The original of extracts from *Sketches in the Life of John Clare by Himself* will be found among the Northampton Mss., and those from the *Prose* and the *Life* (1932), unless otherwise stated in the footnotes, are among the Peterborough Papers. Poem sources are the Peterborough and Northampton documents, unless differently noted. And with new quotations we again 'take liberty' to present Clare as he almost always refreshingly is.

A word about new material: since the writing of the 1932 *Life* our information has grown steadily. There are still gaps, as well as still-untraced papers such as the Emmerson letters, the Elizabeth Kent letters, and the Inskip letters. But responsibility for the book's inadequacies and imperceptions, however sad or shocking, must be our own.

We could not fail to express our deep gratitude to all those writers, whose books we have read, without whom this one could not have been so much as attempted. We have tried wherever necessary to make clear our debts, without, we hope, alienating student and general reader from Clare's enlivening story by too cumbersome notes.

Our acknowledgments and continued thanks are due to the Curator and Committee of the Peterborough Museum, for unfailing kindness and help, and for permission to publish facsimiles of manuscripts; to the Chief and Staff of the Northampton Public Library for equally unfailing kindness, and leave to reproduce the Behnes bust. We thank the Physician-Superintendent of St. Andrew's Hospital for his pamphlet of 1953, and Leicester Reference and Lending Libraries. We are particularly grateful to Mr. Andrew Kean, of the Institute of Education, Leicester University College, for his reading of this book in type and for many useful suggestions. To the *Peterborough Citizen and Advertiser* we owe thanks for the reproduction of Clare's last manuscript, and to the National Portrait Gallery and Sir Leonard Woolley for the new portrait of Clare by William Henry Hunt. The Superintendent and Staff of the Reading Room at the British Museum have been unfailingly diligent and helpful on our behalf and we record our gratitude. We take this opportunity of thanking, too, all those who have been patient over our often pertinacious queries. And we are indebted to our son, R. N. Tibble, for the rest of the photographs.

University College of Leicester, 1954.

CHILDHOOD IN A PRE-ENCLOSURE
VILLAGE 1793-1809

I

BETWEEN winding Welland and Clare's 'willow banks of Nen', in the north-east corner of Northamptonshire, travellers today in the Flying Scotsman can observe for themselves two vividly different types of scenery. The two actually meet at the village of Helpston. Neither is spectacular. Each is essentially English. The originally treeless fen, now intensively farmed, has wind-breaks of Lombard poplar, conical gold corn-stacks, and far-seen lingering sunsets; a few of its once characteristic white plough horses may still be seen. In Camden's day it was 'overspread with water' for much of the year. It still retains a faint air of amphibiousness. After successive drainings since Roman times, farmers can still bring more wheat out of it, acre by acre, than cultivators of any other wheatland in the world. Peat-black earth is intersected by ruler-straight roads that meet each other at right angles. Along dykes as straight, threateningly higher than surrounding homesteads, swans and wild geese fly with their strange wing-music, to nest on reedy platforms by blue-grey water-shallows. Over all, sky and far horizon spread that 'faint shadow of immensity'. Sense of loneliness can be as profound as on an illimitable expanse of ocean or a mountain-top. For Clare the fen was quite often simply 'a paradise of earth's delight'.

But it was the other type of country which he often said 'made up' his 'being'. To the south and west of Helpston the oolitic limestone of the county is at its best. Undulating midland pasture is flanked by that hanging line, just beyond the bounds of what was once Rockingham Great Forest—Royce's[1] Wood, Hillywood, Simon's, Oxey's 'hazel bowers', Open Copy, and Castor Hanglands. These are still, as in his day, green-

---

[1] 'Rice' on Ordnance Survey. Clare spelt it as it still locally is pronounced.

verged for gipsy or picnic. But their trees are mostly scrubby striplings. He tells how, in his part of England, the land was peeled of the great oaks and elms that had stood till the end of the eighteenth century.

Both fen and rolling 'woods and vales' are dotted with church spires of Ketton stone or Barnack rag. These can be seen for miles soaring into the sky. Villages in this Northamptonshire limestone belt are not much less comely than are Cotswold villages: here are Kingsley's Barnack with octagonal spire, West Deeping's crocketed pinnacle, Maxey tower set to catch the sun, Uffington's shapely outline, Glinton's tallest and most slender flèche-silhouette against the sky; and on that march we have described—Helpston, or as it was in the late eighteenth century, Helpstone. Here, on the 13th of July, 1793, John Clare was born.

The times were as profoundly disordered as times now are said to be. The promise of 1789 across the Channel had produced disillusion by 1793, horror and fear enough for the suspension of habeas corpus the next year, and prosecution of anyone who dared express sympathy with the French rebels soon after. Fresh campaigns were being thought of. Armies were soon to begin marching and counter-marching once more. From one angle events were stirring, glorious. From another, impenetrable fate and fury hung over Europe. And concurrently, over England, the Industrial Revolution was gathering impetus.

Nineteenth-century philanthropic zeal saw Clare's 'home of homes' as a 'narrow wretched hut, low and dark, more like a prison than a human dwelling'; it saw the fenny side of Helpston's 'mud hovels' as a 'dark gloomy plain . . . overhung with mists during the greater part of the year'.[1] Dr. Bowles had written almost two centuries before that, that North Northamptonshire was 'as fine a place for variety of wild plants as ever I beheld'.[2]

Mud hovels in Helpston at the end of the eighteenth century there undoubtedly were. Cobbett's eagle eye, during his Tours, as late as 1830, searched out labourers' dwellings in the Midlands, of mud and straw, with floors of broken brick or bare

---

[1] Frederick Martin: *The Life of John Clare*, 1865, p. 5.
[2] Quoted from J. E. Lousley: *Wild Flowers of Chalk and Limestone*, p. 133.

ground. But the cottage in which Clare was born, still standing at the Royce Wood end of the village, and in shape a little like the clay cottage in which Burns first saw light at Alloway thirty years before, is of the beautiful local stone. With its thatched and now whitewashed row, it went up for sale or demolition just before 1940. Tenacious local tradition preserves many hints of what it may have been like in Clare's day, but our nearest reconstruction of it, outside, is the frontispiece sketched by the Yorkshireman Cowen, for the re-issue of *The Village Minstrel* in 1823. Even this is misleading: the original cottage had been bought in 1778 by a retired yeoman, Edward Gee. When Parker and Ann Clare, Clare's parents, came as Gee's tenants, they had the whole house except for the one or two rooms lived in by the old Edward Gee, and Parker had the whole of the spacious garden at the back. It was

> large for a poor man & my father managed to dig it night & morning before the hours of labour & lost no time. He then did well.[1]

The cottage was apparently neat and trim, though later, we know, the sparrows built in the thatch. Other cottages and farms of the ancient village were already less well-kept. Bachelors' Hall, home of the Billings, was soon to become, under the last two bachelor brothers, a dilapidated old ruin. Most village houses were set in their own crofts or gardens. Next to the Clares' close was that of *The Blue Bell*. Parker Clare kept no pig, cow, goat, or fowls; he had no corn and bean patch at the bottom of his garden. The majority of villagers in easier and earlier days had usually had at least one of these. But the whole face of the land was altering as well as its character. Change, both before and after Clare's birth, followed rapidly on change. In 1792, the young farmer who bought the cottage on the death of the Clares' old landlord Gee, raised their rent, and the next year, adding to the building, made four 'tenements' of it

> leaving us a corner of one room on a floor for three guineas a year & a little slip of the garden which was divided into

<hr>

[1] *The Prose of John Clare*, 1951, p. 12.

four parts but as my father had been an old tenant he gave him the choice of his share & he retained our old apple tree. Tho the ground was good for nothing yet the tree still befriended us & made shift to make up the greater part of our rent.[1]

The apples were the excellent old English golden russets; but the room-partitioning and rent-raising the Clares endured in 1792, though widespread and in point of fact illegal, was but a little of the hardship in this period when costs of living advanced between 1750 and 1790 one-third, but wages of agricultural day-labourers only one-seventh.

The cottage, so comfortable according to Clare, and later so dear to him, had a red-tiled floor, and a ladder staircase to the bedroom above. The bedroom, even after being halved, was spacious enough to permit, later still, of its being curtained into three. The living-room contained a good grandfather-clock, and a well-made oak table, as well as Ann Clare's spinning-wheel. It cannot but remind us of the 'Peasant's Nest' which Cowper used to view so nostalgically for its peace and solitude, as he walked from Capability Brown's rich landscape garden at 'Weston Wilderness', back to smaller 'Orchard Side' at Olney. The Clares' water came from the street pump. Cowper would have found his 'Peasant's Nest' supremely uncomfortable, as well Cowper knew.

The family of Clare was a large one in the district round Helpston; the name, originally perhaps Clayer, and indicating an agricultural heritage, was common. John's father, Parker, born on the 14th of January, 1765, was 'one of fate's chancelings who drop into this world without the honour of matrimony'. Yet Parker's mother had been the daughter of 'John Clare-Clark', whose flowing signature in Helpston parish registers during the years of his clerkship, in days when not all England's yeomen could read or write, is all the trace of him we have found. Parker's name was in memory of his father, a Scots fiddler who came to the village and stayed a short time as schoolmaster.

John Donald Parker strolled away again for ever from Helpston at the inconvenient birth of his son. But Clare's grandmother's love, he tells us,

[1] *Prose*, p. 12.

was not that frenzy which shortens the days of the victim of seduction, for she liv'd to the age of 86, and left this world of troubles, Jan. 1, 1820.[1]

Those were coarser, more unself-consciously gay, certainly more hard-bitten days than ours. It is difficult to find a comprehensive picture of that teeming century, with its final sensational whip-up and overturning of previous order by three revolutions. Most difficult of all is it to catch a glimpse of the daily lives of that secret people, the fascinating, unglamorous poor, among whom one of our poets was to germinate his gift, and in the next century to bring it to flower.

Against the time's brutalities and complacencies had come the inevitable championships: *The Rights of Man*, *The Rights of Women*, and, a little later, the indefatigable, eccentric M.P. for Galway, 'Humanity Dick' Martin, was to wage his *Rights of Animals* campaign. Till then, pastimes like cock-fighting, dog-fighting, bear-baiting, badger-baiting, and bull-baiting, though dying since the prohibitions of 1647 and 1654, provided spectacles horrible enough for the Press to denounce. All classes shrieked their bets solemnly—(French travellers observed the English always to take their pleasures thus seriously) in a small amphitheatre. Such travellers, making the then-recognised cultural expedition to England, might, we are told 'have concluded the assembly to be all mad'. Bare-fist pugilism was about to see its heyday: James Figg, the friend of Hogarth, had helped to formulate its rules: 'Gentleman' John Jackson, champion from 1795 to 1800, was to make it fashionable. But even aristocratic patronage failed to make it legal. Fighting places were usually secret, the fights being of Homeric length in which contestants fought toe to toe for sixty or seventy rounds! It was not until about 1860 that gloved and legal fights began to capture popular as well as moneyed and commercial interest.

The rustic equivalent of this had for centuries been wrestling in hob-nailed boots. Country people, except for squires opulent enough to travel by coach or chariot to Westminster Pit, were entirely dependent for amusement on their own invention:

---

[1] *Sketches in the Life of John Clare by Himself.* Ed. Edmund Blunden, 1931, p. 46.

> . . . the noisy rout, their sports to crown,
> Form round the ring superior strength to show,
> Where wrestlers join to tug each other down,
> And thrust and kick with hard revengeful toe,
> Till through their worsted hose the blood does flow:
> For ploughmen would not wish for higher fame,
> Than be the champion all the rest to throw:
> And thus to add such honours to his name,
> He kicks, and tugs, and bleeds, to win the glorious game.[1]

The September Feast of Statute, of Nassaburgh Hundred, had been held at Helpston since the days of Edward the Third; Deeping had a Mayfair, and Stamford its more important rout. These revels, survivals of paganism, incorporated with the yearly re-hiring of labour, still helped to join country craftsmen with nature and their primitive past. At these hiring festivals, emblems of service were worn in hats, and young men in smocks, and young women in white cotton dresses, white stockings, and bright beribboned bonnets, on their annual day of freedom, offered themselves for re-hiring. The tradition was what has been called the essentially English one—really, an essentially agricultural one—of outdoor song and dance, ale-drinking, and good companionship.

Puritan legislation had marked the beginning of the end of these rustic revelries in England a century and a half before this. From Crabbe, in *The Village* and *The Borough*, we might form an austere impression that by about 1800 every man jack of the peasants had turned poacher, smuggler, drunkard, or pauper. Defoe had spoken, some seventy years before, of the roughness, especially of women, at market and fair, and the fears of the prudent were particularly directed on the troupes of ballad singers about this time, said 'to disseminate sentiments of dissipation' in minds which 'should have been bred to principles of industry and sobriety'.[2]

In his youth of great strength, Parker Clare, whose usual work was day-labouring at flail-threshing, was locally noted at Mayday, Statute, and Whitsun games. He was both one of these ballad singers and a rustic wrestler. Having 'a tolerable

---

[1] *The Village Minstrel*, 1821. Poems, 1935, p. 387.
[2] See W. Hasbach: *A History of the English Agricultural Labourer*, New Ed., p. 84.

good voice' he was 'often called upon to sing at those convivials of bacchanalian merry-makings'.[1] In later years he was proud to show his wrestling scars.

This 'chanceling' son of the daughter of the village clerk could read a little in the Bible. He was 'very fond of the superstitious tales hawked for a penny'. Desire to read was advancing among certain of the poor in this period at a heady, phenomenal rate; shoemaker James Lackington, later one of the first purveyors of cheap books, observes in his *Memoirs* of about 1791, that the sale of cheap books had increased by more than four times in the twenty years previous. Practical Divinity, all kinds of 'useful information', comprised two-thirds of available reading matter for the vulgar. Cheap quarto histories, smaller, badly-printed chap-books such as Pepys collected, cookery recipes, dream-interpretations, riddles, and fortune-telling, made up most of the rest. The comparative popularity of Chatterton's poems among the poor was proof, not so much of their author's precocity in poetry, nor of what Keats called his 'purest English', as of natural human wonder at his story. Garlands of Burns's poems, broadsheets of the Percy Ballads, sold by 'flying' stationers along with bear's grease and elixirs for rheumatism and renewal of youth, helped preserve a folk-tradition as yet almost unimpaired. Parker Clare could sing or recite over a hundred of these songs and ballads. His wife, too, had a store of traditional tales.

Parker had married Ann, daughter of Elizabeth and John Stimson, 'town-shepherd' of the neighbouring ancient village of Castor, or Caistor, where Roman Durobrivae once stood. Ann, baptised on the 17th of April, 1757, was thus eight years older than her husband, thirty-five when they married, probably in 1792, and thirty-six when her son was born. Ann did not so much as know her letters. Yet she was prudent, thrifty, and of course superstitious in an age when witches, no longer burnt, were ducked, and merchants of London Town still took their wives to Tyburn for a jaunt to see hanged an idle apprentice or a woman who had stolen a turnip. Ann showed courage and endurance under the dropsy with which she early became afflicted but for which she was never treated.

These were the parents of Clare—reasonably hale country

1 *Sketches*, p. 46.

people. The stock tends to longevity. The family was closely knit, Church of England, and traditional or Tory in outlook. Within it there was a sense of fallen fortunes since the days of 'John Clare Clark'. The completely unknown element in the situation is, of course, the fiddling, vagrant schoolmaster, John Donald Parker.

Clare was the eldest of four and the elder of premature twins. The other twin was a 'fine lively bonny wench'. John, small enough to have gone into a pint pot', was 'waukly', and 'my mother told me she never could have dreamt I should live to make a man'. The bouncing girl died within a week or two. There is record of neither her birth nor her death in the spasmodically-kept parish books of the period. Another child, Elizabeth, was christened on the 7th of July, 1796. She did not live to grow up. A third daughter, born on the 1st of April, 1798, and ten days later christened Sophy, remained with her father, mother, and brother, in the partitioned cottage at Helpston until at least 1824.

Clare's childhood was as well cared for as his father's flail-thresher's pay of about eight shillings a week would allow. Certainly it was profoundly happy. The games which he and his earliest village companions played were those which have persisted, like country customs and songs, down the centuries: leap-frog, hare-and-hounds, ducks-and-drakes, nine-peg Morris 'nicked upon the green', hopscotch, clink-and-bandy, crook-horn, duck-under-water, and chock-and-taw. Serious employment for such country children was taking dinners to hay- or harvest-field, after which they

> ran behind the loaded wain,
> for the mere joy of riding back again:

or they refilled empty bottles for their elders at 'old Eastwell's boiling spring'. Intimations of the French Terror incited them to get corncockles for 'a wild cockade', and 'kecks for bugle horns'. They hunted 'pooties'—those varnished, black and yellow or moth-patterned snail-shells so numerous in limestone country. They sought birds' and rabbits' nests:

> poking sticks into the rabbit-holes & carefully observing
> when I took it out if there was down at the end which was

The Fen's 'faint shadow of immensity'

'long waving rows of willow grey
And clumps of hawthorn shade'

THE CLARE COUNTRY: FEN AND MIDLAND

'THE BLUE BELL'
NEXT DOOR

THE TENEMENT IN WHICH
CLARE WAS BORN

THE ORIGINALLY DETACHED CLARE COTTAGE

(*left foreground*) Drawn by Cowen, 1823

a sign of a nest with young then in went the arm up to the elbow & then fear came upon us that a snake might be concealed in the hole our bloods ran cold within us & started us off to other sports we usd to chase the squirrels in the woods from grain to grain that would sit washing their faces on the other side & then peep at us again we usd to get boughs from the trees, to beat a wasps nest till some of us were stung & then we ran away to other amusements.[1]

Some 'I remember' verses not only tell of childhood games, but reveal, in the child depicted, an ambition, even then, to excel:

> Our pride to reason would not shrink
>   In those exalted hours;
> A giant's were a pigmy link
>   To statures such as ours.
> We even fancied we could fly
>   And fancy then was true:
> So with the clouds upon the sky
>   In dreams at night we flew.
>
> We shot our arrows from our bows,
>   Like any archers proud,
> And thought when lost they went so high
>   To lodge upon a cloud:
> And these seemed feats that none before
>   Ourselves could e'er attain,
> And Wellington with all his feats
>   Felt never half so vain. . . .
>
> And carriages of oyster shells,
>   Though filled with naught but stones,
> Grew instant ministers of state,
>   While clay kings filled their thrones.
> Like Cinderella's fairy queen,
>   Joy would our wants bewitch;
> If wealth was sought, the dust and stones
>   Turned wealth and made us rich.[2]

Only a few years before Clare's birth, the gibbet had creaked and groaned in the sweeping fen wind, just outside the village. The Lodge House on the Heath, where an evil deed had been

1 *Prose*, p. 16.
2 *Poems*, 1935, II, p. 28.

done, before the wild cat made her lair there, was haunted. Witches, fairies, wood and water elves, shagged foals, will-o'-wisps, and good and evil spirits of many kinds, all that Celtic lore—'leased upon the fickle faith of men' and now lost to our literature—was still believed in. The enlightened were already beginning to disdain it as vulgar rubbish.

Old cow-women[1] on Helpston Heath were lively receptacles of superstition and warning. They told stories to the children gathered round in sun-checked shade or bushy storm-shelter, while 'tented' animals pursued their grazing: of Jane, ravished by her master, and having laid ungodly hands on herself, being allowed by Christian charity the public cross-roads as the best place for her last bed; of Amy's and Crazy Nell's almost equally sinister fates; of the workhouse orphan's sad lot.

But it appears to have been Clare's mother whose animistic fancy supplied most of the same kind of Northern fairy-tale lore as that on which Burns, Coleridge, Shelley, and Scott, were nourished in their earliest days. On winter evenings, sewing or knitting, her burring wheel stilled, firelight saving the farthing rushlight, Ann Clare would recount:

> Witches' dread powers and fairy feats:
> How one has oft been known to prance
> In cowcribs, like a coach, to France,
> And ride on sheep-trays from the fold
> A race-horse speed to Burton-hold,
> To join the midnight mystery's rout,
> Where witches meet the yews about:
> And how, when met with unawares,
> They turn at once to cats and hares,
> And race along with hellish flight,
> Now here, now there, now out of sight!
> And how the other tiny things
> Will leave their moonlight meadow rings,
> And unperceived through key-holes creep,
> When all around have sunk to sleep,
> And crowd in cupboards as they please,
> As thick as mites in rotten cheese,
> To feast on what the cotter leaves—

[1] Martin's Granny Bains may or may not have been authentic. Martin was nearer to local tradition since lost. According to Clare's own account, his parents were chief almoners of his early fancy.

Mice are not reckoned greater thieves . . .
And foul, or fair, or dark the night,
Their wild-fire lamps are burning bright,
For which full many a daring crime
Is acted in the summer time;
When glow-worm found in lane remote
Is murder'd for its shining coat,
And put in flowers, that nature weaves
With hollow shapes and silken leaves,
Such as the Canterbury bell,
Serving for lamp or lantern well;
Or following with unwearied watch
The flight of one they cannot match,
As silence sliveth upon sleep,
Or thieves by dozing watch-dogs creep,
They steal from Jack-a-lantern's tails
A light, whose guidance never fails
To aid them in the darkest night
And guide their plundering steps aright,
Rattling away in printless tracks . . .
The children—silent all the while—
And e'en repressed the laugh or smile—
Quake with the ague chills of fear,
And tremble though they love to hear . . .
Till the old clock, that strikes unseen
Behind the picture-pasted screen
Where Eve and Adam still agree
To rob life's fatal apple-tree,
Counts over bed-time's hour of rest,
And bids each be sleep's fearful guest . . .
The children steal away to bed,
And up the ladder softly tread,
Scarce daring—from their fearful joys—
To look behind or make a noise;
Nor speak a word, but still as sleep
They secret to their pillows creep,
And whisper o'er, in terror's way,
The prayers they dare no louder say,
Then hide their heads beneath the clothes,
And try in vain to seek repose;
While yet, to fancy's sleepless eye,
Witches on sheep-trays gallop by.[1]

[1] *Poems*, 1935, I, pp. 293–4.

II

One day in summer, this child of five or six years, with brightly sparkling blue eyes, set out on a solitary expedition. (One recalls Samuel Taylor Coleridge at the same age wandering down to the River Otter.) Later the second wanderer was to record:

> I had often seen the large heath called Emmonsales stretching its yellow furze from my eyes into unknown solitudes . . . & my curiosity urgd me to steal an opportunity to explore it that morning I had imagind that the world's end was at the orizon & that a day's journey was able to find it so I went on with my heart full of hope's pleasures & discoverys expecting when I got to the brink of the world that I coud look down like looking into a large pit & see into its secrets the same as I believd I coud see heaven by looking into the water. . . . So I eagerly wanderd on & rambled along the furze the whole day till I got out of my knowledge when the very wild flowers seemd to forget me . . . often wondering to myself that I had not found the edge the sky still touchd the ground in the distance & my childish wisdom was puzzld . . . when I got home I found my parents in the greatest distress & half the village about hunting me. . . .[1]

The ancient heath was Ailsworth, part of the rough common land of then unenclosed Helpston. It is now a nature reserve, home of the Black Hairstreak, the Large Tortoiseshell, and the Chequered Skipper butterflies. Nearer Helpston in Clare's childhood lay the village's two common fields. Beyond to the east, still undrained fen swarmed with quail, snipe, bittern, ruff and reeve, avocet, crested grebe, besides still commoner pewit, crow, rook, 'caudy-maudy', landrail, and many another Clare later tells of. With its gnarled whitethorn, Langdyke Bush round which the ancient folk-court used to meet, and its hollow Lea Close Oak that could shelter a family, Ailsworth Heath was probably much the same when the small Clare first visited it as it had been for five or six centuries.

[1] *Prose*, p. 19.

This questing son of a peasant has given, in an astonishing bulk of verse and poetry belonging chiefly to his earlier years, almost the only, certainly the most vivid and revealing, pictures of scenes and men during that astonishing sweep of early nineteenth-century Parliamentary Enclosure which helped to produce modern rural England. Sense of freedom before the days of our green hedges and patchwork fields now taken as so characteristic was evidently tremendous:

> No fence of ownership crept in between
> To hide the prospect from the gazing eye;
> The only bondage was the circling sky. . . .[1]

The bustle of a waking village—except on the Sabbath, best of days, whose 'light hours fly swift on easy wings'—gave as evident a sense of mirth and toil united:

> Cocks wake the early morn with many a crow;
> Loud-striking village clock has counted four . . .
> The bird-boy's peeling horn is loudly blow'd;
> The wagons jostle on with rattling sound,
> And hogs and geese now throng the dusty road,
> Grunting and gabbling in contention. . . .[2]

Milkmaids call 'Come Mull'. The motley group of harvesters and gleaners goes to the harvest-field. Cow-women and boys take flocks and herds along road-sides thick with wild-woad, medicinal betony, mullein, and many another flower:

> While distant thresher's swingle drops
>   With sharp and hollow twanking raps;
> And nigh at hand, the echoing chops
>   Of hardy hedger stopping gaps.[3]

Ann Clare, the shepherd's daughter, might be 'illiterate to the last degree'. She might believe the higher learning, seeing the alterations it could produce not always for her own or her village's good, 'blackest arts of witch-craft'. But she maintained that she had 'experienced enough in her own case to avoid

---

[1] *Poems*, 1935, I, p. 415.
[2] *Poems*, 1935, I, p. 56.
[3] *Poems*, 1935, I, p. 171.

bringing up her children in ignorance'. From the very first, her 'hopeful ambition ran high' of making her only son a scholar. Nor did the child's father interfere, 'till downright necessity forced him to check her kind intentions'.

By this, the price of flour had risen steeply as well as rents. For the next thirty years, what with the French war and its aftermath and the advancement of agriculture, Government was forced to turn deaf ears to minor injustices against peasants. In the Clares' most penurious periods the child John, in spite of a 'waukly constitution', went to thresh with his father, who made him a light flail for the purpose. But until he was eleven or twelve, never less than three months out of the year were 'luckily spared' for 'improvement': first with hornbook from 'an old woman in the village', 'mourning for sunshine liberty'; next, freely and eagerly, with a master at Glinton two miles distant. Eight weeks' work paid for one month's schooling. At this second school, under a master 'white with years', very different from his own grandfather, Clare learnt to read and write: an advance on Stephen Duck, the Wiltshire thresher whose verses had been patronised by the University of Oxford and Queen Caroline about the middle of the century. Duck had taught himself in adolescence by reading *Paradise Lost* with the aid of a dictionary. Clare's lot was an advance, too, on James Hogg's, who proclaimed that he did not begin to be able to write down his own verses till the age of twenty-six. Even George Stephenson, the railway genius, made a beginning only at seventeen.

Clare's sister, Sophy, too, must have gone to school, since in 1820 she wrote a very fair hand. Seaton's school was in the roomy vestry of Glinton church, over the gravestone of John Wing. Graveyard and road were the children's playground. Seaton, whose 'peal'd wand' hung above the blackened chimney, rewarded the bright-eyed little boy for progress during absence, and the child was encouraged to study further at home. On the cottage table made by John and his father when the boy was about twelve, pens, ink, and paper began to jostle barley loaf or dish of potatoes. The mother would stop her wheel. Both parents felt that their son would 'one day reward them for the trouble they had taken to give him schooling'.

Attending Seaton's vestry classes with John was the younger daughter of a Glinton farmer—'the stillest and most good-natured girl in the school': 'I was a lover very early in life', Clare confesses in his Autobiography:

> my first attachment being a schoolboy affection was for Mary who . . . was belovd with a romantic or Platonic sort of feeling if I coud but gaze on her face or fancy a smile on her countenance I went away satisfyd we played with each other but named nothing of love yet I fancyd her eyes told me her affections we walked together as school-companions in leisure hours but our talk was of play & our actions the wanton nonsense of children yet young as my heart was it would turn chill when I touchd her hand & tremble & I fancyd her feelings were the same for as I gazd earnestly in her face a tear woud hang in her smiling eye & she woud turn to wipe it away her heart was as tender as a birds.[1]

Apparently the children wandered by brook and hedgerow, watching for moth, bird, and flower. We do not know what Mary was like, except that she had fair hair and blue eyes. We do not even know that she was interested in reading. It was her self-effacing sympathy that was important.

Appetite for reading in Clare himself had small sustenance other than the Bible and Church Prayer Book of his parents' faith. Worse than this, rheumatism, scourge of the fens, began to overtake his father. Seaton's idea of the boy's qualifying for an usher in a school dimmed, like his parents' undoubted ambitions for him, into castles in the air. Reluctantly John was taken away from day-school: though on a new master's exhortation—Seaton died about 1806—he continued his studies for some time at Glinton 'night-school'. James Merrishaw, the night-school master, was old and white-haired, too. But both Seaton and he fostered the love of reading in the boy with the extraordinary memory. It is said that when eight or nine Clare could repeat whole chapters of *Job* by heart. While Merrishaw lived, he had the run of the old man's small library.

But the puzzle is, surely, why this boy, eager and sensitive as he may have been, should set out to write poetry. He himself

[1] *Prose*, p. 44.

always said that his first entry into that other universe was when one of his mother's brothers, a drover, brought 'Pomfret's Poems' back from London. This was perhaps the 1808 edition of that much-reprinted poet who, as Johnson says, was always "a favourite with that class of readers who, without vanity or criticism, seek only their own amusement". It was the wood-cuts which had attracted drover Stimson. It was the poem 'Love Triumphant over Reason', which, when his father read it aloud, spoke to the boy.

Up to this time Clare had not a single book of his own. In 1806 as we know both from the volumes themselves in his library at Northampton, and from his own account, he managed to acquire two. One was a copy of the popular *Hymns and Spiritual Songs* of Dr. Watts. The book was purchased of 'J. T. Drakard, Printer, Bookseller, Stationer, Binder, Music Seller, Dealer in Genuine Patent Medicines, Perfumery, Umbrellas, Hat Cases, Bonnet Boxes, Trinkets, etc.', of Stamford. Clare's second book was one of what James Montgomery in his *Lectures on Poetry* of 1833 called 'the four universally and permanently popular long poems in the English language'—Thomson's *Seasons*. Either his friend Tom Porter of Ashton, or another young man, a weaver, and older than himself, first showed Clare it and allowed him to dip into it. 'I can't say the reason but the following lines made my heart twitter with joy:

> Come gentle Spring, ethereal mildness come,
> And from the bosom of yon dropping cloud,
> While music wakes around, veil'd in a shower
> Of shadowing roses, on our plains descend.'

He 'teazd' one and sixpence out of his father—nearly a quarter of a week's wages—with which to buy the book. Next day he started for Stamford:

> but when I got there, I was told by a young shop boy in the street (who had a book in his hand which I found to be 'Collins' Odes and Poems') that the booksellers would not open the shop on a Sunday. This was a disappointment most strongly felt, and I returned home in very low spirits; but having to tend horses the next week, in company with

other boys, I planned a scheme in secret to obtain my
wishes by stealth, giving one of the boys a penny to keep
my horses in my absence, with an additional penny to
keep the secret. . . .

Again:

> I got to Stamford. . . . On my return the sun got up,
> . . . and as I did not like to let anybody see me reading on
> the road of a working day, I clumb over the wall into
> Burghley Park, and nestled in a lawn at the wall side.[1]

Small, frail, and intelligent, but 'shanny' and reserved—if
Clare was not to be an usher when schooldays were over, then
other employ than 'coarsest chance' of thumping corn with a
flail must be thought of. Already his parents' ambitions were
being crushed by the enormity of odds against them. Worse,
the boy was growing so fond of being alone that his

> mother was feign to force me into company for the neigh-
> bours had assurd her mind into the fact that I was no
> better than crazy . . . my reading of books (they woud
> jeeringly say) was for no greater improvement than quali-
> fying an idiot for a workhouse.[2]

How ruthless an unlettered community can be towards any
tendency to difference from the herd is by now a commonplace.
Shoemaking was mooted. The boy 'turned a sullen eye'. And
the small premium could not be spared. He weeded wheat, or
helped haymakers and harvesters. But as enclosing of land
crept on apace, agricultural employment grew scarcer. He
gathered firewood or cazons (dried cow-dung), or idled with
one-time herd-boys. In spite of smallness and diffidence, he
was not without prowess and its usual escapes: climbing after
a buzzard's nest and losing his foothold, to hang thirty feet
from the ground; falling into deep water when his bundle of
bulrushes used as a raft shot from under him. Rebelling against
church-going, in spite of 'strong snubbings',

[1] *Sketches*, pp. 58, 59.
[2] *Prose*, pp. 15, 16.

of a Sunday morning I have been out before the sun
delving for worms on some old weed-blanketed dunghill
& sliving off across the wet grass . . . till I came to the
flood-washd meadow stream . . . & my heart woud
thrill with hopes of success as I saw a sizable gudgeon.[1]

But it was an unsatisfactory time. His parents were disappointed, the boy restless and thwarted. He pursued fruit-
less arithmetical studies with the aid of Bonnycastle and
Fenning on the cottage table during winter evenings as before;
he devoured the ill-printed chap-books, saving his pence for
*The Babes in the Wood, Valentine and Orson, The Seven Sleepers, The
King and the Cobbler, Long Tom the Carrier.* His three-farthings
meant a sheet of paper. His mother had begun to take the
sugar-bags he usually wrote on, for fire-lighter or kettle-holder.
His stock of pencils until adolescence was 'a bundle I had of a
Jew at Stamford for a shilling'.

He had a childish companionship with Richard Turnill, the
unusual son of a neighbouring farmer. But Richard died of
typhus. Richard's brother John, also of studious and inventive
turn of mind, who had been away at boarding school, then
pored over mathematics with him; they read the newspaper;
the night sky in Turnill's telescope sent Clare home puzzled
and alarmed. They strove to improve their copperplate. But
in turn the acquaintance with John was broken by Turnill's
going into the Excise.

It was during this period of first frustration that, helping at
harvesting as team-leader for Richard and John's father, Clare
witnessed a loader, Thomas Drake, fall from his wagon and
break his neck. Shock precipitated a kind of fit. The boy
'swooned away without a struggle'. For a time, each spring
and autumn after that, he was attacked with a

chillness and dithering that seemed to creep from one's
toes till it got up to one's head, when I turned senseless
and fell.[2]

These fits were 'stopt' by a Mr. Arnold, M.D., of Stamford.
Quite likely they would have ceased without the ministrations

[1] *Sketches*, p. 50.
[2] *John Clare: a Life*, 1932, p. 36.

of Mr. Arnold. It has been stated that the fits were epileptic; but all that can finally be said from the evidence before us is that they were 'epileptiform'.

After this period of 'idle leisures', 'doing jobs as I could catch them', he went to drive plough at Woodcroft Castle. Mrs. Bellars, the mistress, was kind, but the boys had to wade the flooded moat and work wet-shod all day in bad weather, and Clare stayed only a month. Disappointment again. He was ashamed. His parents began to think he would 'make nothing but a soldier'. A 'bragging fellow named Manton' offered to apprentice him as a sign printer and stone cutter. This time the boy was willing, even eager, but again, the small premium demanded could not be found. His parents were relieved when another brother of Ann Clare's, Morris Stimson, came over from Wisbech, where he worked as footman for Councillor Bellamy, to say that his master needed a boy in his office. Morris Stimson was certain that John was scholar enough for a lawyer's clerk. John's father and mother were equally certain. All were—except the shy and retiring John. His mother found

> a white neckcloth & got me a pair of gloves to hide my coarse hands but I had overgrown my coat and almost left my sleeves at the elbows & all my other garments betrayed too old an acquaintance with me.[1]

A century of sporadic but steady Enclosing, high farming, and expanding overseas trade had seen the widening and deepening of most navigable English rivers. Pack-horse and foot traffic along muddy, deep-rutted roads had given place to the possibilities of water-freightage. The brief era of canals was at hand, and the even briefer heyday of turnpike roads and Tantivy coaches. Walking to Peterborough, Clare made his first journey, as Hazlitt went in his youth to see the farm where his mother was born, down the River Nen, by one of the two packet-boats: twenty-one miles for eighteenpence. The timid aspirant for the post of lawyer's clerk, head down, was received and interviewed by Councillor Bellamy—and naturally rejected. Morris Stimson was told by his mistress to keep the boy till Sunday, and then to pay his return back on the boat—but not

[1] *Prose*, pp. 20, 21.

before Clare had had a look at the town's book-and-picture shop, which was displaying E. V. Rippingille's *Village Ale-house* and *Letter Carrier*.

At last, probably in May, 1809, Francis Gregory, the Clares' neighbour at *The Blue Bell Inn*, next door, hired Clare for a year. Gregory, an ageing bachelor, though of poor health, was cheerful and kindly, and treated John as a son. But the boy had to do much of the tending of the horse and the one or two cows by himself, and both his love of solitude as well as his sensitive fears were accentuated. He hated to take the animals to graze on the heath in the spring dusk because of the inhuman squealing of badger and vixen. On his two-mile weekly journeys to Maxey for flour, 'haunted spots' forced on him the habit of spinning stories 'without a ghost'. Being overheard muttering to himself did not improve his village reputation, and 'thoughts became troublesome in company': 'I felt the most happy to be alone'. Yet he later calls Gregory's the nursery of his rhyming. Up to this 'I knew nothing of poetry': it was 'felt and not uttered'.

The truth was that everything in nature was making intense and lasting impression:

> No matter how the world approved
> 'Twas nature listened, I that loved.

The spirit in storm and wind, as well as the 'little chumbling mouse' 'spoke' to him.

So, too

> the tall poplars peeping above the rest like leafy steeples the grey willows shining chilly in the sun as if the morning mist still lingered on its cool green I felt the beauty of these with eager delight the gadflys noonday hum the fainter murmur of the beefly 'spinning in the evening ray' the dragonflys in spangled coats darting like winged arrows down the thin stream . . . I lovd to see the heaving grasshopper in his coat of delicate green bounce from stub to stub I listend the hedgecricket with rapture. . . .[1]

This lively and delicate perception, that rejoiced so in the spirit of life within and without, would be difficult enough to

[1] *Prose*, pp. 25, 26.

balance against the rough knocks of experience. And the boy
had other talents which might have helped in easier circumstances but which would almost certainly hinder in straits like
these. At the end of a year he left Gregory 'with the restless
hope of being something better than a ploughman'.

Was this the period, between 1809 and 1810, when he was at
Gregory's, that he renewed his comradeship with Mary Joyce?
He was nearly seventeen. Mary was four years younger. He
tells us she was thirteen in *A Daydream in Summer*. If what Clare
says, too, in a still-unpublished sonnet, is fact and not fancy,
they met after schooldays at a village party at Martinmas, when
Mary, in rustic fashion, betrayed preference for him in a game
of forfeits, and 'paid with joy a kiss for every fine'.[1] They seem
to have revived their childhood enthusiasm for stream and
hedgerow secrets. How long this second phase prospered we
do not know. But when Mary grew toward 'womanhood', she
'felt her station above mine at least I felt that she thought so'.
Elsewhere he says the 'world' caused her frown, 'choked the
hopes' he had of her, and 'made thee haughty, Mary'. Mary's
father, James[2] Joyce of Glinton Manor, has been blamed for
separating the young lovers. In those days of rapidly fluctuat-
ing agricultural fortunes, and in face of yeoman ambitions to
belong to the gentry, it would have been a queer farmer
who would look with favour on his daughter's alliance with a
landless labourer's son. But James Joyce's favour was probably
never asked. Clare's later pre-occupation with the subject of
'secret' or untellable love sprung partly from the fact that
his love for Mary remained unspoken. But the idea had, by
then, an altogether wider and deeper significance. Meanwhile,
from his explicit statement we know that Mary

> knew nothing of my fondness for her, no more than I did
> of her inclination to forbid or encourage me.[3]

Yet

> I felt a hopeful tenderness that I might one day renew the
> acquaintance & disclose the smotherd passion she was a

---

[1] Peterborough Mss. 16.

[2] Given as 'William' Joyce in *John Clare: a Life*. But in the list of names in
the Enclosure Award of 1809, there is only one Joyce—'James', with some
seventy-five acres of land dispersed in the common fields. From a descendant
of Mary Joyce's sister Ann, we know, too, that he was 'James'.

[3] *Sketches*, p. 87.

C

beautiful girl & as the dream never awoke into reality her beauty was always fresh in my memory. . . . I cannot forget her little playful fairy form & witching smile even now.[1]

He wrote that between 1820 and 1824. If he finished at Gregory's in May, 1810, satisfactory or even continuous employment was as far off as ever. The only friendship which prospered, and that but in a very limited way, was with an older boy, Tom Porter of the neighbouring village of Ashton. Porter's grandfather had been steward at Walcot Hall, and Porter had inherited a few books like Sandys' *Travels* and Parkinson's *Herbal*. These Clare devoured, as well as others on Porter's special interest of gardening. The two rambled about seeking bee-orchis and spider-orchis at Swordywell and in the many disused quarries of the neighbourhood, and fly-orchis and butterfly-orchis in Helpston's ancient pastures.

III

Burghley House by Stamford town, seat of the Marquis of Exeter, is four miles north of Helpston. Its spacious wooded park and gardens look toward the spires and towers of what was the scene of much Cecil pomp in Elizabeth the First's time. Stone-built Stamford was perhaps at its most prosperous in those days immediately before the coming of the railways. Mentioned by E. V. Lucas as possibly the original home of Charles Lamb's family, Stamford lies on the great North Road, and was then a day's posting from London. Coaches rattled through its narrow streets. Its inns were always full of travellers. Though after the making of railroads, it settled down in sleepy, respectable beauty as a small market town, watching Peterborough with its more favourable contours outstrip it in commercial importance, in Clare's youth it would be a kind of metropolis near the great domain of Burghley.

Tom Porter told Clare that the master of the kitchen gardens there wanted an apprentice: John and his father went at once to see the head gardener. Finding him 'in white stockings' the two Clares pulled off their hats to him, 'as if it had been the

1 *Prose*, p. 44.

Marquis himself'. The boy was taken on for three years, his work being to take fruit and vegetables to the Hall twice a day. But it was not long before the gardener showed himself in his true colours—'swearing in his passions' at the boy, whom at the same time he found 'still and willing', for things 'too trifling to be called faults'. He sent Clare errands at all hours of the day and night, chiefly for ale. On other occasions the gardener's wife bade him fetch her husband from an inn. Rather than face the music at either end, Clare took to sleeping in the Park, waking covered with rime, which affected his 'side with a numbness'. At other times the under gardeners, locked in the garden-house to prevent their stealing fruit, would climb out of the window and over the wall, treating the penniless youth with them, to 'midnight revels' at *The Hole in the Wall*. This was a 'drunkards' den' famous for its ale when 'Barnaby Harrington' visited Stamford early in the seventeenth century. When Clare and his elder companions frequented it, it was kept by a former servant of Burghley.

By the autumn the boy had had enough. So had the credulous, but kindly foreman, George Cousins, reader of Abercrombie's *Gardening* and the *Bible*, and collector of epitaphs. The two rose early one morning; and, to avoid trouble over Cousins's broken agreement (Clare was not 'bound') stole secretly away. They walked to Grantham, twenty-one miles; they slept at *The Crown and Anchor*; and Clare had time to repent of his rashness. Next day they tramped to Newark-on-Trent. There they found work with a nurseryman named Withers, lodging at a lame man's house, whose son was celebrated for making fiddles. They stayed some months; but continued heavy digging taxed the boy's strength, and he 'became so ignorant in this far land that I could not tell which quarter the wind blew from'.[1] Withers's method as employer was by no means auspicious, either. He paid them one part of the wages, but promised them the rest 'after a further trial'. Homesick and restless, Clare 'got fresh' at the village feast at Bostwick,[2] and 'took the King's bounty' for the militia. He was still but seventeen, but England was fighting 'almost all

---

[1] *Prose*, p. 28.
[2] Mss. has 'Baldwick', and so given in *Life*. But Bostwick is the only village within walking distance of Newark.

Europe' at that moment. Recruiting was carried out crudely
and hastily at festive gathering and in bars. Fortunately, as
he himself knew afterwards, he was 'too short' when he went to
Nottingham to be sworn in.

By the winter, again he and Cousins were determined to
endure no longer. Again they rose early one morning, and 'not
burdened with luggage', 'easily stole away undetected' from
Newark. They reached Stamford that night, but not daring
to show themselves at any inn, slept under a tree in Burghley
Park, to wake next morning 'covered as white as a sheet' with
frost.

Home once more, Clare tried gardening with the farmers
round about. But 'the continued sameness of a garden cloyed'.
The truth was deeper and altogether more complex. A 'thought
unceasing mind', cramped and confined, was striving to burst
the bonds of its frustration; a restless imagination was seeking
expression. Two or three years before this, after reading *The
Seasons* hidden in Burghley Park on his way back from buying
the book at Stamford, he had composed what he afterwards
called his first poem. Actually there were dozens of verses
before that, but all destroyed. He afterwards burnt, and then
rewrote *The Morning Walk* many times, correcting it out of all
recognition. But a certain confidence had been reached. The
pleasure such power gave was, of course, also coupled with
Locke's 'disquiet'—the ambition to achieve against all odds, to
have his say in his own way as others had had theirs. But the
satisfaction, even the knowledge, of his gift must remain for
the moment locked in his own heart. The shock of Enclosure's
revolution was over his village. Under the unrest this caused
in him, 'poetry was for a season thrown by'.

II

CATACLYSM 1809–1819

I

IN 1809, before Clare left Helpston for the first time, to work in Burghley gardens, the Act of Parliament had been passed, '49. Geo. III', 'for enclosing lands in the parishes of Maxey with Deepingate, Northborough, Glinton with Peakirk, Etton, and Helpstone'. This was one of those batches hurried through every Parliament of George the Third, assemblies, as Trevelyan remarks, 'not otherwise famous for radical legislation'.[1] Although the actual Award bears the later date 1820, already, when Clare returned from Newark, those changes were afoot which altered the structure of his village, and radically affected the lives of its people, obliterating traditions which had survived since the thirteenth century.

Even if, long before the social hierarchy of the Middle Ages, some of the very earliest agricultural communities *were* made up of roughly equal free men, could Freedom and Locke's 'natural' equality ever have been known to us except by their opposites, domination and slavery? Certainly down English centuries one hears the first of the key-words so stubbornly upheld by Clare grow resonant, accumulating echoes.

There can be no doubt that the open-field system of our early agriculture, which remained in Helpston till the end of the eighteenth century, was wasteful of time and energy, as well as what we now call unscientific. Nor, equally, can there be doubt that, under Enclosure, small yeomen and cottagers were deprived, not only of their land, but of traditional rights, and were left, far too often, without just recompense. No criticism, so far, has competently countered J. L. and Barbara Hammond's facts and figures, or their thesis that much of the injustice was unnecessary. If only the far-sighted, the indus-

[1] *English Social History*, p. 376.

trious, and the progressive, could have filled, as Locke advised, no more than their pitcher with the water of the spring! But both rich and poor, whom H. J. Massingham so rightly called 'natural allies', were swept along at this time in a powerful drama greater than themselves.

The Helpston Enclosure Award of 1820, typical of its kind, betrays to any modern disinterested scrutiny that the Commissioners saw themselves paid; the larger landowners and the Church did not suffer. Those who could make a claim were not without redress even if it was not always to their liking as to commonable rights. But those who could not afford, or did not know how, to write a claim, naturally stood to lose any recompense that was going. The practical, energetic, and shrewd, as ever, did not fare badly: the thriftless, the illiterate, or the peace-loving rustic who detested the haggle of voices, often received less than his clearest dues.

Those upheavels which impelled Davies, Eden, Young, and later, Cobbett, to their ignored remedies, had come to a crisis in 1795. Instead of the suggested minimum wages and allotments, the remedy known as the Speenhamland plan was adopted: that wages should be made up to livelihood level by parish relief. This deprived the indigent among the agricultural poor of the last shreds of prized independence. Such a system of pauperisation was intended to be, and might even look, philanthropic. But agriculture was thriving, rents soaring, and landowners, farmers, shopkeepers, and new bankers and money-lenders, all sharpened their wits, as the French War dragged on, in a fierce, but now familiarly understood and accepted, need for luxury and higher standards of living.

Home again in the changing village, Clare at eighteen, found that his father, 'strongly knitted with independence', preferred to potter about road-mending for his five shillings Poor Law award, 'fancying he was not so much beholden to their forced generosity, as if he had taken it for nothing'. But five shillings, even in those days, would not keep wife, daughter, and Parker Clare himself. Responsibility for the four of them fell on John: while at either gardening or field-work, there was hardly sufficient employ to keep two, let alone four.

In 1812 there came one of England's periodic invasion scares. Under Castlereagh's army-reform, each regiment of the Line was attached to a county. Of each two battalions, the first was for the Line; the second for defence at home. These second battalions were to be raised for a term of service of seven years from an army of reserve of two hundred thousand men between the ages of eighteen and forty-five. They were to be called-up and trained for a month. This was the 'national scheme' under which, in the general panic, Clare took the bounty of two guineas, rather than the 'cross-grained choice of being forced to enlist'. Rumour in Helpston had it that the French had reached London, even Northampton. Sworn in at Peterborough, Clare went with a neighbour's son to Oundle, the place of quartering. There he was lodged at *The Rose and Crown*, a 'good place'. But 'a more motley multitude of lawless fellows," he declares, "was never seen in Oundle before."

'One of the shortest'—he was probably about five feet two— Clare was in that residue of the battalion 'nicknamed bumtools for what reason I know not'. The Captain of his Company, the 5th, was 'a good sort of fellow'. We may suppose him not an advocate of army flogging, lately exposed as an atrocity by two ardent reformers, John and Leigh Hunt. Twenty years before, at the beginning of that same war, Coleridge, as Private Comberbacke of the Light Dragoons, had been awkward in the art of learning to ride. Clare in his turn was 'terribly teazd by a little louse-looking corporal who took a delight in finding fault with me & loading me with bad jests on my awkwardness as a soldier'.[1] Clare admits that, though he took 'more than necessary pains' he was not particularly soldierly as to dress or habits. Nor was he 'apt at learning' his exercise. Being then a 'ryhmer', his thoughts were often fatally absent when the word of command was given. When, therefore, the corporal rapped him over the knees 'in a sneering sort of way' and declared he would "learn me how such fellows as I were dealt with by soldiers", Clare could stand it no longer. Throwing aside his firelock, and

> seizing him by the throat I hurled him down and kicked him when he was down—which got the fellow fame; for those that had been against him before lifted him up and called him a good fellow and me a coward.[1]

[1] *Sketches*, p. 104.

Threats of the 'black hole' followed, and of 'tying up to the halberd'. But the captain intervened. Clare escaped with an 'addition on guard'; and the corporal wisely left the unsatisfactory recruit alone after that.

It is probable that Clare served a month in the summer of 1812, and since he speaks of being called up a second time, another month in the summer of 1813. On this occasion he took a further bounty for service abroad, but heard no more about it. Soon after the Peace Declaration of 1814, the Northamptonshire militia was disbanded.

With this, still leaner years set in. Till 1813, the Continental System had kept prices up, masking, by the top-layer of prosperity, the condition of the mass of the disinherited. After Cobbett's *Rural Rides*, after the last labourers' revolt of 1830, agricultural labourers' conditions were villainous—till the time when, as J. S. Mill said, "the poor came out of leading strings" and the country's future depended "on the degree in which they can be made rational beings".

Our unusual village boy, determined at all cost to be a poet, had, by about 1818, the same startlingly clear, directly glancing blue eyes which he had had as a child. It has been recently said that he was short-sighted, because he wrote that he had 'no eye to kill anything'. More likely he meant that neither eye nor heart was interested in learning to use a gun. His hair, blond when he was a child, was in his adolescence a pale chestnut, fading again later. Two inches taller than John Keats, he was still small, like Hartley Coleridge, Thomas De Quincey, Robert Bloomfield, and William Blake. He was delicately made. His forehead, so often commented on by those who saw him, was, as one of his doctors described it later, 'of great breadth and altitude . . . such as we are in the habit of associating with . . . the highest order of intellect'.

An only son, an only child until his sister Sophy was born when he was five, Clare had been, in his own words and in a cottage context, 'coddled up' by his parents. His unusualness as a child and his brightness at school had been indulged as long and as far as possible. Modern psychology might say that the family was affected by the current scramble between subsistence and luxury: that the sense of fallen fortunes in both Stimsons and Clares instigated parental ambition, and the parental admiration for the boy's precocity helped give him an 'ego-ideal' which drove him all his life and beyond his strength. But this is to explain only the spur to genius.

He had been for some years, though 'with all secrecy possible', venturing to commit his musings 'readily to paper'. Receiving a somewhat grudging assent from Tom Porter that he, when shown some verses, at least understood them, Clare had, also some time before this, begun to preserve what he thought best. He hid them in an old unused cupboard, then in a recess in the kitchen wall, then in the box his mother had given him for his clothes and possessions when he left home for Burghley. On that occasion Ann had sadly bade him: 'leave off writing' and 'buy no more books; tho' I own it's better than spending your money in beer'.[1] His problem was to find a disinterested judge for his verses. 'Quite in the suds' from a further remark of Porter's on the necessity of spelling and grammar, he had, probably before militia days, bought a 'Spelling Book'. Had not Dr. Johnson firmly established the hitherto individual matter of orthography, once for all, by his Dictionary of 1755? Had not Lord Chesterfield written to his son in 1750 that

> orthography . . . is so absolutely necessary for a man of letters, or a gentleman, that one false spelling may fix a ridicule upon him for the rest of his life. And I know a man of quality who never recovered the ridicule of having spelled *wholesome* without the w. . . .

Alone in Helpston, Clare turned from the discouragingly intricate new laws of orthography and grammar. Ignorant of Burns's defiant

> Gie me ae spark o' Nature's fire,
> That's a' the learning I desire;

but feeling the breeze of romanticism, he advised himself:

> If I could talk to be understood, surely by the same method, writing might be made out as easy and proper. So in the teeth of grammar (and in these last shifts of standing out against poverty) I pursued my literary journey as warm as usual, working hard all day and scribbling at night, or any leisure hour, in any convenient hole or corner I could shove in unseen.[1]

[1] *Sketches*, p. 69.

Imitation of his favourites among the ballads his father sang were his first compositions, long before *The Morning Walk*. These had at first caused the laughter of both his parents, which had driven him to 'a process of cunning', the 'necessity of a lie to try the value of their criticisms'. He had pretended to copy the verses out of a borrowed book. Remarks then, 'unadulterated with prejudice' had been 'Aye, boy, if you could write so, you would do'. And with this encouragement he 'scribbled on unceasing for 2 or 3 years', still without divulging his secret, reciting the songs every night when they were all seated by the fireside.

> At some things they woud laugh, here I distinguished affectation and conceit from nature. Some verses they woud desire me to repeat again, as they said they could not understand them; here I discover'd obscurity from common sense, and always benefited by making it as much like the latter as I could; for I thought if they coud not understand me, my taste should be wrong founded, and not agreeable to nature. . . . My own Judgment began to expand and improve, at least I conceited so, and thinking my criticisms better than theirs, I selected my pieces approved of by them, and even found most of 'em fit for nothing but my mother's old purposes; for as I kept sorting them over and over, there was few that escaped that destiny in the end.[1]

Approval from neighbours and villagers was less easy to win. His disposition was to wander alone, among 'stillness and wildness', learning nature by a sensitive vision that gave rise to excessive horror as well as to the resilient happiness that lasted him all his life. This combined in Clare with a deep need, such as Coleridge and Shelley had, for understanding. He sometimes wondered that, whilst *he* was bound to pause over the quantities of pleasing things, another should pass, 'as careless as if he were blind'. And

> the laughs and jeers of those around me, when they found out I was a poet, was present death to my ambitious apprehensions . . . the labouring classes remain as blind in such matters as the slaves in Africa.[2]

[1] *Sketches*, pp. 63, 64.
[2] *Sketches*, pp. 63, 69.

Moreover, in the Clares' 'dilemma of embarrassment' oc-casioned by Parker's almost complete disablement, both parents began to distrust their son's love of books and learn-ing in which, when he was younger, they had taken such pride. Naturally they felt it useless, worse than useless—a positive stumbling-block—if he must 'stick at hard labour'.

Employment became more and more difficult. Labourers, herded into 'catchwork gangs', were liable to be sent where required. Clare worked in a 'motley set', 'setting down fences and planting quick-lines'—hedges, that is. Rootless, poverty-stricken, deprived of aim, and under a smarting sense of bewildered injustice, these early nineteenth-century labour-gangs became a criminal liability over the countryside. The Government's stern answer was more and more severe laws and sentences for the next two decades. Offences punishable capitally had already leapt to nearly two hundred.

What Clare calls his 'irregular habits' began at this time. At Burghley he had been only a boy. Now he was

> with partners whose whole study was continual striving how to get beer . . . such as had got drunk the oftenest fancied themselves the best fellows. . . . But . . . though I joined my sixpence toward the bottle as often as the rest I often missed the tot that was handed round for my constitution would not have borne it.[1]

Fond of music in days when music was no affair of listening only, he learnt to play the violin, in the hope of picking up a trifle at feasts, merry-makings, or what Thomas Bewick called 'hoppings'. His acquaintances, the gipsies, taught him. He was at home with Boswells and peg-making Smiths. 'Superiors' could make him feel awkward, his freedom in danger. He was occasionally tempted to go off with 'the quiet pilfering unpro-tected race', whose incursion into village crowds often caused the law to be summarily called out. A number of poems and a shrewd prose account of this untameable people have 'within-ness' of sympathy rather than the external judgment audible in Crabbe's attributing to them so much of 'misery, vice, deceit'. Clare did not find the gipsies miserable, or very vicious, or more deceitful than the run of mankind, or thieves, except in

---

[1] *Prose*, p. 34.

small matters. They were ignorant, dirty, and almost totally unreflective, and hence no good as permanent friends; and he found the meat they ate very unpalatable. Yet

> No matter where they go or where they dwell
> They dally with the winds and laugh at hell.

II

It is not likely that, once free of militia, 'dabbling in rhyme' was thrown by for long, though dates and events become vague between 1814 and 1818. We know that by 1819 Clare had well over a hundred poems written. This is remarkable merely as proof of the peculiar energy that is always a part of genius. Most of this early work was naturally clogged with a great deal that was not poetry.

The fragmentary *Morning Walk*, as we know it from manuscript, is not in Thomsonian blank verse, as we might expect from a poem inspired by *The Seasons*. It is in traditional three-and four-stressed couplets, but its poetic climate is eighteenth century.

> Look yonder! see the rising sun
> His daily course has just begun
> Let's lightly beat the dewy grass
> And mark each object as we pass
> There the unheeded daisy grows
> There the golden kingcup blows
> There the stinking bryony weaves
> Round the hazel her scallopt leaves. . . .[1]

There is nothing here beyond a juvenile experimentation with trisyllables and tetrasyllables that was in the very air round poetry after a century of that strict attention to poetic laws which Blake had condemned as 'niggling formalism'. Clare's *Morning Walk* has points of comparison and contrast with Coleridge's early *Songs of the Pixies*. Where Coleridge was indebted to Milton, Gray, and Collins, the literary creditors of Clare's youth were Pomfret, Parnell, John Cunningham, and

[1] Peterborough Mss.

of course Thomson. But in the quotation above, already the close 'living' picture of white bryony suggests unusual perception, if nothing more.

Every penny he could save from this time onward he bought books or paper with. In 1814 his celebration of his twenty first birthday was privately to purchase a 'blank book' from a bookseller at Market Deeping. He had met J. B. Henson while listening to the Congregational dissenters, the Independents, at Helpston chapel. For this blank book Clare paid Henson the considerable sum of eight shillings—a week's wages. He paid by instalment, and at first refused to satisfy Henson's curiosity and 'side-wind enquireys' about what he could possibly want such a book for: 'I had kept the secret too long to be so easily persuaded to let it go'. Into this book he copied those of his verses which, after sifting, re-sifting, copying and altering, he thought worthy of final preservation.

Slowly he had given up his other studies—mathematics, astronomy:

> I considered walking in the track of others, and copying and dinging at things that had been found out some hundreds of years ago, had as little merit in it as a child walking in leading strings.[1]

His library consisted of Abercrombie's *Gardener's Journal*, *The Seasons*, a shattered copy rebound at home of *Paradise Lost*, *Fisher's Young Man's Companion*, *Robin Hood's Garland*, *Bonnycastle's Mensuration*, *Death of Abel*, *Joe Miller's Jests*, a *Collection of Hymns*, with some odd Pamphlets of Sermons by the Bishop of Peterborough.

This was no great equipment for a would-be poet—though Burns's Masson, Bible, Spelling Book and Grammar were little better. Clare had borrowed *Robinson Crusoe*, soon after he could read, from a boy at Glinton school, promising to return it next day. But 'in the night a great snow fell'. 'I had it a week instead of a day'. *Pilgrim's Progress* had also pleased him 'mightily' as a child. His father's reading of the Rev. John Pomfret had seemed to voice his own boyish convictions about some deep matters. He had read Gibbon's 'indefatigable traveller' Sandys, at Tom Porter's. He knew Chatterton's

[1] *Sketches*, p. 67.

'verses on Resignation' from a pictured pocket-handkerchief his mother brought him from Deeping fair. John Turnill had read him David Mallet's sad *Ballad of Edwin and Emma* while they were weeding, and he had begun an 'equally true and tragic' village story of his own under its influence. This was *The Fate of Amy*. Besides Cunningham, Pomfret, and Thomson, he knew Erasmus Darwin, Robert Bloomfield's *Wild Flowers*, and Goldsmith in extract. He read and re-read 'the prophetical parts of the *Bible*', 'the fine Hebrew Poem of Job'. He had added Izaak Walton's *Angler* to his store from the bookshop at Stamford, not long after *The Seasons*.

There is a longer list of books of perhaps a year or two later than 1814. This has some very curious items: 'Martindale's *Landsurveying*, Ball's *Astrology*, Culpepper's *Herbal*, Ray's *History of the Rebellion*, Sturm's *Reflections*, Hervey's *Meditations*, Wesley's (John Wesley's father, Samuel) *Philosophy*, L'Estrange's *Fables of Æsop*, a book on Comets, Lee's *Botany*, King's *Tracks of London Laid Open*, and *The Father's Legacy* or *Seven Stages of Life*'. His sister Sophy seems to have had one book only—*The Female Shipwright*, a 'true story' and 'a winter evening favourite' of both Clare and Sophy. Besides all these were the *Poems* of Parnell, Waller, Cobb, Fawkes, Broome, and Mrs. Hoole, and *Life* of Bampfylde Moore Carew.

He spent puzzled hours over Lee's *Botany* before abandoning its 'dark system' for practical flower-hunting with John Billings or Tom Porter. Ray, Parkinson, and Gerard, after Lee, were 'fresh air & balmy summer of a dewey morning after the troubled dreams of a nightmare'. His taste in novels was 'very limited'. *Tom Jones* and *The Vicar of Wakefield* were his staple, and *The Vicar* was re-read each winter with delight. He could not 'plod through every book in a regular mecanical way . . . but . . . I read Thomson's *Seasons* and Milton's *Paradise Lost* thro when I was a boy'. It is interesting, if idle, to speculate what a mind of the calibre of John Stuart Mill's would, in completely isolated self-dependence, have made of the 'old books of motley merits' we have given. Clare has long been accredited with an undeveloped intellect, even an insufficiency of it. Outside his own self-deprecation, and a vernacular simplicity of expression, his story holds little proof of either undevelopment or insufficiency of intellect.

But the important provenance was folk-literature, besides the popular *Seasons*, *Paradise Lost*, the *Bible*, *Pilgrim's Progress*, and *The Vicar*. Thus a relentlessly Olympian recipe for 'making a poet out of a man' might have prescribed much that Clare actually had—not forgetting his early freedom in the open-field village, least of all forgetting the cataclysm of his depriva-tion of it.

III

But it was as scholar rather than poet that he was known in Helpston during this early period. He would still 'as leave have confessed to be a robber as a rhymer'. His habits of spending Sundays in the woods called forth further adverse comment. Some now put 'criminal interpretations on my rambles'. Game-laws in those days when man set traps for man in English forests were to reach a severity, Romilly declared, unparalleled in any country. The difficulty was, as Thomas Bewick said, to convince intelligent countrymen that the fowl of the air, 'God's plenty', was created only for the rich. Much less could he be convinced about fish in flowing rivers. To this day in the fens, mobile and industrialised as the people have become, boys with bent pins like to catch their dinners by fishing in Brown's or Jones's 'drain'. Rabbits, rooks, pigeons, and eggs of larger birds had all been numerous enough to leave the villager something of his deeply rooted privilege before the eighteenth century. Yet most lordships had had game rights bestowed on favourites since the days of Norman kings. But in this, as in other country matters, when lords should take, as Crabbe said, 'such dreadful vengeance for a hare', the situation became well-nigh intoler-able. And all helped to deepen what Disraeli was later to call the 'great rift' between rich and poor which made, by the mid-nineteenth century, 'two hostile nations' of our one England.

   With temperamental readiness in the cause of the weak and unjustly oppressed, Clare championed the Billings brothers—'slandered' he declares, as poachers. He was nearly taken for a poacher himself. He had been many times in fear, reading or writing in

> . . . the briary thicket, where
> Echo keeps her mocking voice.

> . . . arguing with myself how vain
> An afterthought, 'still to keep free,'
> Made me to seek the road again,
> And own the force of liberty.

Lenient Earl Fitzwilliam might be; Clare himself had, as we
have said, 'no eye' to kill anything. When an old firelock burst
in James Billings's hand, it was prudent to go no more to the
woods 'crow-shooting'.

But at Bachelors' Hall or *The Blue Bell Inn* he could always
puzzle the village schoolmaster, 'one of the most pretending
and ignorant of men', over a pint.[1] Other neighbours, however, thought it folly in him to continue at hard work. The
parish clerk, a man of 'busy merits', offered to accompany him
to ask Lord Milton for help or advice. They were told Lord
Milton would see them, but though they waited hour after
hour, 'night came on and told us we was dissapointed'. The
porter bade them try again tomorrow, but the clerk had a
better idea and he importuned Lord Milton at a farm near
home next day. With his own axe to grind first, he produced
an 'antique box with several farthings of King Charles the
Second's reign'. There was a lively traffic in these finds
brought to light by ploughing under Enclosure. Lord Milton,
with his usual kindliness, bought box and farthings of the
worthy clerk, and promised to do something for Clare. This
may have been the time when Parker Clare was sent to the sea-
bathing infirmary at Scarborough. Unfortunately, to save
expense, Parker walked part of the way home, and spoilt the
benefit from his change.

Under the frustration of this period, Clare's companionship
with Mary Joyce finally ceased:

> fearing to meet a denial, I carried it on in my own fancies
> to every extreme, writing songs in her praise, and making
> her mine with every indulgence of the fancy.[2]

In *Sketches* he says it 'was nothing but love in idea' and

> other Marys, &c., excited my admiration, and the first
> creator of my warm passions was lost in a perplexed

[1] *Prose*, pp. 32, 33.
[2] *Life*, 1932, p. 58.

multitude of names, that would fill a volume . . . ere a
bearded chin could make the lawfull appology for my
entering the lists of Cupid.[1]

The poets whom literary criticism calls romantic all placed
great faith in human love. In Western civilisation Eros and
Agape are intricately entwined. These poets probably over-
stressed human love, coming, as they did, after a century of
insistence on Reason as Nature that had ended in a holocaust
of blood.

Clare knew, either from his attention to Pastoral or from his
own temperament the connection between suffering and understanding. As early as this he was glimpsing a possible eternity
between the everyday and the ideal. In one of his many poems
to Mary, a sonnet written soon after his determination to write
of her no more, he first stated the paradox:

> I met thee like the morning, though more fair,
> And hopes 'gan travel for a glorious day;
> And though night met them ere they were aware,
> Leading the joyous pilgrims all astray,
> Yet know I not, though they did miss their way,
> That joyed so much to meet thee, if they are
> To blame or bless the fate that bade such be . . .
> Posession has not cloyed my love, nor cursed
> Fancy's wild visions with reality. . . .[2]

Mary Joyce died unmarried at Glinton in 1838. The family,
with the gipsy's curse on it apparently fulfilled, that its male
heirs should die out, left the village soon after that year. But
between this parting in their youth and 1838, except for one
occasion in 1821, there is no evidence that these two saw, much
less spoke with each other, though they lived only two miles
apart.

His second love was Elizabeth Newbon of Ashton. In another
fragment he calls Elizabeth 'my first love really' as if the love of
Mary were on an altogether different plane. He discusses
Elizabeth in terms of country practicality and realism. 'She
was no beauty but I fancyd she was everything & our court-
ship was a long one'. Eventually Elizabeth charged him with
'sins of changing affections'. Her father, one surmises, had a

[1] *Sketches*, p. 87.
[2] *Poems*, 1934, I, p. 529.

D

fascination for Clare almost as strong as Elizabeth's. Newbon was a wheelwright, 'happy and harmless', like Cousins, the Turnills, John Cue the one-time shepherd of Ufford, one of those real country characters. Though he did not attend church, Newbon yet set great store on his Bible. He knew it 'almost by heart', applying Napier's *Key to the Revelations*, and delighting to test Clare's knowledge. He was the original of the poem *The Cottager*.

By this time Clare had added to *The Morning Walk*, *The Evening Walk*, possibly *The Fate of Amy* and *Helpstone*, though these two were not in their final form till some years later. He had tried the sonnet, after reading Miss Mitford's 'landscape poet' Charlotte Smith, in one of the eleven editions of her 1784 *Sonnets*. Early examples of this favourite among verse-forms with which he experimented later were *The Primrose* and *The Gipsy's Evening Blaze*. He wrote *The Village Funeral* in 1815. An early satire was on a certain Doctor Touch, who at Deeping gave out that he could work cures by laying his hands on the sufferers. Parker Clare was taken, in hopes of having his rheumatism alleviated, but, Clare says in his prose notes, 'the fellow did not cure them by touch but by blisters which he laid on in unmerciful sizes at half a guinea a blister.'

Other verses of the period are *To a Violet*, *The Robin*, *Reflections in Autumn*, *The Universal Epitaph*, *Noon*, and *Winter*; *The Lodge House* is a long discursive tale concerning an old haunted ruin, and *Dobbin* a rambling, still-unpublished account, many times recast, of 'an old cart-horse which was in great fame in the village for his gentleness & strength & readiness for all sorts of jobs'. There are probably many other first drafts among Clare's manuscripts that had been written by this time.

There is little to halt us in this amateur writing. 'Rhapsodies in rhyme' will hold an obvious pitfall if not disciplined in some way. The particularity of some of the images is what is striking, as well as a dawning pre-occupation with those matters which were absorbing the greatest among his contemporary poets in one form or another—freedom, love, and joy.

Meanwhile;

Poetry was a troublesomely pleasant companion annoying & cheering me at my toils I coud not stop my thoughts &

often faild to keep them till night so when I fancyd I had
hit upon a good image or natural description I used to
steal into a corner . . . & clap it down . . . upon the crown
of my hat & when I was more in a kip for thinking than
usual I usd to stop later at night to make up my lost
time. . . . My heart burnt over the pleasures of solitude &
the restless revels of rhyme that was eternally sapping my
memorys like the summer sun over the tinkling brook till
it one day shoud leave them dry & unconscious of the
thrilling joys busy anxietys & restlessness which it had
created.[1]

Of his method:

As I found nature then so I made her if an old pond with
its pendant sallows fringing its mossy sides happend to be
in the pleasant nook where I sat concealed among the
blackthorns drawing its picture I calld it a pond & so my
feelings were stirred into praise . . . then these moods often
repeated grew unperceivd into quantity on paper & then
I indulged my fancy in thinking how they woud look in
print. I . . . hid the others out of shames way as laughing-
stocks for the crowd who think it a childs occupation to
indulge in such feelings & inexcusable in a man.[2]

Circumstances, including hostile ones, combined with temperament to fix in Clare a devotion to the realities of his youth
which became so prominent a feature of his poetry:

There is nothing but poetry about the existence of childhood real simple soul-moving poetry laughter and joy of
poetry & not its philosophy & there is nothing of poetry
about manhood but the reflection & the remembrance of
what has been.[3]

IV

For the next five years his production was intensely local and
parochial—as Constable's was during these very years in East
Anglian meadows round Dedham. But behind all Clare's

[1] *Prose*, p. 32.
[2] *Prose*, pp. 52–3.
[3] *Prose*, pp. 44–5.

early evocations of country life the ring of his three pre-occupations, freedom, love, and joy, is heard. Blake, Burns, and his
contemporaries, Coleridge, Shelley, Wordsworth, and Keats,
all stress these three problems of our humanity. Each of the
three words has endured the ceaseless ebb and flow of controversy, and each is earthed in primeval myth and pre-
Christian philosophy.

Pastoral poetry is said to have ended in England with Andrew
Marvell. And so it may have done as a poetic artifice. Johnson,
assuming the pastoral genre to be some kind of apprenticeship
for poets, thought its element in *Lycidas* 'easy, vulgar, and therefore disgusting'. Theocritus the court poet of the third century
B.C. was trying to state something of what men must leave
behind them in their journey. Clare and his early poetry stand
at a much nearer, but in some ways similar, road-fork of older
and newer life.

Under the eighteenth century's determined urbanising,
through Pope himself, Ambrose Philips, the Wartons, Pomfret,
Dyer, Green, John Cunningham, and Shenstone, only a des-
sicated mock-pastoral had flourished. Yet what is important
to perceive is, not so much any unprecedented cleavage or
'dissociation of sensibility', as that never for long does the un-
remitting search among poets cease for what they conceive to
be the most direct, deep, and uncontaminated sources of both
thought and feeling.

Such search was certainly responsible for *The Seasons* as early
in the eighteenth century as 1725. Thomson achieved popular
success. But his landscape description, solemn and clamant,
gives an undeniable sense of the lonely destroying vastness of
mountain scenery almost completely annulled in a view from a
comfortably distant town-window.

Crabbe, promptly condemning Goldsmith's picture of Lishoy,
undoubtedly sought to redress what he saw as a looming senti-
mentality in poetry. And, likewise condemning the century's
'smart antithesis richly trimmed with rhyme', declaring that
except for Lady Winchilsea's *Nocturnal Reverie*, and a passage or
two in Pope's *Windsor Forest*, there was not 'a single new image
of external nature', Wordsworth proposed, in his fighting
preface to *Lyrical Ballads*, to adopt for his poetry 'the very
language of men'. Coleridge, in 1817, countered this dogma

as both impractical and useless. Remarkably soon after his secret beginnings, we find Clare determined to reinstate the nettle, thistle, and henbane of Crabbe's wasteland of 'stinking' weed into a fresh garden 'free for all'. He was aware of a cleavage between poetry's deep sources and culture: Shenstone's Pastorals 'are improperly called so'.[1] And almost from the birth of his own poetry, certainly well before his first publication, he was determining its relationship, not with any intellectual cult, but with the reality of country life. That reality, of 'hope, love, joy' came to be for him the essence of 'poesy'.

In order to hold such a reality in sight a price had to be paid, of course. By about the end of 1816 Clare was twenty-three, thoughtful and silent, expansive only after a pint of ale. And he was becoming conscious of a second paradox, in the change called 'progress' as he saw its workings all round him. 'Ye injured fields, ye once were gay'. Parts of Helpston Heath and the whole of Cowper (Copy) Green were being ploughed up: 'scarce a greensward spot remains'. Trees were being felled at an astounding rate—Round Oak, Lea Close Oak: 'Old favourite tree! art thou too fled the scene?' The woodman made him a ruler from the wood of Lea Close Oak. Landyke Bush (he usually called it Langley Bush) lasted a few years more, its store of legends a little longer still. Other places are made to lament their own degradation: 'My name will quickly be the last That's left of Swordy Well'. Rites which used to 'crown the swain's merry toils', when labour had been linked with enjoyment—of Plough Monday, Candlemas, Breakday, Maytime, Shearing, Midsummer, Lammas, Harvest, Martinmas, and Hallowe'en—were at last being swept away for good. Realising its uselessness—knowing the cause already lost, Clare could not prevent his grief. But evocations of the happy toiling country life of his childhood begin already to take on a new poignancy. The Helpston of his young manhood was a different community from that of his childhood. So we get verse about a greedy spoliation of the land in the name of progress, with a modern ring that tends to cover up its originality, and we get verse about things vanished and valued in this double sense.

Thus, his early work has at least three distinct thematic back-

---

[1] Letter to I. K. Holland of 1817: *Letters*, p. 25.

grounds: there is the closely and lovingly depicted community of pindar, hayward, shepherd and harvester, gooseherd and cow-tender, 'Gossips and Grannies'. Gleaners, nutters, herb-gatherers, woodcutters, mole-catcher, village doctress, and cress-gatherer, are all there from the days when

> master, son, and serving man and clown
> Without distinction daily sat them down.

There are the happy pictures of a teeming nature that progress could never plunder of its beauty. And there are the bitter verses—to culminate later in *The Parish*—of the tree-stripped land which enclosure evidently produced at first, and of freedom lost:

> banished now with heaths once wild and gay
> As poet's visions of life's early day . . .
> In little parcels, little minds to please,
> With men and flocks imprisoned, ill at ease.[1]

v

About the spring of 1817, acute lack of employment, as well as his secret ambition, sent him seeking work outside the 'imprisoned' catchwork gangs. He and a neighbour, Stephen Gordon, went to burn lime for a man named Wilders of Bridge Casterton, about seven miles from Helpston.

Arriving penniless, they obtained lodgings at 'a house of scant fame'. They were 'troubled with threble fares in each bed', an inconvenience Clare at least 'had never been used to'. He toiled at first night and day to collect a little money to send home—and to buy a new olive-green coat, 'a colour I had long aimed at'. At the end of the year he and Gordon went to another of Wilders's kilns, in 'a hamlet which seems . . . to have been a town of some magnitude in past times, tho' it is now nothing more than a half solitude of huts and odd farm houses scatter'd about some furlongs asunder'.[2]

---

[1] *Poems*, 1935, I, p. 420.
[2] *Sketches*, pp. 74·5.

Old Pickworth is truly one of Rutlandshire's lost villages. It is said to have been demolished by Lancastrian rebels whom Edward the Fourth defeated at Losecoat Field on the Great North Road nearby. Dr. Hoskins tells us in his essay on deserted villages of the Midlands[1] that at Pickworth traces of old floors and fireplaces have been found in casual excavation; Clare says he and Gordon dug up quantities of human bones. But, Dr. Hoskins regretfully adds: 'one cannot trace any proper report on the subject'.[1] It was a sense of the forgotten, forsaken village's past that roused Clare to his *Elegy on the Ruins of Pickworth*. Here he first voices his scepticism over Pope's triumphantly ambiguous 'Whatever is, is right'. The Pickworth verses have little in common with John Cunningham's pastel description in *Elegy on a Pile of Ruins*, though this title no doubt prompted Clare, and he borrowed the stanza of Cunningham's *Day* for many of his early pastorals. The *Elegy on the Ruins of Pickworth* indicates an horizon of sceptical inquiry, towards which, from now onward, Clare was frequently to lift his eyes.

A time was once, though now the nettle grows
    In triumph o'er each heap that swells the ground,
Where they, in buildings pil'd, a village rose,
    With here a cot, and there a garden crown'd. . . .

Mysterious cause! Still more mysterious plann'd
    (Although undoubtedly the will of heaven);
To think what careless and unequal hand
    Metes out each portion that to man is given. . . .

Almighty Power!—but why do I repine,
    Or vainly live thy goodness to distrust?
Since reason rules each provident design,
    Whatever is must certainly be just. . . .[2]

VI

To Henson of Market Deeping's repeated, inquisitive questions, Clare, on one of his visits to pay an instalment on his blank book, and 'fresh from a free application of ale at the

[1] *Essays in Leicestershire History*, p. 70.
[2] *Poems*, 1935, I, p. 53.

fair', at length disclosed something of the tremendous secret of his writing. The front page of this beautiful manuscript reveals the burning ambition. In neatest copperplate is an imitation of the title-page of a book: *A Rustic's Pastime in Leisure Hours*: *Helpstone*. 1814.

Henson had asked to see some of the poems. Clare had taken him *The Setting Sun*, and *To a Primrose*. Approving, Henson had offered to print a volume of poems by subscription. Since people must be informed before they would subscribe, Henson promised to print 300 prospectuses for one pound. The problem was—who should write the information on the prospectus. Clare thought Henson should know best what was required. Henson was emphatic that Clare should write it. In the deadlock which occurred Henson offered to print as an alternative Clare's verses on the Death of Chatteron in a pamphlet to sell to hawkers. But doubtful of both the merits of those particular verses and of penny broadsheet notice, and suspicious now of Henson's judgment concerning either prose or poetry, Clare promised to tackle the prospectus himself.

The public-house where he was staying at Casterton was anything but a place for study. But he had a three-mile walk night and morning in the clear pale atmosphere above softly swelling contours of Rutlandshire's limestone country, to yet another of Wilders's kilns at Ryhall. Here he worked alone. Already five or six attempts at the troublesome address to subscribers lay behind him. As Coleridge knew 'exuberance of mind' could hamper composition. Image and feeling in Clare pressed so abundantly as to produce a sense of chaos if much impeded by deliberation. Deliberation became too aware of inadequacy. His mind was thus considerably less well-fitted, he felt, for prose than verse. Yet new solitudes after the boundless flat of the fen had already inspired him to a fresh burst of 'rhyme'. Furthermore, he had fallen 'over head and ears' in love a third time, and the most urgent of incentives was given to publication.

On Sundays and holidays he frequented *The Flower-Pot Inn* at Tickencote. Except that this pleasant stone cottage no longer sells beer, the lovely hamlet on the banks of the Gwash rivulet must have looked for Clare much as it does today. Restoration of its famous quintuple Norman chancel arch would just have been completed. The end of the 'century of Reason' saw many churches in decay. On one of these expeditions between Pickworth and Tickencote, the sight of a young girl going across the fields sent him hastily 'to the top of a dotterel to see which way she went'. A few weeks afterwards, he met the girl again 'when going to fiddle at Stamford', and escorted her home. That summertime, among the woods where wild lilies grow, Clare and the daughter of William Turner of Walk-herd Lodge wandered in peace—except that there was a rival already in the field. Patty's parents, who, like so many in those times, had seen better days, when they knew the situation, encouraged the shoemaker as a steadier proposition than the poetry-writing lime-burner.

At long last—still working night and day at Pickworth or Ryhall—Clare saved the pound J. B. Henson demanded for printing the prospectuses—an aim 'I never lost sight of'. All that was necessary was the *Address to the Public*. Dropping down under a hedge on one of his early-morning walks to Ryhall, Clare thought of his parents' distresses, of 'labouring so hard and so vainly to get out of debt'; he pondered his 'still added perplexities of ill-timed love'. But again, instead of reasoning steadily in what Sir Herbert Read has called the 'lower tension' of prose, he was assailed by the same involuntary question as assailed Shelley in his visionary last poem: *What is life?* He 'hastily scratted down' two verses:

And what is Life?—An hour-glass on the run
A mist retreating from the morning sun
  A busy, bustling, still repeated dream;
Its length?—A minute's pause, a moment's thought;
  And happiness?—A bubble on the stream,
That in the act of seizing shrinks to naught.

What are vain hopes?—The puffing gales of morn,
That of its charms divests the dewy lawn,
  And robs each flow'ret of its gem—and dies;
A cobweb hiding disappointment's thorn,
  Which stings more keenly through the thin disguise.

The poem was later published in *Poems Descriptive of Rural Life and Scenery* with five stanzas, deformed in the final one by a change of pattern and a dragged-in moral in the approved eighteenth-century manner. Clare probably added this stanza after the subconscious sense of the poem's rhythmic unity had left him, and conscious technique alone proved unequal to its task.

Reaching Ryhall that morning with the address still un-written, before he began work, he sat down on a lime-scuttle, determined to complete one of some sort. At the end of his day, setting out with what he had composed to walk the three miles to Stamford, feeling himself 'adrift on the broad ocean of life', half-swamped by uncertainty and self-distrust, he yet decided that he could not be worse off than he was, even if the whole project were engulfed. Resting on a stone-heap, he re-read his 'Proposals for publishing by subscription a Collection of Original Trifles, on miscellaneous subjects, religious and moral, in Verse, by John Clare, of Helpstone'. Burns, we remember, had published his Kilmarnock *Trifles* by subscription, in 1786. Clare had certainly seen this by some time in 1818. In Clare's final production a quotation from Allan Ramsay is followed by the conditions of publication: the book was to cost three shillings and sixpence, and to be printed 'on a superfine yellow wove foolscap paper, in octavo size'. The matter had plainly been well thought out. Such requirements reveal Clare's interest in the layout of books, and his distrust of Henson's ideas of excellence in print, as well as in prose and poetry. Then came the Address that had cost so much labour, to three hundred as yet visionary subscribers:

> The public are requested to observe, that the Trifles humbly offered for their candid perusal can lay no claim to eloquence of composition, (whoever thinks so will be deceived,) the greater part of them being *Juvenile* produc-tions; and those of a later date offsprings of those leisure intervals which the short remittance from hard and manual labour sparingly afforded to compose them. It is hoped that the humble situation which distinguishes their author will be some excuse in their favour, and serve to make an atonement for the many inaccuracies and imper-fections that will be found in them. The least touch from the iron hand of *Criticism* is able to crush them to nothing, and sink them at once to utter oblivion. May they be allowed to live their little day, and give satisfaction to

those who may choose to honour them with a perusal, they will gain the end for which they were designed, and their author's wishes will be gratified. Meeting with this encouragement, it will induce him to publish a similar collection, of which this is offered as a specimen.

When he reached the post office at Stamford, a penny was demanded as late-postage fee. Disclaiming ownership of the precious letter, Clare 'with some shame' got it in that way,

> directed with a pencil, printed on a sheet of paper that was crumpled and grizzled with lying in one's pocket so long, and to add to its novelty sealed with shoe-maker's wax.[1]

But it brought a hundred printed Proposals within a week.

A letter from Henson demanded that Clare should meet him at *The Dolphin*, an inn in Stamford Broad Street much frequented by farmers and cattle-dealers. Clare found Henson, though he had printed a sonnet for him to see, altogether less enthusiastic, and stipulating five shillings more for the Proposals than the pound agreed on. But after a few minutes, overhearing Henson's talk, Clare's first subscriber had materialised —the Rev. Thomas Mounsey, second master, and teacher of the Greek and Latin languages, at the Stamford Free Grammar School.

For a while a mirage of possible success glittered brightly. Clare distributed his papers. There is a draft of a letter to Henson, speaking of a list of subscribers, one of which was apparently a baronet.

> Good God! How great are my Expectations! What hopes do I cherish! As great as the unfortunate Chatterton's were, on his first entry into London . . . and undoubtedly, like him, I may be building "castles in the air" but Time will prove it.[2]

Henson, Clare says later, pretended he *had* a hundred subscribers: so—'I lost a week's work to go home and arrange matters'. But the next time they met, Henson was demanding

---

[1] *Sketches,* p. 77.
[2] Peterborough Mss.

fifteen pounds before he would begin the book. And the truth about the matter of subscribers, we learn from a letter in the British Museum Correspondence, stuck at an obstinate seven. Since he had neither '15 pence nor 15 farthings' to his name Clare, for the time being, gave up all idea of publication.

Twice in his frustration he attempted to enlist in the artillery. But, being 'fresh at the time', he was let off by paying the expenses of the drink. As he was 'wanting in height', he decided later, this might be 'a better plea than the sergeant's honesty'. He would sometimes walk miles, go half a day's journey in order to write unmolested, and to avoid the shame of neighbours' questions about this failure of his high plan.

Yet—despite what must have looked like mountains of difficulty, he went on preparing poems for a possible volume. But he 'could not help playing the fool and running unnecessary expenses'. These particular expenses seem to have been taking *The Enquirer* during that winter when lime-burning was impossible and he had no other work.[1] He owed fifteen shillings for them. Tom Porter agreed to take one of the prospectuses to Thomson the bookseller who had let Clare have *The Enquirer* and who kept the New Public Library in Stamford High Street. But Thomson treated prospectuses and slender subscriber-list, intended by Clare as earnests of future payment, with contempt, and demanded his money.

At this depressing moment Edward Drury enters on the scene. Drury was about to take over the New Public Library from Thomson. He prided himself on being descended from the Elizabethan family in whose honour Drury Lane was named, and had arrived in Stamford only a few months previously. He was the son of a Lincoln printer, whose sister was the mother of John Taylor, a London bookseller and publisher. After listening to Porter's story and reading one of the leaflets so summarily rejected by Thomson, Drury promptly paid Clare's debt. Accompanied by Robert Newcomb, proprietor of *The Stamford Mercury*, he visited Helpston the following Sunday to enquire of Clare's landlord, a farmer named Clark, about Clare's character as well as his reputation as a poet:

---

[1] There is no evidence for further prolongation of Martin's story that Wilders or any other employer dismissed Clare for selling prospectuses.

'The former was open to every meddler but the latter was a secret'.[1] Announcing themselves as subscribers the two descended on the cottage. Sophy ran for Clare at Bachelors' Hall. Drury at first said little. Newcomb investigated. Clare confessed to disappointment with Henson. Whereupon Drury declared that if the poems could be honourably retrieved, not only would they be printed but he himself would pay Clare for the transaction. Newcomb invited Clare to dine with him the next day, but 'cautiously opend the door to remind me that unless I brought the Mss. I need not come'.[2]

Newcomb no doubt meant his speech lightly. But the sensitive and independent poet 'felt insulted'. In the more considered account of *Sketches*:

> I was hipt most cursedly at what ended their visit, and wish'd I had not come home . . . I have a heated spirit that instantly kindles in too hasty bursts of praise. . . . When I fancy myself injured, I cannot brook it, no more than stifle my gratitude, when I am under obligations: one flows as freely as the other, nor do I repent it.[2]

'The Autobiography', however, says Clare spent most of the next day with Drury, who looked over some poems he took, gave him a guinea, and promised to pay the rest of his debts. Henson returned the manuscript with 'some reluctance' when Ann Clare went over with a note to demand it later that week. Soon after this, Henson 'did some dirty doings with Satan', and left Deeping.[2]

Once the whole of the manuscript was in Drury's hands, he invited the opinion of the 'Rev. Mr. Twopenny', of Little Casterton. Mr. Twopenny returned the packet with a 'cold note'. He had no objection to 'raising the poor man a small subscription'. The poems appeared to him to possess very small merit. A more favourable critic was Sir John English Dolben, of Finedon Place, Northamptonshire, ancestor of the poet who was Bridges' friend. And Clare resumed work in Wilders's garden in the spring of 1819 with hope on his horizon.

[1] *Prose*, p. 61.
[2] The accounts in *Sketches* (pp. 81, 82, 83), and in *Prose* (pp. 61, 62) differ as to when Clare first went to see Drury.

During the next few months he spent much of his leisure, on Sunday mornings and in wet weather when lime-burning was not possible, reading at Drury's, or getting 'new tunes for my fiddle'. He collected about a hundred and fifty tunes in his music books, old dances and songs, eighteenth-century horn-pipes and jigs and a sprinkling of waltzes, marches, and songs by Dibdin. Every poem he wrote he took to Drury. There was some kind of agreement which Clare admits he signed. At Drury's he met Dr. Bell, an acquaintance of 'Peter Pindar' (John Wolcot). Bell was evidently of like character with the author of *Apple Dumplings and a King*. This editor of *The Banisher of the Blue Devils* provided Clare with the humorous name for the melancholy later to assail him. Another friend of these months was Isaiah[1] Knowles Holland, Nonconformist minister of Deeping; but unfortunately this sympathetic adviser left for St. Ives in October of this year.

Clare worked for Wilders till November, when a drop in wages—'from eighteen pence to fourteen pence per diem' *The London Magazine* of January, 1820, tells us—made him leave, though he liked both place and employer, and left with regret. Drury had already told him his poems were in the hands of the London printer, his cousin John Taylor. He had read from Taylor's letters high praise of them. The day Clare left Casterton, he called on Drury, and was invited to Octavius Gilchrist's to meet Taylor.

Octavius Gilchrist, a genial Stamford grocer, was not only an authority on the Elizabethan dramatists and a contributor to Leigh Hunt's *Reflector*, but a friend of that enigma of human character, William Gifford, and a contributor to Gifford's savage and influential *Quarterly Review*. Here was possible luck from a curious angle. During the next year or two Gilchrist became one of the most loyal and disinterested of Clare's friends.

Gilchrist's guest that day, John Taylor, was the son of a small Retford publisher of Scottish extraction. The enterprising young Taylor had gone to London in 1803. He had spent some time, first in the House of Lackington, at the famous 'Temple of the Muses', and then with Vernor and Hood, where he had met that firm's country author, Robert Bloomfield. James

---

[1] *Not* 'Isaac', as given in *Life*.

Augustus Hessey, also an apprentice in the flamboyant Lackington House in Finsbury Square, had been no more satisfied with it than John Taylor. In 1806, these two serious young men formed a partnership to set up a new bookselling and printing house at 93 Fleet Street. By 1819 they had built up a progressive business. Not content merely to meet the supposed demands of the growing reading public, they had already published for Hazlitt, Henry Francis Cary, and John Hamilton Reynolds. Taylor was soon to add Lamb, De Quincey, and Landor to their list. They had a new poet—John Keats. Taylor was himself an accurate scholar and a writer, though of strange tastes. He had a turn for vexed questions. His was the solution of 'Junius' as Sir Philip Francis—that riddle that seems so unimportant now. Later Taylor became an authority on Currency, and a student of Theology, evolving theories about the Great Pyramid. According to his early friends, the ruling features of his mind were 'order, precision, exactness and fact'.

But on 'bull-running day' at Stamford, at which traditional festival (according to William Hone's *Every-Day Book*) a bull was jostled into the river by a crowd of completely unarmed men and finally slaughtered for the poor, John Taylor was much taken with what he called Clare's 'meekness and simplicity'. He told the shy guest that his poems were already in the press. Indeed, Taylor hinted—much might be expected of them.

VII

At Helpston, whilst Clare had been away, the family fortunes had reached a disastrously low ebb. Two years' rent was owing. The cottage was to be given up. Parker and Ann were to move to the parish house. The officer had already branded their goods and set them down in the parish books. This miserable matter of rent was settled by Drury—and years after exacted as part of Clare's debt to him.

On returning to Casterton and lime-burning in the spring of 1819, Clare had resumed his love for Patty Turner. Patty, too, was deeply involved. When she saw John coming, she would run and rescue her clean gingham from the hedge, and put it on, 'whether it was dry or not'. But at home, during the previous winter, Clare had met Betty Sell, a field-working girl of sixteen from the neighbouring village of Southorpe, whose black ringlets he commends. His verses of this year, *To Patty under a Cloud*, and *The Adieu*, betray a variety of minds, an unashamed lustihead, and a natural reluctance to be trammelled just at the point when escape might be possible. His youth could not help fancying 'woman made for joy', nor feeling that at the moment life had all manner of possibilities. 'Long smothered affection for Mary revivd with my hopes & as I expected to be on a level with her bye and by I thought then I might have a chance of success'.[1] So that, when Patty was unable to conceal her situation, 'which marriage alone coud remedy', her parents declared that 'as she had made her bed hard she shoud lie on it'. Clare, like Burns toward the Armours, felt 'stubbornly disposd to leave them the risk of her misfortune'.

Moral pressure was at once exercised, not only in this matter of women, but about drinking; certainly by Drury, probably by Gilchrist and Holland. It was partly Clare's own fault. The gay self-mockery of the 'poor rude clown' who 'like the Poet Marvell had not sixpence to bless himself' could too easily become a thong from others. Burns had rapidly found himself unable to support the myth of the 'heaven-taught ploughman'. Clare's situation of finding the one avenue of possible escape lined by friends who insisted on assuming roles of adviser and patronising benefactor was difficult enough. But he had, among those dramatic contradictions which make up personality, that which often goes with self-effacing gentleness—obstinacy; and beneath that, well concealed, the element of iron we have noted—inflexible determination and independence.

Yet desire in him was strongly linked with affection and loyalty. When Patty told him of her parents' harshness to her, he 'could stand out no longer'. 'I gave her money till we should be married'. In *Sketches*, the account for John Taylor's eye written about a year after this, Regency realism combined with individual forthrightness to sum the situation thus:

[1] *Prose*, p. 64.

WOODCROFT CASTLE IN 1812

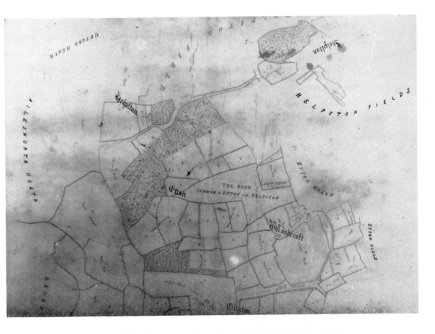

SKETCH-MAP OF HELPSTON UNENCLOSED, 1772

STAMFORD IN 1794

BURGHLEY HOUSE IN 1782

I was little fit or inclined for marrying, but my thought-
less and ram-headed proceedings, as I was never in all my
life anything else but a fool, committing rashly and repent-
ing too late ... and ... my easy nature, either in drinking
or anything else, was always ready to submit to persuasions
of profligate companions ... when ... not only health
but my life has often been on the eve of its sacrifice, by an
illness too ... disgusting to mention.[1]

Two notions may emerge here according to the reader's way of
looking at things. The first is of some looseness in Clare's which
might have continued since his spell at Burghley or at least
since catchwork days. A second notion from *Sketches* may be of
a Rousseau-like zeal for confession. Besides belonging to the
Regency period, Clare had the natural convictions in social and
sexual matters of the deeply pastoral. We shall be able to
observe this instinctive outlook in conflict with experience as
well as with a grimly retributive strain in the religious confusions of the day, until eventually his strange compromise was
made. If we want proof of contradiction in his mind over his
dilemma, we have them in two poems of this period; from *An
After-Repentance*:

> But parsons' lessons fools deceive:
>   Their pocket fees their preachings suit:
> Without we wed, they'd make's believe
>   To taste of love's forbidden fruit.
> Good Lord! I tremble at the crime,
>   A sinful, sad, unruly lout;
> I quake, I quake at gossip time,
>   Whose tongue blabs every secret out.[2]

Country Sweethearts, freer from attitudinising, is perhaps better
evidence of both man and poet:

> I'll ne'er walk at even grim,
>   When the night is glimpt wi' grey;
> When the light is waxing dim;
>   Deeds are done at closing day.
> Ever sin' by blossom'd bean

[1] *Prose*, p. 86.
[2] *Poems*, 1935, I, p. 243.

E

While the gnats were dancing by,
Ye did on my bosom lean,
Aye the tear's bin in my eye.

Ever sin' ye pass'd the morn
    When ye little dreampt a spy,
Meeting Dolly 'hind the thorn,
    Aye the tear's bin in my eye.
Ever sin' ye vow'd to wed,
    And I prov'd wi' many a sigh
Ye'd the vow to many made,
    Aye the tear's bin in my eye.

Sweet the tear shines on thee, love,
    Which I soon will wash away;
Tenderness has won me, love,
    Fear thou not the even grey.
Sin' we sat by beans in bloom,
    I have bin the ring to buy;
Think no harm from that shall come,
    Wipe the tear from either eye.[1]

There was a scheme in the winter of 1819 for him to go to London for two months' training 'in the capacity of a schoolmaster'. But already Taylor, so unerring in his knowledge of genius, so poor a judge of men, was writing of the high moral character necessary for such a position. Clare a village schoolmaster? It flashes a moment. Daring to ruminate no more beneath the forest's 'wind-shaken trees'? Income, if small, assured. But the plan for training was forgotten, and it was not to be.

On practical, common-sense, and economic grounds—'I had been as well off if I had married five years earlier than I did'—persuading himself he deeply wished it, he married the Maid of Walkherd on the 16th March of the following year. Two months later their first child, a daughter, was born. The marriage did not turn out a conspicuous failure. Patty did not furnish Clare with any 'exact and copious Recipe of "How to make a Husband compleatly miserable"'. Once, in the inauspicious beginning, he feared his wife might 'turn out a termagant' being one of the 'most obstinate of womenkind'.

[1] *Poems*, 1935, I, p. 248

But about a year after this, he could report to Taylor that he had found out he possessed 'a more valuable article' than he at first expected, and that 'Pat & myself now begin to know each other & live happily'.

Patty, who could read but not write, was in general good-tempered, active, and later, a great talker—a typical Martha. Under her management the cottage was spotless and her 'coil' was economical; but even had the age been more auspicious, good housewifery alone could not have saved them from the worst poverty. In time, we know, Patty joined the moralists, to impress on Clare that his ills were due primarily to idleness and weakness of nature; yet we do not hear of help asked that was not given. There was, however, a wealth of emotion in Clare's temperament that Patty could neither share not fulfil, nor, from the first, even hope to comprehend. A fount of good sense and reason in him mingled strongly with ardour and idealism. Only after a long struggle did the spring of emotion finally go underground into that dark alembic of the mind, to emerge distilled in the purity of the later lyrics.

ESSAY IN POPULARITY 1819–1824

I

POEMS Descriptive of Rural Life and Scenery, by John Clare, a Northamptonshire peasant, was published by Taylor and Hessey, and E. Drury, on the 16th of January, 1820. The first edition of a thousand copies disappeared like lightning. The story of the peasant-poet was in every poetry-lover's thoughts. His name was on every literary sensationalist's tongue-end, in London. A second edition, also of a thousand copies, vanished in the same way. In May a third followed that. Before the end of the year a fourth edition was printed.

Clare's friend Holland brought the first tidings to Helpston. He opened the door eagerly; 'laughed as he shook me by the hand'; Clare read the astounding news on his face.

A new era began in this hitherto quiet life, in which events crowded and strange faces jostled. In February Clare was invited to Milton Park. Drury sent one of his own shirts, advising him not to pay the visit in his Sunday clothes, which were, Drury said, "more suitable to a Squire of high degree than humble John Clare". In the servants' hall at Milton Clare could neither eat nor drink 'for thought', but Lord Milton's quiet unaffectedness, when he sent for his guest, soon set him at rest. Milton bade him 'beware of booksellers', and on his departure

> they gave me a handful of money the most that I had ever possesd in my life together & I felt almost sure I should be poor no more there was seventeen pounds.[1]

A few weeks later Henry Manvers Pierrepont, brother-in-law of the Marquis of Exeter, brought an invitation to Burghley for

[1] *Prose*, p. 68.

the following Sunday. When Sunday came it was snowing un-
mercifully, and, fearful that his shoes would be in 'a dirty condition for so fine a place', Clare put off the five-mile walk till
next day. When he arrived, the porter informed him he should
not have delayed for hail nor snow, nor yet 'tho it rained knives
and forks with the tynes downward'. Cursing his hard-nailed
shoes along the marble corridors and oak floors, Clare was
ushered into the presence of the Marquis, who received him
kindly, regretting that Lady Sophia his sister could not see
him, as she was very ill and had sat up too long expecting him
the day before; he told him that he had no room in his gardens
for work at present, but that he would allow him '15 guineas a
year for life', and, seeing Clare's embarrassment, suggested he
had better go, or he would lose his dinner in the servants' hall.

A month or two after this he was invited to Holywell Hall,
the seat of General Birch Reynardson, descendant of that Lord
Mayor of London in 1649 who suffered imprisonment for his
loyalty to the cause of King Charles. At Holywell, dining again
in the servants' hall, Clare at first mistook the governess for the
General's wife. Sensing his blunder, he was later embarrassed
to find the 'pretty impertinent girl', 'mischievously familiar to
a mind less romantic than my own', loitering in the path of his
way home. She begged him to write to her; but

> fancying that she only wanted me to write love letters to
> have the pleasure to talk about them my second mind
> wrote a very cold one in which I inserted the "Second
> Address to a Rosebud in Humble Life".[1]

Still another host was Mr. Hopkinson, a magistrate, of the
village of Morton. That country potentate sent a note saying
that a horse would be at the cottage at nine in the morning,
leaving Clare 'no option wether I chuse to go or not'. Soon
after his arrival at Morton Mrs. Hopkinson

> took me upstairs to show me a writing desk which she
> told me to consider as my own & showd me at the same
> time all the draws & their contents of Paper Pens Ink
> saying that she expected I woud make use of it & hoped
> I woud write something every day she woud find me

[1] *Prose*, pp. 73–4.

plenty of paper but when the upshot came & after I had
exhausted my whole budget of thanks for the present she
begd to caution me that I shoud not take it away with me
that it was mine every time I came & as long as I staid
but she coud not part with it.[1]

Mrs. Hopkinson next insisted on taking her prize the round of
the village. Clare, seeing that the busily spinning housewives
were interested in neither himself nor his hostess, was 'obliged
to tell her I was not fond of such visiting'. Back in the magis-
terial drawing-room, her daughters having quarrelled with her
and retired upstairs, the lady proceeded to a criticism of *Poems
Descriptive*. With suggestions for inclusions in the list of bene-
factors, and for improvement of some of the verses, she read
aloud

> in a loud confident voice like the headboy in a school who
> is reckoned a good reader & tho she met with words
> frequently that she did not understand [she] woud jar
> them over with an unnecessary mutter as if she thought
> you woud take no notice or did not understand.[2]

At dinner that night, Mr. Hopkinson voiced his intention of
'mentioning' Clare to Lord Milton and Lord Exeter. Then he
revealed himself as the—fortunately not common—type who,
'if you told anything as an interesting story or fact' next day
repeated your story 'word for word as his own'. On a walk to
Belvoir Castle with this arch-bore, a whistling labourer excited
his suspicion, and Clare was commanded to go the other side
of the plantation to watch which way the 'poacher' went. 'I
tryd to convince him that the whistle was a song tune but it was
no use . . .'

At home letters rained. Mrs. Eliza Louisa Emmerson, wife of
a London picture-dealer and collector, began her long friendship and 'poetic communing' on the 7th of February, praising
his poems and his 'genius' and sending a copy of Young's *Night
Thoughts*. On the 12th Taylor enclosed a letter from Admiral
the Hon. William Waldegrave, first Baron Radstock, with a copy
of Blair's *Sermons*, and a recommendation from the Admiral to

[1] *Prose*, p. 76.
[2] *Prose*, p. 76.

'peruse those Sermons on Prosperity, on Adversity, and on Humility'. The Admiral himself had derived valuable instruction from them. As Naval Governor of Newfoundland, Nelson's old friend had quelled a mutiny on board H.M.S. *Latona* by nicely mingling threats to blow the ship out of the water with exhortations to his sailors to repent. Radstock was also author of *The Cottager's Friend* or 'A Word in Season to him who is so fortunate as to possess a Bible or New Testament and a Book of Common Prayer', a manual in its twentieth edition in 1816. His other book was *The British Flag Triumphant*. Very soon the fire-eating old Admiral, with characteristic energy, had begun a subscription list for Clare to secure him at least a measure of independence:

> Taylor & Hessey inserted a hundred pounds in their name at the top of the list & the good Lord Fitzwilliam gave me a hundred pounds from a letter which Taylor sent who . . . mentioned Keats . . . to whom his Lordship gave £50.[1]

Another correspondent was Dawson Turner, botanist, antiquary, and friend of John Sell Cotman. Turner saw in Clare the herald of a cultivated peasantry, but warned him against any misguided attempt to escape from his humble station. Still another was Captain Markham Sherwill, author of *Ascent to the Summit of Mont Blanc*, 1825, and of *Poems*, 1832. Sherwill importuned the newly-made baronet Sir Walter Scott about Clare. Scott sent two pounds by Sherwill, and a copy of *The Lady of the Lake*. Probably disapproving of anything that looked like an attempt to revive a patronage happily defunct, Scott refused to write his name in it. Rebuffed, Clare wrote a letter from the standpoint of what he now hoped was for him poetry's franchise:

> . . . If the pride in notice of great men be a greater vanity I have it sure enough.[2]

To make sure against charity, he enclosed a copy of *Poems Descriptive*. As far as we know, Scott did not reply. The article which Radstock urged him to use his influence for with Lock-

1 *Prose*, p. 71, Peterborough Mss.
2 Peterborough Mss.

hart further recommended Clare to remain a happy peasant rather than waste time striving to become a mediocre poet.

New friends who appeared nearer home were Herbert Marsh, Bishop of Peterborough, and his German wife Marianne. Marsh had studied at Leipzig, translated between 1793 and 1801 Michaelis's *Introduction to the New Testament*, and stood up fierily to those who condemned his efforts to renew historical controversy in the Church. Mrs. Marsh's notes to Clare, covering almost the next score of years, and accompanying comforts, medicine, books, invitations to the palace, but never advice, are refreshingly free from the least hint of class-conscious patronage.

But not all whom Elia might have punned off as 'knock-eternal' visitors were as tactful or as welcome as Marianne Marsh. There was Preston, with a portmanteau of his own unpublishable Mss. There were those who arrived at nine o'clock on Monday morning, in the midst of Patty's washing or cleaning:

> carriages . . . filld with gossiping gentry . . . was tempted by curiosity more than anything else to . . . know wether I really was the son of a thresher & a labouring rustic as had been stated . . . & on finding me a vulgar fellow that mimickd at no pretensions but spoke in the rough way of a thoroughbred clown they soon turnd to the door.[1]

One 'dandified gentleman' proceeded to catechise Clare on his reading, hoping the poet 'had a fondness for books' as he wished to have the pleasure of making him a present of some:

> he then begd my walking stick & after he had got it he wanted me to write my name on the crook . . . he then asked me insulting liberties respecting my first acquaintance with Patty & said he understood that in the country the lower orders made their courtship in barns & pigsties & asked me whether I did I felt very vexd & said it might be the custom of the high orders for aught I knew as experience made fools wise in most matters but I assured him he was very wrong respecting that custom among the lower orders . . . after he had gossiped an hour he said "Well I

---

[1] *Prose,* p. 69.

promised to give you a book but after examining your library I dont see that you want anything as you have a great many more than I expected".[1]

Chauncy Hare Townshend, Hartley Coleridge's friend, whose *Jerusalem* had been the Cambridge Prize poem of 1817, and who was still a student at Trinity Hall, paid Clare two visits in the spring of 1820. The first was not a success because Clare, caught shabby and dirty, was embarrassed, with too many 'hums and ha's'. But on the second occasion, inspired 'with a pint of John Barleycorn', and in one of his 'sunshiny moments', 'a new man' with 'too many tongues', Clare broke through Townshend's youthful affectation of dandyism, and they had a rallying talk about poetry and poets. Over forty years later, countering a story in Martin's best manner of how the 'perfumed' visitor at first mistook Clare for a ferocious highwayman, Townshend recalled the 'fine intellectual countenance' of the poet and the pleasure of their conversation.

But least imperfect sympathies of all were with the butler-archæologist, Edmund Tyrell Artis, discoverer of the Roman site at Castor, and with Henderson, the gardener-botanist. Artis was busy with *The Durobrivae of Antoninus*; Castor had the most extensive archæological remains then known in the country. He was also author of *Antediluvian Phytology*. Both these two beautiful books are now rare. Through these men Clare received a second invitation to Milton:

> they were . . . well-informed men not unacquainted with books & I never met with a party of more happier & heartier fellows in my life there was Artis up to the neck in the old Roman coins & broken pots of the Romans & Henderson never wearied with hunting after the emperor butterfly & the hornet sphinx in the Hanglands Wood & the orchises on the Heath.[2]

II

Most reviews of *Poems Descriptive* were following the lead given by John Taylor in his able and disarming Introduction.

[1] *Prose*, p. 72.
[2] *Prose*, p. 75.

Having spoken of the attention due to the poems' intrinsic merit, Taylor pronounced the poet 'the least favoured by circumstances, and the most destitute of friends, of any that ever existed'. Clare, Taylor then suggested, was in the position of the early poets who had no traditions to guide them. His innovations followed that 'mode of procedure, by which all languages have been formed and perfected'. Many of these unfamiliar expressions were indeed not new, but were among the oldest in the language, preserved by oral tradition. Then he extolled Clare as 'a child of nature', a phrase bound to excite both literary and popular interest. It linked what Taylor had just said with Wordsworth's 'very language of men' in his preface to *The Lyrical Ballads*, and with Coleridge's countering of Wordsworthian dogma in *Rustic life and Human Diction* of *Biographia Literaria*, in 1817. Such a phrase worked on popular as well as literary curiosity, since the two were still undivided in our modern sense. The Burns sensation, as well as Chinese travel, Pacific and Nile exploration, had given rise more than ever to contradictory ideas about primitive man. Here was a titbit savouring of Dryden's 'noble savage' controversy popped cunningly down with the best morning papers.

The *London Magazine* for March 1820, reviewed *Poems Descriptive* next to Smart's *Song to David*. The article in the *Quarterly* for May, prepared by Gilchrist but rounded off by Gifford himself, gave generous praise to both poems and poet. The *Gentleman's Magazine*, the *Antijacobin Review*, and the *Monthly Magazine* were willing to pass over Clare's 'vulgarisms'. The *New Monthly* compared him to Theocritus, and praised his acquaintance with 'that least known of languages, that of the human heart'. The critic of the *Eclectic Review* wisely scented danger: 'If, instead of thinking them "very clever considering they are by a day-labourer", our readers agree with us in conceding to them a high degree of poetical merit quite independent of the circumstances of their author, they will be prepared to enter with the requisite sympathy into the details of his history.' In the *Morning Post*, through Lord Radstock's influence, poems, news of Clare, and letters from his admirers, appeared almost daily for some months. In America the *Analectic Magazine* reviewed the *Poems* with approval.

There existed in 1820 a considerable poetry-reading public.

It had grown steadily among the middle class of the previous fifty years, nourished by wider education, by circulating libraries fathered by the bookseller-poet Ramsay, by book-clubs, debating societies, and lectures. It was exploited by enterprising purveyors of cheap books, such as Bell, Cooke, and Lackington. The genius of Scott in 1805, and the genius of Byron in 1812, had captured popular imagination, and the genius of Constable and Murray had exploited both to the full. Astonishing prices were being given for copyright, a host of new periodicals appeared to 'guide' the public, poetry became a fashion and a rage, and the author of *Childe Harold*, the most popular poet, was at once the hero and the scandal of the day.

It is not surprising that this zest for poetry, genuine enough potentially, should be erratic, limited, and by no means com-mensurate with any considered estimate of either the more immediately perceptive or of posterity. It gave Scott and Byron full measure of praise and reward. But it naturally failed to recognise some greater, and it applauded many less. Taylor wrote to Clare in August, 1820, of *Lamia*: 'We have some diffi-culty in getting through 500 Copies of his [Keats's] work, though it is highly spoken of in the periodical Works.' Shelley's circle of admirers was lamentably small. The five hundred copies of Wordsworth's *Excursion*, 1814, were not sold out till 1820. Southey, that prodigy of industry, said he would be sur-prised if five hundred copies of *The Curse of Kehama* sold within seven years. Yet many besides Scott, Byron, Moore, and Camp-bell reaped rich rewards. Murray could give Crabbe £3,000 for his copyrights in 1819. Ten thousand copies of 'Croesus' Rogers's *Pleasures of Memory* sold between 1801 and 1819. Milman had five hundred guineas for *The Fall of Jerusalem*. The success of *Poems Descriptive* was partly due to this wide-spread interest in poetry, partly due to good publicity, only a very little to how fresh and original a voice Clare's really was. A vogue in 'country' poetry had been increasing since the turn of the century. Besides Bloomfield's *The Farmer's Boy*, there had been *The Happy Villager* by Richard Wallis, *The Distressed Village* by William Golden, *A Village Romance* by Jane Elson. Clare's publisher undoubtedly realised that he had found his peasant-poet rather late, and that the popularity of 'village literature' might not last much longer. Those who, when prodded by a youthful Taylor, applauded this volume of Clare's apprentice verse could hardly be expected to catch, among a host of 'mock-birds', the authentic lyric of a finer note. Would John Taylor, growing ever more cautious as he grew older, distinguish it himself?

Besides the earlier verse already mentioned, *Poems Descriptive of Rural Life and Scenery* contained the *Address to Plenty*, as well as *Dawnings of Genius, Familiar Epistle to a Friend* in the Fergusson and Burns manner, and descriptive pieces like *Falling Leaves, Summer Morning*, and *Summer Evening*; poems of an experimental realism were *Dolly's Mistake, My Mary, A Country Girl*, and *Lubin*; about a dozen other songs and ballads are now of little importance; and there were some twenty-four interesting sonnets. Frugality of epithet, vigour and originality of verbs, and an instinct for crisp vowels to produce sharply etched images, give directness and direction to much of the verse. Written in the same rhythm as *Lines from among the Euganean Hills, The Address to Plenty* has not, as Sir Herbert Grierson points out, Shelley's misty splendours and vastness of vision. It has instead a naïve sincerity and humorous balance. Clare has tasted success. This is what he asks of it:

> Leaves are fled, that once had power
> To resist a summer shower;
> And the wind so piercing blows,
> Winnowing small the drifting snows,
> The summer shade of loaded bough
> Would vainly boast a shelter now. . . .
>
> Oh, how blest 'mid these alarms,
> I should bask in Fortune's arms,
> Who, defying every frown,
> Hugs me on her downy breast,
> Bids my head lie easy down,
> And on winter's ruins rest.
> So upon the troubled sea,
> Emblematic simile,
> Birds are known to sit secure,
> While the billows roar and rave,
> Slumbering in their safety sure,
> Rock'd to sleep upon the wave,
> So would I still slumber on,

Till hour-telling clocks had gone,
And from the contracted day,
One or more had click'd away.
Then with sitting wearied out,
I, for change's sake, no doubt,
Just might wish to leave my seat,
And, to exercise my feet,
Make a journey to the door,
Put my nose out, but no more. . . .

Troubles, then no more my own,
Which I but too long had known,
Might create a care, a pain.
Then I'd seek my joys again,
Pile the fire up, fetch a drink,
Then sit down again and think. . . .[1]

Clare's attitude from the first to John Taylor's cautious over-editing (a caution so curiously at variance with expressly-uttered and excellent theory), is important. Most of the manuscripts which we know went up to Taylor for the first two volumes are clearly-enough copied, and except for 'No Stops or Punctuation Attempted', need not surely have proved so very troublesome. About emendation Clare was emphatic:

Bad spelling may be corrected by the amenuensis, but no word is to be altered.[2]

And while the book was in the press:

'Eggs on' in the *Address to the Lark*—whether provincial or what I cannot tell but it is common with the vulgar (I am of that class) & heartily desire no word of mine to be altered.[2]

The word "twit-a-twit" (if a word it may be called) you will undoubtedly smile at but I wish you to print it as it is for it is the Language of Nature & that can never be disgusting.[2]

Condemning the 'old threadbare epithets of "sweet-singing cuckoo", "love-lorn nightingale", and "sparkling brooks"', he added, in a letter to Taylor of about this time, that he thought

[1] *Poems*, 1935, I, pp. 46, 50, 51.
[2] Peterborough Mss.

Southey's 'mouthings' had something of this effect of choking poetry's deep springs. His poetic aim, instinctive for only a short time, was growing clearer. Its intention was, and this he was claiming as his own particular angle in the Wordsworth-Coleridge outlook, by using the countryman's traditional words for unashamed invigoration, but not for artificial simplicity, to set sharply-seen, piercingly-felt images in poetry as close as possible to their originals—nature being 'the very essence & soul of Poesy'. His reading was still vestigial and unmethodical. That could never be other. But constant cross-reference between poetic reading and the stuff of folk-experience around him— once he claimed poethood through his first publication— rapidly made his aim conscious. Wordsworth's far richer, far more widely-ranging and intellectually self-confident originality could not have been practised with clearer immediacy. Most of the pieces in *Poems Descriptive* do not rise much above the level of *The Idiot Boy*, *Goody Blake*, or of Coleridge's *The Three Graves*. The pitfalls of this kind of poetry were different for Clare; but the simplicity and directness of his vision did not fade with the years. It grew, if narrower, keener, more and more penetrating.

III

The Regent stage-coach conveyed passengers from *The George Inn*, Stamford, to *The George and Blue Boar*, Holborn, within fourteen hours. At six one morning early in March, Clare left *The George*, Stamford, in company with Octavius Gilchrist. As they 'glided along in the heavy sweeing coach', Clare, feeling 'as if some stranger soul had jumped into my skin', saw Oliver Cromwell's birthplace at Huntingdon, Cowper's 'mellancholy-looking garden' at Olney, and amused himself with watching the varying features of scenery. As they approached the City, lamps lining the roads 'diminished in the distance to stars'.

On the night of their arrival, Madame Vestris was singing *The Meeting*, a song of Clare's set to music by Haydn Corri. Too late that first evening for Covent Garden, where Madame Vestris was, Clare, with Gilchrist and their host, Gilchrist's brother-in-law, the jeweller Burkhardt, walked to Westminster

Bridge. Clare was disappointed. He found the Thames 'less in my eye than Whittlesea Meer'.

He saw Kean and Macready in plays adapted from *Ivanhoe*, at Drury Lane and Covent Garden; and Munden and Amery in 'bad' farces accompanying the plays. Dining with John Taylor, he met the perennially black-coated Hessey, who sang, played the violin, and was a favourite with young ladies. Taylor introduced him to big, blunt, roughly-dressed, piously evangelical Lord Radstock. Radstock, in turn, presented him to Mrs. Emmerson. 'Emma' or E.L.E., had a large circle of literary acquaintance; she had befriended several young writers besides Clare, and she contributed much trivial rhyme to the lesser periodicals of the period. Her visitor's shy direct-ness soon broke through her veneer of affectations. At Taylor's, too, Clare met H. F. Cary, the translator of Dante. He met, too, the witty J. H. Reynolds, who had already published *Safie, an Eastern Tale*, and *The Naiad*, but who was later to for-sake poetry, counting his fame sufficient in being Keats's 'affectionate and steady friend'. Clare was taken to see Peter De Wint, landscape painter of cool, grey fenny distances and warm wheatfields; to meet William Hilton, recently elected to the Academy, and accounted by some the first historical painter of the age. Hilton's portrait of Clare, painted on this visit to London, is now companion to Hilton's Keats in the National Portrait Gallery. Clare wears his green coat, yellow waistcoat, and bright loose tie. The brilliant blue of his eyes and the waving light brown hair add to the eloquence of colouring. The nose is delicately moulded beneath the high forehead, the mouth sensitive but tranquil; the chin not so firm as Keats's chin, nor as Lamb's in Hazlitt's Elizabethan-ruffed portrait; but firm. The whole is a vivid impression, pastoralist, peasant, and poet welded as they should be; 'C in alt', as Hood said; no 'noble in disguise', which Clare at no time had ambition to simulate. But certainly Lamb's 'princely Clare'.

He was at home again at the end of the first week in March. Marriage with Patty at the church of Casterton Magna took place on the 16th. John Turner, Patty's uncle, and Sophy Clare, signed as witnesses. Martha Turner Clare made her mark. There was no room in the cottage at Helpston, and Patty remained at Walkherd till the birth of her child Anna

Maria on the 1st or 2nd of June. A project that Lord Milton was to build the poet a cottage encouraged Clare to a poem about essentials: the cottage was to be thatched, so that sparrows could build in the eaves, and swallows paste their nest beside the chimney-tops; sand sifted on the floor would be as comfortable as carpets; the garden with sweet-brier 'and old man's beard' must not be too fine: and there were to be shelves all round and a corner-cupboard 'for the books'. But the cottage proposal was still-born.

Yet in the next few weeks, for the briefest of spring-times, Clare came near realising that intellectual freedom, out of which alone, Quiller-Couch assured us a hundred years later, great writing can emerge. By the end of April Radstock had collected a hundred pounds. With Earl Fitzwilliam's hundred, and the hundred 'advanced' by Taylor and Hessey, this, with smaller subscriptions amounting in all to three hundred and seventy-five pounds, was invested in Navy Five per Cents. The investment was held in trust to Clare by Taylor, who took Richard Woodhouse, lawyer and friend of Keats, as joint trustee in September. The half-yearly dividend of £9.7.6., which fell to £7.17.6. in 1823, was paid through the publisher. In May the second Earl Spencer, collector of the finest library in Europe of its date, by the good offices of Clare's friend Dr. Bell of Stamford, gave him an annuity of £10, also to be paid through his publishers. Relating these facts with benevolence's occasional lack of reticent manners, Taylor could announce in the preface of Clare's next book that the poet's income was £43.15.0.

The modest dream of *The Address to Plenty* seemed realised. Clare felt independent, secure as to money-matters: he would not therefore, he said, 'be much in love with field-labour for some time to come'. He was reading Dryden, and Johnson's Dictionary, Lord Milton's gifts. Pope for 'harmony of numbers' surpassed all he had ever known. Determined to 'care no fig' for poetic 'fashion', he could not quite understand the so emphatic reaction of Wordsworth, Lamb, Hunt, and Hazlitt, to Pope's 'cuckoo couplets'. He wanted to see Bloomfield's *Banks of Wye*. Returning Gilchrist's 'Wordsworth', he begged the loan of a 'Byron'. He was writing at a great rate—already he had enough for a second volume. He begged Gilchrist:

"Please to put James Simpson in mind of a good fair jar of ink." He thought 'Currie's Burns', which Radstock had promised, a good book to have; Burns was so much better a poet than Ramsay. Gaily he instructed Taylor not to charge Hilton for frame and glass of the portrait, but to 'pay him at my account'. He was afraid that his new long poem *The Peasant Boy*, already completed, might be thought plagiaristic: it had some likenesses to James Beattie's *Minstrel*, which he was reading for the first time.

Spring passed into summer. Clare and Patty were installed in the adjoining tenement to the old cottage at Helpston. And gradually Clare became aware that the 'small fortune' which benevolence had assured to him was in fact little more than the £25 a year he might have earned as a day-labourer. But the earnings of a day-labourer in 1820 were not sufficient for more than the barest of needs. From the first Clare supported his parents as well as his own family, while the little more of his income was swallowed by those necessary expenses, unknown to the peasant, which he incurred as a writer. His friends imagined that he could easily add to his income by part-time work at his old occupation. But—*improbus labor*—these two are the hardest to mix, especially if the manual work is compulsory. What employer, with labour over-plentiful, would hire a man on those terms? Naturally it was by writing that Clare hoped to win freedom from the struggle that had recently over-shadowed his life and his parents'. Hence his business relations with his publishers soon became a matter of first importance.

Those relations were complicated from the first by the fact that the poems had been published by Taylor and Hessey with Drury. Drury had discovered Clare, advanced small sums of money and considered himself prime mover in the affair, and the poems as he said in a letter, as his 'property'. But John Taylor was by no means content to be regarded merely as his cousin's agent in the business. Even by March the partnership between Drury and Taylor had become strained. Their letters to Clare show them skirmishing for position: 'Have you any Letters of his wherein he speaks of the Share I took in bringing out the Poems? or any later letters referring to the agreement?' Taylor inquired on the 28th. On the same day Drury wrote that he could not consent to give up the Ms. book for which

F

Clare had sent: 'It is so importantly useful to me towards clear-
ing up a mischievous understanding between me and Mr. Jn.
Taylor of London . . .' This book contained Clare's receipt
for the £20, though what else Drury ever gave other than the
first fifteen shillings' debt and the six guineas' rent that was
owing when Clare returned from Casterton we do not know.
By April Drury was commenting to Clare on the 'dilatory
twaddling habits of J.T.', and to Taylor on 'a most disingenuous
and dastardly manner' of Clare's acting, and announcing his
intention of going to London to clear his and Taylor's disagree-
ment up. Taylor explained to Clare the result of that visit,
which marked a temporary truce to discord:

> We have settled to give E.D., on condition that he sends
> up the agreement (the one about a quarter profits) for us
> to destroy it, one half of whatever profit we derive from
> the present or future Poems, retaining in our own Hands
> the sole management, and perfectly uncontrolled in what
> we think proper to give the Author. E.D. has been repaid
> the Copyright and all the other expenses and I have
> charged nothing for my Trouble as Editor so far. . . . You
> shall have at least half of all the profits, and he shall
> sustain no loss by our advancing any sums we may deem
> right to you. These Things I state for your Information,
> for I have no Disguise.[1]

For a short time affairs ran a shade more smoothly. Clare
continued to take Drury poems for the new volume. But Drury,
while full of complaints about Taylor's reticence, was about
that time sending his cousin a specimen of another local poet,
'a second Clare'. Taylor, however, was facing difficulties at
that moment as a result of generosity to John Keats. In
September the firm was £130 out of pocket over *Endymion*, and
Lamia had not yet paid the expenses of its publishing. In an
unsent letter to Keats, Taylor wrote: 'If I were rich enough to
do without the whole sum that you might want, I would gladly
give it to you, but if I wanted it I know nobody who would
let me have it.' Though we know George Keats later paid back
all which Taylor felt he was owed, yet here, perhaps, is some
explanation of that hundred pounds which in the Preface to

---

[1] *Clare Correspondence*, British Museum.

The Village Minstrel was made to look like a *gift* to Clare, but which was later retracted. Clare might certainly have resented matters less if he had known that, in effect, the profits on his first book were being used to help a fellow-poet in dire stress, and that poet John Keats.

But the dispute between Taylor and Drury placed him in the kind of position he particularly disliked. Both men of the world knew instinctively what they might have called in their own minds a childishness in him. They battered at his loyalty. He hated dissension. And not only were Taylor and Drury at loggerheads, but almost immediately there was friction elsewhere. The realities the writer faced were as sharply practical as, and more tormenting than, those of the peasant.

As early as February Taylor had written to his father admiring the pains Lord Radstock was taking over selling *Poems Descriptive*, but announcing his hate of 'Patronage for its Selfishness'. Radstock was apparently 'proposing by broad Hints a better Bargain' for Clare's next volume—that they should divide profits equally with the author. This Taylor expressed his willingness to consent to, if anyone would 'do the office of editor *gratis*'. He would have been interested to see Gifford or Murray decipher and edit, and would make no objection if the latter would offer '£500 or £1,000 for the next Volume'. About the same time Taylor told Clare that Radstock disapproved of certain poems and was demanding that they should be omitted from the third edition. These were *Dolly's Mistake*, a rollicking ballad about the too-trusting Dolly and deceptive young Ralph at the wake, and the refreshingly original description of *My Mary*. As in none other of the 'Mary' poems—all of which have unattainable or renounced love for their subject—in this one Clare was looking through the enchanted hedge, trying to unite pastoral truth, with the ideal that tantalised. The picture of the rough hard-working servant girl has both vigorous realism and delicate sympathy. But *My Mary* was not Lord Radstock's idea of a love poem. Besides, there were other passages in the book that excited even greater disapproval. In *Dawnings of Genius* Clare describes the ploughman as

That necessary tool of wealth and pride:

and eight lines in *Helpstone* begin:

> Accursed Wealth! o'er-bounding human laws
> Of every evil thou remain'st the cause.

Mrs. Emmerson wrote, urging Clare to agree at once to the omission of these 'highly objectionable' passages, these 'radical and ungrateful sentiments'. Radstock had instructed her:

> Tell Clare if he has still a recollection of what I have done, and am still doing for him, he must give me unquestionable proofs of being that Man I would have him to be—he must expunge—expunge![1]

Clare was 'bothered' as he wrote to Taylor. His freedom as a writer hung on the matter. He suggested leaving asterisks at the omitted passages for the 'open-minded and enquiring'. *My Mary* and *Dolly's Mistake* he was prepared to stand by. Taylor suggested that for the sake of the Subscription-List Radstock should be given way to; 'when the Follies of the Day' were past they would restore all as in the original edition. *My Mary* and *Dolly's Mistake* were omitted in the third edition, but not the 'radical sentiments'. In a letter to Hessey, 'the Judgment of T.' was 'a button hole lower' in Clare's opinion. In the fourth edition both poems and excerpts quietly disappeared, together with *The Country Girl* and *Lubin*. Well before the fourth edition Clare reminded Taylor of his promise, begging him again to heed no 'frumpt up, false delicacy'. But it is a simple matter to ignore in letters what one does not want to answer.

Taylor's policy of dignified reticence soon brought the truce between him and Radstock to an end. Radstock's interest did not cease with the closing of the Subscription-Fund. He had a scheme whereby Clare was to visit a clergyman who would improve his external conduct to make it accord with his inner delicacy. By November a new crisis loomed. Mrs. Emmerson passed on Radstock's complaints about Taylor's secrecy and lack of respect to him. Radstock then wrote to Taylor, stressing the need for a written agreement between Clare and his publishers. In his reply of the 11th of December, Taylor stated he was actually benefiting Clare more than he would have been

---

[1] *Clare Correspondence*, British Museum. See also *Letters*, pp. 89, 334.

bound to do under any half-profits scheme: 'But my Lord, if you think your arbitration will be advantageous to Clare—I as a Publisher can have no objection to it; in the meantime I shall suspend those labours which are not within the province of a publisher.'

Radstock's riposte was immediate. He did not doubt the publisher's goodwill

> but still I apprehend that in matters of real business, no man's word, however well established his integrity, would be considered sufficiently binding, unless accompanied by some written document. As the case now stands between you and Clare, I understand that no terms whatever have been offered, he would therefore I think be to blame to resign his manuscript to any Publisher whatever, without a specified security for his labours.[1]

As to the labours of editing, if

> no Lord Radstock had stepped forth in support of the Work, my own private opinion is, that a second edition of the Poems would not yet have shewed itself. That your labours were great respecting the little volume in question, I most willingly allow, but that you were amply remunerated I am equally convinced.[1]

Taylor's next move was an ultimatum: 'I will write to Clare to know whether I am to treat with him or your Lordship for the Copyright of his next Volume.' Then he turned his attention to Helpston: 'Unless you commission Lord R. to interfere in this Matter I know of no Right that he has to write to me on the Subject . . . I would resign the Mss. rather than acknowledge his Agency after what he has said.' If, however, Clare wished to go on as before, he must insist on an agreement being executed between them on a basis of half-profits, as the only way to avoid 'meddling interferences'. Mrs. Emmerson wrote that Lord Radstock had broken with Mr. T., whose impetuosity had done Clare real injury. She urged him to press for a written agreement, but advised him not to withdraw his manuscripts, since that would delay the new book. On the 24th of December Taylor consolidated his strengthened position:

---

[1] *Clare Correspondence*, British Museum.

he was busy selecting poems from the wealth of manuscripts Clare had sent him, and intended to publish two volumes under the title *Ways of a Village*. He also sent the first half-yearly dividend—Clare had had nothing, of course, the whole year so far from the Funds. Taylor suggested how pleasant it was to receive £20 a year free of obligation to anyone. Mrs. Emmerson's letter of the 31st of December believed Taylor's intentions were honourable, but he had not been 'either candid or liberal'. Clare was to send a copy of the agreement to Lord Radstock.

Taylor's letter of the 1st of January 1821 marked his victory. Clare had expressed his confidence in his publisher: he was willing not only to sign an agreement for the forthcoming book, but one binding him for future publications. Taylor thanked him, but could not accept such wild generosity.

> I know we cannot be more secure of your Goodwill than we are without any such Bond, and should a Difference arise between us . . . it would be unjust to tie you fast. . . . That foolish Lord R. has no Conception of such Sentiments as these; what a wretched world he moves in, to have learnt no better at his time of life than thus to estimate his Friends as he pretends to call them——[1]

'Very unjust' Clare commented in pencil beside the description in this missive.

Meanwhile Drury was still carrying on a guerrilla warfare on his own account. He expressed grave concern to Clare about Taylor's conduct, advising him to support Lord Radstock in demanding an exact statement of his position, but warned him not to be too friendly with that patron. Then we hear that Radstock had written Drury a 'flaming appeal' about Taylor's disingenuous ways. Whereupon, since 'hawks mustn't peck out hawks' eyes', Drury wrote back to persuade Radstock he was mistaken about Taylor, setting his private dudgeon aside, and in the process taking some blame on himself, and scattering a few spots on Clare. In his opinion, he explained to Radstock, both published and forthcoming works were entirely Clare's property, and Clare would be justified in demanding the *whole* profits on them if he felt inclined.

And there the matter remained. The agreement, suggested

[1] *Clare Correspondence*, British Museum.

by Radstock to save Clare from Taylor, then insisted upon by Taylor to save Clare from Radstock, then accepted by Clare but refused by Taylor to save Clare from himself, was never drawn up.

IV

During the greater part of 1820 Clare, short of money, had been writing with the feverish activity that was becoming habitual with him, waiting in vain for either some of the half-profit on *Poems Descriptive* or for an instalment from the Fund money. Taylor, whose mind was analytic and corrective rather than creative, had suggested as a new subject *A Week in a Village*. On this Clare was busy, as well as, remembering Burns, on songs for music setters, and on a long poem: 'When I am in the fit I write as much in one week as would knock ye up a fair size Vol', he wrote to Taylor in May. *Village Scenes*, its fair copy dated 21st of August, contains sixteen poems. Six were included in *The Village Minstrel*, three in *The Shepherd's Calendar*, two were published in 1934, and the rest remain. Clare did not work easily to a set formula. The poems have his freshness of outlook, his hardy energy, but they lack form. He copied and re-copied, always achieving greater clarity in detail, yet insufficiently capable of reducing multiplicity to its necessary poetic unity.

Exhilaration from the success of *Poems Descriptive* kept him going. But as early as the previous January Drury's jeremiad on the subject of his creative fury had reached his cousin in London:

> He has no other mode of easing the fever that oppresses him after a tremendous fit of rhyming except by getting tipsy. A simple pint of ale very often does this, and next morning a stupor with headache and pains across the chest afflicts him very severely. Then he is melancholy and completely hypochondriac—you will easily suppose how true is my account when I assure you he has rhymed and written for 3 days and 3 nights without hardly eating or sleeping. I therefore watch with a degree of fear Mr. Gilchrist's proceedings.[1]

[1] Northampton Mss.

Octavius Gilchrist, an easier and more genial man than Drury, maintained that Clare had fine balance and innate common sense. But even he thought the headaches the 'denunciation threatened by Scripture: "woe unto them that drink strong drink" '. By April of 1820 all were alarmed by a rumour that the poet had been attacked by a fit 'of a dangerous kind'. He had rested, during a seven- or eight-mile walk, outside Stamford, under Uffington Bridge, and had only recovered consciousness in great alarm (fearing the occurrence of his childhood attacks) next morning. Taylor wrote immediately in considerable anxiety to recommend blistering for the 'ague' in the chest. And Sherwill advised: 'we all eat too much—two-thirds of what is usually taken would be sufficient . . .' Dr. Fenwick Skrimshire attended him—'that curious man who collects the eggs of English birds', Clare noted.

He himself, his pre-occupation with the writing of the long *Village Minstrel* obvious from his words, reported to Taylor that he was 'worse in health than you can conjecture or than myself am aware of '. But writing continued. Clare's eager letters of the whole of the period between the publication of his first book and that of his second show, against the alarums of his friends, an alert calling back of balance after lionising and a rapid maturing both in practical responsibility and long-term poetic aim.

On the 27th of June, Hessey wrote that Keats was very ill. Three days later he sent a copy of *Lamia* with further news:

> A Blood Vessel in his Lungs broke last week and he has been under Dr Darling's Care ever since. By copious bleedings and active medicines the evil is at present reduced, but the prospect of its return & the evidence it affords of the state of his Constitution make me feel the greatest concern for him. I think the simplicity of "Isabella" will please you much. "Hyperion" is full of the most sublime poetical Images & the small Poems delight me very much.[1]

Taylor wrote in August that Keats would have to spend the winter in Italy, and he appended some of his critical theory, always so excellent. (Or was Taylor echoing Lamb, whose way of discommending was always silence, and whose strong

[1] *Clare Correspondence*, British Museum.

praise of *Lamia* must have led to discussion of Gifford's crab-apple censure?):

> You are now a richer Man than poor K. and how much more fortunate . . . but what is most against him it has been thought necessary in the leading Review, the *Quarterly*, to damn his Poems for imputed political opinions—— Damn them (I say) who could act in so cruel a way to a young man of undoubted Genius—I hate Criticism at all Times except when it is of that enlarged kind that takes entire Surveys of a Subject, and conceiving old writers to be new and new ones to be old awards to each his proper Share of Commendation. Besides in Poetry I think Praise should be given where it is due, and that Silence is sufficient Dispraise——[1]

On the 27th, Taylor wrote that Keats was on his way to Rome:

> If he recovers his strength he will write to you. I think he wishes to say to you that your Images from Nature are too much introduced without being called for by a particular Sentiment—— To meddle with this Subject is bad policy when I am in haste, but perhaps you conceive what he means; his remark is only applicable now and then when he feels as if the Description overlaid and stifled that which ought to be the prevailing Idea——[1]

Clare had missed meeting Keats by a few hours on his first visit to London. The cross-criticisms of these two, both of informal literary training, illumine the aims being fought for at this time in poetry. Clare wrote of Keats in a letter-fragment:

> He keeps up a constant alusion or illusion to the Grecian mythology & there I cannot follow—yet when he speaks of woods Driads & Fawns & Satires [satyrs] are sure to follow & the brook looks alone without her naiads to his mind yet the frequency of such classical accompaniments make it wearisome to the reader where behind every rose bush he looks for a Venus & under every laurel a thrumming Appollo—— In spite of all this his descriptions of scenery are often very fine but as it is the case with other inhabitants of great cities he often described nature as she appeared to his fancies & not as he would have described her had he witnessed the things he describes—— Thus it

[1] *Clare Correspondence*, British Museum.

is he has often undergone the stigma of Cockneyism &
what appears as beautys in the eyes of a pent-up citizen
are looked upon as consciets by those who live in the
country—these are merely errors but even here they are
the errors of poetry—he is often mystical but such poetical
liscences have been looked on as beauties in Wordsworth &
Shelley & in Keats they may be forgiven. . . .[1]

Keats used nature as an illustration of his central human
emotion. For Clare nature was the source of that emotion.
His repugnance was for cult, fashion. Any sentimental or any
intellectual 'sham' killed for him the freshness and hence the
'truth' of the image.

His long poem and *Village Scenes* finished and sent to London,
this 'more fortunate' and 'richer man than poor K.' was suffering great agitation of mind. He was troubled by 'nervous fears'
and 'phantasies of the brain'. John Taylor, grieved to hear of
some fresh 'fit of drinking', warned anew against Stamford.
Drury, on the other hand, was now convinced Clare would
never be well until he abandoned his 'low-minded companions'
at Helpston. Nervous depression was emphasised before the
winter was over by further Enclosure destruction:

> My two favourite elm-trees at the back of the hut are
> condemned to die—it shocks me to relate it but 'tis true.
> The savage who owns them thinks they have done their
> best, and now he wants to make use of the benefits he can
> get by selling them. O was this country Egypt, and was I
> but a caliph, the owner should lose his ears for his arrogant
> presumption; and the first wretch that buried his axe in
> their roots should hang on their branches as a terror to the
> rest. I have been several mornings to bid them farewell.
> Had I one hundred pounds to spare I would buy them
> reprieves—but they must die. Yet this mourning over
> trees is all foolishness—they feel no pains—they are but
> wood, cut up or not. A second thought tells me I am a fool:
> were people all to feel as I do, the world could not be
> carried on,—a green would not be ploughed—a bush or
> tree would not be cut for firing or furniture, and every-
> thing they found when boys would remain in that state
> till they died.[2]

---

[1] *Prose*, p. 223.
[2] Cited from Introduction to *The Village Minstrel*, 1821.

In March news came of Keats's death: 'You know how I reverence him,' Clare wrote to Taylor at once in reply. From *Lamia and other Poems* of the poet who 'mounted pegassus without saddle or bridle' he had copied such lines as 'Then in a wailful choir the small gnats mourn', '& joy whose hand is ever at his lips Bidding adieu', and 'Let the maid Blush keenly as with some warm kiss surprised'. He sent a sonnet:

> . . . When Rancour's aims have passed in nought away,
>   Enlarging specks discern'd in more than thee,
> And beauties 'minishing which few display—
>   When these are past, true child of Poesy,
> Thou shalt survive. . . .[1]

Winter was over. In one of his most encouraging letters, Taylor had suggested a prose account of earliest adversities at Helpston. By April Clare had sent the 'Sketch'. Though Taylor made use of its information, this waited till 1931 to see the light of publication. Taylor, praising Clare's prose, had proposed just such a sketch for the *London Magazine*, but it is probable that the effort lacked the emphasis on humility which Taylor felt necessary to provoke moneyed interest. He had just bought that brilliant periodical, the two-year-old *London* (intending to edit it himself), on the death of its first editor, John Scott. Scott had died after a duel with Jonathan Christie, John Gibson Lockhart's second, during that furious war of politico-journalistic rivalries then raging amongst *London* and *Blackwoood's*, *Edinburgh* and *Quarterly*.

Busy again, Clare's disappointment lifted: 'I am not uneasy at your delay but am by times very fluttered with impatience when vanity tickles me.' But Taylor, with the *London* venture, an array of talent—Lamb, De Quincey, Cary, Hazlitt, and Coleridge—round his dinner-table, and 'Elia' and 'The Opium Eater' in his office, had little time for *The Village Minstrel*. Yet, for Clare, once the 4,000 copies of his first book had gone, delay was serious. First manuscripts, and then proofs, had already been lying about for weeks. The season was slipping by. Within a month, as Mrs. Emmerson wrote, all the families of consequence who had patronised the first book would be out of town. Radstock had been successfully silenced. His 'Puffings'

[1] *Poems*, 1935, I, p. 283.

in the *Post* and *New Times*, so 'disgraceful 'to a publisher, as well as 'injurious to Clare's fame' were at an end. Clare himself had been weaned almost entirely from Gilchrist and Drury. Except for Mrs. Emmerson, the Marshes, Artis and Henderson at Milton, he could look to no one except Taylor. And in the midst of anxiety about the book a family trouble broke. Patty's second daughter, born on the 24th of June, 1821, died soon after.

On the 23rd, Hessey wrote, apologising for delays. The book was ready except for the Introduction—which Taylor was too busy to write. In July Hessey sent three copies for the Marquis of Exeter who had been enquiring; but they lacked the still-unfinished Introduction. Hilton's portrait was used as frontis-piece for the first volume, but De Wint's drawing of the cottage was omitted as unsatisfactory for the second. In August Taylor was still trying to complete the Introduction. He thought that as the season was past it was of little consequence whether the book came out then or a month later. Weeks ago Clare in desperation and against his better judgment had conceded:

> I am not against having my humble occupation, mean parentage, & scanty Education—or anything of the like hinted at in your preface—just what you think suitable so you may do.[1]

On the 29th of August, Taylor wrote that the Introduction was finished at last. It had taken him four months. But he was being fired on by many authors, and he supported an alarming burden of correspondence during these few years. Some armour was necessary: 'I am overworked', he stated 'and have much more reason than you to think of dying'. He wanted to delay publication until November. But Clare's

> I think nor compose nothing—my soul is in a Lethargy my warmth for rhyming has left me my poetical spirit is no more—— Get the book out as soon as you can I long to know my doom—the sooner the better[1]

decided him to issue at once. He bade Clare rest satisfied. 'You have now £45 a year, and reckoning one page monthly in the *London*, £57.' Two poems had already been printed in the July

[1] Peterborough Mss.

and August numbers. And about thirty appeared in the *London* during the next three years. But a later note in one of Clare's memorandum books at Peterborough informs us: 'This year I commenced writing for *The London Magazine* & was to have £12 in addition to my income but I have had nothing allowed me as yet'. Taylor entirely forgot that *London Magazine* promise.

Better in the summer as he always was, and busy in August in the harvest field, Clare, too, in his almost filial affection for the older man, could now detach himself:

> Your delay makes me swear cursedly at times—that is grumbling at oneself—for I say little elsewhere   Still I am yours sincerely & affectionately & ever shall be.[1]

At last, on the 22nd of September, he received a dozen copies of *The Village Minstrel*. 'The season is sadly against the sale,' Mrs. Emmerson wrote. There were no 'Puffings' from Radstock this time. Taylor had printed 2,000 copies. By December, 800 had been sold. In March, 1822, Hessey wrote: 'I am happy to tell you that *The Village Minstrel* continues to sell as well as we could expect.' Taylor was less cheerful: 'It is certain that the last work does not take like the first.' Even by December, 1821, the book's comparative failure was obvious enough.

It was to be expected that those who had been attracted in 1820 chiefly by a genuine 'peasant-poet' would be less interested to find that the peasant was now, as one reviewer put it, possessed of 'a small fortune', 'passing rich with forty pounds a year'. Charles Churchill's 'To pray and starve on forty pounds a year' might have been fitter. Goldsmith's parson of 1770 would have been much less comfortable by 1820. Yet the sale of 800 copies in three months—Keats's *Lamia* managed much less than this figure—seems small but incontrovertible evidence that Clare had a possible public. Had Taylor been able to dispense with leading strings—when it was a question of Radstock's patronage he could exclaim: 'Take your own Course; write what you like;'—had he taken a risk, published as quickly as Clare wrote, or at least more quickly than he actually did publish, Clare might possibly have established himself in the modest way he wished between 1820 and 1830.

[1] *Life*, 1932, p. 168.

The popularity of village verse actually survived till the mid-
century, with the indefatigable, self-assertive Howitts, and
Thomas Miller's *Language of Flowers* and *Pilgrimage of Love*.

But a glance at the growing bulk of Clare's manuscripts since
about 1819 is more profitable than idle speculation. There are
drafts, often four or five in number of the same poem, and often
hard to distinguish from the final form which he intended.
Pictures of changing village and villagers beside 'changeless'
nature are rich, haphazard. All is seen from within, never
merely from outside. The portrait of the cottager, of this date,
makes this clear:

> A simple-worded plain old man
> Whose good intents take errors in their plan
> Oft sentimental and with saddened vein
> He looks on trifles and bemoans their pain,
> And thinks the angler mad. . . .
>
> *The Pilgrim's Progress* and the *Death of Abel*
> Are seldom missing from his reading table,
> And prime old Tusser in his homely trim,
> The first of bards in all the world to him,
> And only poet which his leisure knows;
> Verse deals with fancy, so he sticks to prose. . .[1]

In spite of its background differences which we have noted, and
of an interesting progress from realism toward romantic idealism
that is discernible, this early bulk of verse has to be forgiven for
its faults and redundancies before the occasional fire in it, that
refuses to go out, can be felt. Perhaps we must first be interested
in the things Clare was writing about, in heroes like an old
cart-horse, in the 'brown clod' of the hare 'the harrows failed
to break', in the 'white-nosed bee', before we can appreciate
the verse. If, like Millamant, we 'loathe the country and everything that relates to it', we shall be as lost before Clare's evocations of a rural England that has vanished, a countryside in
process of change, and an inexhaustible nature, as through
similar predispositions and other ignorances, we should be at
a first reading of Theocritus's Fourth Idyll or *The Waste Land*.

Reviews of *The Village Minstrel* appeared in the *New Monthly*,

[1] *Poems*, 1935, I, p. 385.

the *Literary Chronicle*, the *Literary Gazette*, the *Gentleman's Magazine*, the *European Magazine*, and the *Eclectic Review*. They were
more critical, as was to be expected, but all recognised that
Clare had more than fulfilled the promise of *Poems Descriptive*.
Adverse considerations were directed chiefly on the poet's use
of provincialisms, 'vulgarisms', 'low and insignificant' words.
A review, intended for the *London* but rejected by Taylor and
sent to Clare, by comparison of handwritings is shown to be the
work of Allan Cunningham. Cunningham found much that
was extraordinary and beautiful in the book, but noted
obscurity and wordiness, and thought the imagery too confined. He disliked the glossary, curiously assuming that the
words in it were the poet's coinings, and suggested that Burns
and Ramsay furnished no excuse since they were using their
own tongue. He seems to have been unaware that Clare was
deliberately using a dialect akin to that which Shakespeare did
not disdain. He wished to see more event, more pruning and
selection, and greater elegance and use of the 'established
language of poetry'. Clare's comment is valuable:

> There are a many just faults found in this Criticism
> among some trifling the censures are generally just & the
> praises in one or two instances more than I dare or can
> believe I deserve his observation that Poets should conform
> their thoughts or style to the taste of the country by which
> he means fashion is humbug & shows that he has no
> foundation of judgement for a critic that might be relied
> on his lights lead astray.[1]

Taylor, in his Introduction, having hinted heavily again
about the poet's finances, and oddly asserted that the publishers 'paid Clare £10 for his poems', then, in the excellence
of theory, deplored the illiberal spirit of criticism in late years,
which had 'let slip the dogs of war in the flowery fields of
poesy'. For

> Clare has created more of these never-dying forms, in the
> personification of things inanimate and abstract—he has
> scattered them more profusely about our paths, than
> perhaps any poet of the age except one. (Keats.)

[1] *Life*, 1932, p. 170.

From the quotation Taylor gives to illustrate this praise, it is questionable whether he was valuing Clare for his best qualities. His wincing, spinsterish editing often makes this more doubtful still. He gave himself so much unnecessary trouble altering 'breast' to 'shoulder', 'flowers' to 'posies' or 'blossoms', 'runnels' to 'rills', 'pad' to 'path', and 'naked lad' (of boys bathing in the brook) to 'merry bath'. Yet but for Taylor we might have had the poetry of neither Keats nor Clare. Clare's own criticism (like Scott's on *Tales of my Landlord* in the *Quarterly* for January, 1817) of his second book is as good as any. Quoting Spenser's 'I play to please myself' on the first page of his manuscript, he had written the whole volume in this spirit. Now he was dissatisfied, sorry he had not withheld the title poem much longer for revision: 'The reason why I dislike it is that it does not describe the feelings of a rhyming peasant strongly or locally enough.'

Once embarked on the thorny path up Parnassus, and hoping to make a living, his concern with the development of his art in relation to that had yet to be considered. There are a hundred and twenty stanzas in Spenser-Beattie form of *The Village Minstrel*, the poem which he had begun as *The Peasant Boy*. He was still afraid that the poem might be thought plagiaristic. The fear of plagiarism had been especially common in the eighteenth century. Any line he took from another poet, Clare said, he would openly acknowledge and be proud of it. Blake's words on this matter of plagiarism are as good as any:

> The difference between a bad artist and a Good One
> Is: the Bad Artist seems to copy a Great deal.
> The Good one Really does Copy a Great deal.

The Village Minstrel is, aside from its value as part of the total of Clare's picture of rustic traditions, an original and a quite different thing from Beattie's rhetoric. That Clare owes nothing beyond the stanza-form to Beattie, and little to Ramsay, may most quickly be seen from a glance at Beattie's *Minstrel* or at *The Gentle Shepherd*:

> A more uncouthly lout was hardly seen
> Beneath the shroud of ignorance than he;
> The sport of all the village he has been,

SWORDY WELL

SWORDY WELL'S ORCHID GROUNDS TODAY

GLINTON MANOR: MARY JOYCE'S HOME

WALKHERD LODGE: MARTHA TURNER'S HOME

Who with his simple looks oft jested free;
And gossips, gabbling o'er their cake and tea,
Time after time did prophecies repeat,
How half a ninny he was like to be,
To go on soodling up and down the street
And shun the playing boys whene'er they chanc'd to
    meet. . . .

And he would mark in July's rosy prime,
Crossing the meadows, how many a nameless fly
Of scarlet plumage, punctual to its time,
Perch'd on a flower would always meet his eye;
And plain-drest butterfly of russet dye,
As it awaken'd by the scythe's shrill sound,
Soon as the bent with ripeness 'gan to dye,
Was constant with him in each meadow-ground,
Flirting the withering swath and unmown blossom
    round. . . .

'Twas pleasing too, when meadow's browning swath
'Neath sultry sunbeams withered on the lea,
To mark the ploughboys at the Sunday bath,
When leisure left them at their wading free
In some clear pit hemm'd round wi' willow tree
And brush and brake to screen the dabbling crew,
Tho' bashful milkmaid couldn't help but see,
And doubtless, blushing by the naked crew,
Their bosoms might be warm'd to wish a nearer view.[1]

But *The Village Minstrel's* two volumes were not, on the whole,
sufficient advance on *Poems Descriptive*. Little as we may want
to over-praise, still less can we afford to condescend about this
second book of Clare's. We linger in front of a God's plenty
seeming only less exhaustible than nature is exhaustible. Half-
impatiently we read again poems about rustic fishing, Sunday
walks, and recollections after a ramble, *To an Angry Bee*, *To a
Red Clover Blossom*, and *Winter Rainbow*. Half in delight we
marvel at the difference between these seeings and those of
Byron's 'sternest but best poet of Nature', Crabbe. We linger
over

---

[1] *The Village Minstrel*, pp. 19, 21. Taylor omitted stanza 3. See *Poems*,
1935, I, p. 142.

Here by the arch's ancient wall
     The antique eldern buds anew;
Again the bulrush sprouting tall
     The water wrinkles, rippling through.[1]

We recall Crabbe's

Beneath an ancient bridge, the straiten'd flood
Rolls through its sloping banks of slimy mud. . . .

And we read again from *The Village Minstrel*, accepting Clare's plenitude of images, rarely the mere tabulations they have sometimes been said to be, but always building the atmosphere of day, scene, or season:

Crimp-frilled daisy, bright bronze buttercup,
     Freckt cowslip-peeps, gilt whins of morning dew,
And hooded arum early sprouting up
     Ere the whitethorn bud half unfolds to view,
And wan-hued lady-smocks, that love to spring
     'Side the swampt margin of some plashy pond. . . .[2]

In sixty sonnets, which he soon felt were 'poor stuff', he had tried out thirty-six different rhyme-schemes. He worked 'without rule & compass', not 'as a Taylor cuts out a coat for the carcass'. He was defying formalists, those critics 'who would make readers believe a sonnet cannot be a Sonnet unless it is precisely 14 lines & a long poem as such unless one first sits down to wiredraw out regular argument'.[3] From couplets he worked through Spenserian and Shakespearean forms to combinations as intricate as the Petrarchian model. Such experimental flouting of a highly intellectual and conventionalised form, even though William Lisle Bowles and Cruttwell the printer had made such a captivating success in 1789, was a little hardy. There had been so many, besides the gifted ones like Wordsworth, Keats, and Lamb, who tried to coax success out of inspirations not dissimilar to those of *The Bells, Ostend*. But in view chiefly of his later sonnet assemblies, Clare's *Village Minstrel* experiments are worth remembering.

[1] *The Last of March, The Village Minstrel*, II, p. 120.
[2] II, p. 131.
[3] *Letters*, p. 56.

By December, 1821, he was short of money, and he asked Taylor to advance his Fund dividend. After some delay, Taylor sent the £10 on the 17th, promising Earl Spencer's £5 and 6 guineas for the *London Magazine* poems in a few days. The £5 arrived on the 30th of January, 1822, the money for the *London* writing not at all. Summoning what Eliza Emmerson called his Giant of Resolution, he 'determined in the teeth of vexation to surmount disappointment by unwearied struggles'.

By January he was again 'all madness for writing', but 'how long it's to last I don't know'. He had finished *The Dream*, but felt he must rest from 'terrible' poems such as that. By March, the surge of creativity had spent itself, and he was entering another of his periods of exhausted depression. The ebb and flow of generative mood is observable through Keats's and Burns's Letters as well as Clare's. If we examine, we shall find that most poets work thus. In February Clare wrote:

> . . . the Muse is a fickle Hussey with me she sometimes stilts me up to madness & then leaves me as a beggar by the wayside with no more life than whats mortal & that nearly extinguished by mellancholy forbodings—[1]

And in March:

> this confounded lethargy of low spirits that presses on me to such a degree that at times makes me feel as if my senses had a mind to leave me Spring or Fall such feelings it seems are doomed to be my companions but it shall not overpower me as formerly. . . .[2]

Isolation in Helpston itself had become so much more marked since the publication of his first book:

> I live here among the ignorant like a lost man in fact like one whom the rest seems careless of having anything to do with—they hardly dare talk in my company for fear I shoud mention them in my writings & I find more pleasure in wandering the fields than in mixing among my silent neighbours.[3]

[1] *Letters*, p. 132.
[2] *Letters*, p. 135.
[3] *Letters*, p. 132.

He tried to break the intolerable barrier: 'You tell me' Mrs. Emmerson wrote, 'by an act of inebriety you have made yourself "ridiculous and have been suffering for it for this week past". Why suffer the goodness of your heart to mislead your understanding by taking you into society no longer suited to your situation . . .' But she, from what was to him her lively *beau monde* of friends and writers, could not wholly understand the loneliness of the impressionable mind at Helpston. Clare evidently had a drinking bout on two or three occasions in March and April of 1821, besides on this occasion in December of the same year when Mrs. Emmerson cautioned him not to tell Lord Radstock. There is no doubt that, as Elia said, there are 'robust heads and iron insides whom scarce any excesses can hurt', and there are those 'who feel the want of some artificial aid to raise their spirits in society to what is no more than the ordinary pitch of all around'. There is equally little doubt that Clare's drinking was often to gain the companionship of his neighbours free from suspicion. He frequently drank on an empty stomach; and not only did he feel bound to confess to one or other of his friends on almost every occasion, but he was visited by remorse out of all proportion to the offence. The heavily penitential attitude towards drink of the Evangelical age persisted all through the nineteenth century. In March, 1821, Clare told Taylor how 'confoundedly drunk' he had been; he had 'rolled to Drury's', who would be able to say 'plenty to degrade me if he pleases'. In the long eager letter of the 3rd of April, when he sent the 'Sketch' of his life, he discussed sincerity as an essential to writing, and promised to send *The Last of March*, his poem about Lolham Brigs just finished. Then: 'P.S. I am just got from the blue bell & am damnation drunk & consequently as happy as possibility can make me'. But it is surely needless to labour any further this point of a part-serious, part-rueful, part-frolic awareness on Clare's part, of what, in respect of the tankard, he was about.

v

The poem *The Dream* was written for the *London* of February, 1822. But '—you must not deceive me as you have often done

by saying so and so is to be in the Mag & then nothing of it
when it comes'. He had had the idea of making a collection of
horrific poems, *A Vision of Hell, Shadows of Fate*, and so on,
besides *The Dream*, and publishing them 'under a feignd name'.
This is the first we hear of the kind of ruse that became common
about this time, either to avoid the natural sense of the writer's
exposure, or to escape firebrand criticism and Mohock abuse.
Clare's aim in this collection of poems was to collect enough
ready money to buy Billings's Bachelors' Hall. The brothers
were his 'oldest and now only friends in the village'. Their 'cot'
was under mortgage to a Jew. But Taylor declared it impossible
to touch the Fund money, and Lord Milton came to the rescue
of the Billings with twenty pounds to pay their debt.

Reading in *Confessions of an English Opium Eater* De Quincey's
account of his visions of darkness, fugitives, tempests, caves of
hell, and everlasting farewells no doubt, as Clare said, contributed to *The Dream*. But the poem invites comparison far more
with Byron's *Darkness*. That was a dream, too: of the sun gone
out; no love left on a Nagasaki earth; in hideous terror, their
humanity lost, having burnt their forests and cities for light,
the people died. Two enemies alone were left, who, when they
caught sight of each other—shrieked, and sank lifeless to the
herbless, treeless 'chaos of hard clay'. Clare's poem, by no
means so macabre, nor so melodramatic as Byron's, is yet of a
world dissolving in fury and darkness, with hell yawning for
the souls of the damned. Byron might defy the Judgment
threatened by Anglican and Catholic dogma. Clare was too
intuitively aware, not only of outworn dogma, but of a burden
which increasing human knowledge imposed:

> A gloomy sadness round the sky was cast,
> Where clouds seemed hurrying with unusual haste;
> Winds urged them onward, like to restless ships,
> And dim light faded in its last eclipse . . .
> Fierce raged destruction, sweeping o'er the land,
> And the last counted moments seemed at hand . . .
> Sons from their father, fathers sons did fly,
> The strongest fled, and left the weak to die;
> Pity was dead: none heeded for another;
> Brother left brother; and the frantic mother
> For fruitless safety hurried east and west,

And dropped the babe to perish from her breast . . .
Stars drunk with dread rolled giddy from the heaven,
And staggering worlds like wrecks in storms were driven;
The pallid moon hung fluttering on the sight,
As startled bird whose wings are stretched for flight;
And o'er the east a fearful light begun
To show the sunrise—not the morning sun,
But one in wild confusion . . .
The heaven's blue curtains rent and shrank away,
And heaven itself seemed threaten'd with decay;
While hopeless distance with a boundless stretch
Flashed on despair the joy it could not reach,
A moment's mockery—ere the last dim light
Vanished, and left an everlasting night . . .
The melting glooms that spread perpetual stains,
Kept whirling on in endless hurricanes.
And tearing noises, like a troubled sea,
Broke up that silence which no more would be.

The reeling earth sank loosened from its stay,
And nature's wrecks all felt their last decay.
The yielding, burning soil, that fled my feet,
I seemed to feel, and struggled to retreat . . .
I felt all terrors of the damned, and fell
With conscious horror that my doom was hell:
And memory mocked me, like a haunting ghost,
With light and life and pleasures that were lost . . .
And days misspent with friends and fellow men,
And sins committed—all were with me then.
The boundless hell, where tortures never tire,
Glimmered beneath me like a world on fire. . . .[1]

So much of *The Dream* is not given in order to show Clare's
badness or goodness when he tried a kind of poetry very
different from the one he had so far chosen. The important
point is that he was driven, at least once, to try to put these
forebodings into verse. Certainly his poem has power, and a
warmth Byron deliberately refrained from in his. It bears also
a sense of boomerang effect from the religious questioning that
was opening up in front of him about this time and which his
mind refused to avoid. And both his poem and Byron's, if we
retrace our steps through the tunnel and try to look along with

[1] *The Shepherd's Calendar*, 1827, pp. 210–8. *Poems*, 1935, I, pp. 399–403.

the widening vision of the early nineteenth century, give out
ominous premonitions which reach us with a kind of shock.

But *The Dream* also serves to illustrate the impact on Clare of
personal experience. It shows, not intentionally, of course, how
deeply the failure of *The Village Minstrel* had already sunk into
the limbo of his 'Identity'; what 'assault and battery of the
mind' the well-meant moral patronage of supporters had
become. And we know that he felt the impressionability of this
'Self-identity' as a childish weakness manhood should somehow
have vanquished or chased away.

On the surface, of course, he merely realised how badly he
needed a change of scene and company as well as a rest. Had
he known that William Hazlitt, the 'Slang-whanger' as the
Quarterly called him, had been detained outside Burghley's
fretted Gothic in early February, it could not have brought the
two together. Hazlitt was at this time assuaging 'phrenzy' by
writing *Liber Amoris*. But he was twenty years 'the worse for
wear and tear' since he first visited Burghley, and still too
impatient to listen to another's struggles. Clare wished London
was nearer. In April, Mrs. Emmerson, recently removed to a
house in Stratford Place, wrote begging him to pay them a
visit. He should have the 'most elevated spot in the house'—
his 'sky-chamber' they later called it. Only too eager to accept,
when Hessey sent £5 for expenses, in the third week in May,
Clare set out on his second trip to London.

VI

In 1822 the *London Magazine* was in the hopeful heyday of
brief brilliance. So much has now been well and so accessibly
written on this periodical and the group of men whose talents
gave it life that our task is here to avoid being repeaters. Both
the new poetry and the new criticism, of Wordsworth, Lamb,
Hunt, Keats, Coleridge, Shelley, and Hazlitt, were based on a
wider perception of man's capacity than that which the limited
decorum of the eighteenth century had allowed. The perception would narrow again. Such expansive hope was bound
to dwindle, as knowledge proved once for all our consanguinity
with the beasts. Then only it could safely re-ascend. But in

spite of the justice of the present century's indictment of their miasmic vagueness, it is their sense of dauntless imaginative adventure that links all the English so-called romantic writers together, whatever their period or their individual divergences.

Foremost in the galaxy of contributors which John Scott and then John Taylor had gathered for the *London* was Charles Lamb. Under the editor's eye for genius, Lamb was paid at a higher rate than all the rest. S. T. Coleridge, though not of the contributors, was in 1822, with the Gillmans at Highgate, consolidating his philosophic fame by lecturing, and he came occasionally to Waterloo Place. Leigh Hunt was at that moment on board the *David Walter*, bound with the ailing Marianne and his family, away from Elizabeth Kent, for Shelley and Italy. Second, therefore, of the great spirits more constantly seen would be William Hazlitt. Hazlitt had, in January, 1822, ominously sold the second volume of *Table Talk* to Henry Colburn and the *New Monthly*. His best work of 1819, '20, and '21, Taylor and Hessey had already published. Then there was Thomas De Quincey, whose literary fame had burgeoned with the *Confessions of an English Opium-Eater* in the *London* of September and October, 1821. There was a group of younger men. Thomas Hood, the serious and the punning, usually shone in *The Lion's Head*, and was the rather phantom sub-editor. Allan Cunningham, of the 'dark, flashing, guerrilla eye', the hater of puns and lover of poetry, the hater of things English (De Quincey said) and, according to Clare, lover of all things Scottish—Cunningham contributed songs and ballads and long-winded essays to the *London*. Clare's relations with 'Nalla', giant of six foot four, were of the happiest. So, too, they were with James Montgomery, and with Charles Abraham Elton, translator of Hesiod and Propertius. Bryan Waller Procter as 'Barry Cornwall' produced pleasant Keatsian, Shelleyan, and Byronic imitations which bade fair to make him a popular poet. John Hamilton Reynolds, Thomas Noon Talfourd, and Hartley Coleridge, were also among the outstanding of the *London* contributors.

Most of these upholders of the brilliant rival to Edinburgh's formidable 'Maga' attended the excellent dinners given by John Taylor at Waterloo Place. On these occasions, as Procter remembered, wit and wine flowed, 'all the fences and restraints of authorship were cast off, and the natural human being was disclosed'.

It was with possibility of such delectable company that Clare, the *London's* already famed Green Man, found himself on his second visit. Among it he was welcomed. He was also immediately liked as a man free from snobbery in its many forms. He had hazarded himself to Town alone. Gilchrist was too ill to accompany him. For the first few days, he stayed at Taylor's, entertaining himself at the Fleet Street window with the 'constant successions' that thronged this way and that; Elia's London: ladies cheapening; bucks reeling home; mechanic watchmen. Clare's great amusement, when he walked abroad, was not the silver-smiths' and pastry-cooks' shops, but the book-sellers'; just as they had been when, as a boy, he visited Stamford or Deeping or Wisbech. But greatest amusement of all was the constellation of authors at the *London* dinner-parties. How acutely he discerned at once the self-importance of the 'little vapours', 'dabbling critics who cut monthly morsels from genius'. Who these could be he lets fall no hint: 'it is plain I do not allude to friends'. But it was invariably self-magnification which distinguished for Clare temporary flames from true visionaries, the 'fixed stars in the world's hemisphere'.

His first dinner must have been very soon after his arrival. Hazlitt was at that one. And Hazlitt was in London only a few days at the end of May to correct the second volume of *Table Talk*. He was there, too, to receive the final blow which Letter the Last of *Liber Amoris* had, perhaps that very day, set down in that charged personal prose that somehow out-tops the personal. Had Clare had a hunch of Hazlitt's passion, mutual understanding might have gone easier. As it was, no wonder Hazlitt seemed to him to sit at table 'a silent picture of severity, his eyes as upon empty chairs', like Macbeth's at another banquet. Then about forty-four, Hazlitt to Clare was 'middle-sized, dark-looking', his face already 'deeply lined', his eyes bright, but 'buried under his brows'. 'For the blood of me' Clare could not come near the irascibly great critic who, as one of our present finest poet-scholars notes for us, was 'denied to the end the clear course which should have been granted one so wise in his very confusions'.[1]

[1] Edmund Blunden: *Charles Lamb and his Contemporaries*, p. 177.

Charles Lamb, greatest 'Londoner' in more than one sense, presented, in May, 1822, and we dare guess would have presented, whatever further acquaintance might have been possible, fewer obstacles to understanding. 'Tipsy-joy-and-jollity' Lamb, in his usual sombrest black, his 'immaterial' legs as clerically gaitered, was certainly on the right hand of the Editor on one of these occasions. His 'cousin Bridget Elia' was never far away. The large bronze-coloured snuff-box was on the table in front; and when the cloth was drawn, the tankard. And next to Lamb, Tom Hood remembered in his *Literary Reminiscences*,

> shining verdantly out from the grave-coloured suits of the literati, like a patch of turnips amid stubble and fallow, behold our Jack i' the Green—John Clare! In his bright, grass-coloured coat, and yellow waistcoat (there are greenish stalks too, under the table), he looks a very Cowslip, and blooms amongst us as Goldsmith must have done in his peach-blossom.

The two 'drouthie neebors', Clare and Lamb, discussed poetry. Elia, we all know, avowedly cared little for Pastoral. 'More of House Lamb than Grass Lamb'—eighteen years seniority and his own renunciation of poetry gave him the best leave to banter on certain 'Clare-obscurities'. These originated, he thought, in a contempt for the rules of Priscian. Clare opposed, vehemently denouncing all philology 'as nothing but a sort of man-trap for authors'. There was, not long after, a Magazine dinner at Thomas Griffiths Wainewright's, the *London*'s 'Janus Weathercock'. Did Lamb, who skipped the battle-accounts in Hazlitt's *Life of Napoleon*, and suggested Hampton Court with a tether of forty miles for that superannuated disturber of Europe's peace, mistake his Janus? T. G. Wainewright, brilliant art-critic, was later convicted of forgery and suspected of murder by poison. It was on this occasion at the sumptuous apartments in Great Marlborough Street that Janus's serving man, Hood thought, took Clare for some 'eccentric Notable of the Corinthian order, disguised in Rustic'. Lamb and Clare, returning arm on arm through the Strand, invoked calls of "Tom and Jerry—there goes Tom and Jerry!"[1]

[1] Characters out of Pierce Egan's sports classic, *Life in London*.

Discussion on rusticisms continued out of Town. Clare sent Lamb his books. Lamb, back from his first visit to France with Mary, wrote preferring Clare's 'Grongar Hill kind of pieces in eight syllable lines, my favourite measure', such as *Cowper Green* and *Solitude*. He suggested that the 'true rustic style' was to be found in Shenstone. Where 'nothing is gained in expression' he went on, 'slang' is to be avoided. We already know what Clare felt about Shenstone's pastoral quality. But he knew the unassailability of the argument about gain in expressiveness. Yet not alone by taking thought could Clare ever add a cubit to his poetic stature. Lamb's influence will be best seen in Clare's sonnet to him in the August *London*. 'Elia, thy reveries and visioned themes'. 'Lamb's best poetry is in *Elia*', he later noted, sensing both Lamb's and the *London's* 1825 superannuation. In his second sonnet to Lamb is Clare's last word to him on the argument over rusticisms—time's fulfilling way with words. We shall be reminded, reading it, how Lamb's own books brought him little more money than Clare's brought him; and *Elia* reached no second edition till after its author's death:

> Friend Lamb, thou choosest well, to love the lore
>   Of our old bygone bards, whose racy page
> Rich mellowing time makes sweeter than before
> The blossom left; for the long-garnered store
>   Of fruitage is right luscious in its age,
> Although to fashion's taste austere. What more
> Can be expected from the popular rage
> For tinsel gauds that are to gold preferred?
>   Me much it grieved; for I did long presage
> Vain fashion's foils had every heart deterred
>   From the warm homely phrase of other days,
> Until thy muse's ancient voice I heard,
> And now right fain, yet fearing, honest bard,
>   I pause to greet thee with so poor a praise.[1]

If they had one perfect sympathy at this time, these two, it was their acute perceptions of both romance and reality. Both loved the past. Lamb wrote 'for antiquity', he said. Did not both feel the *toga virilis* sit heavily too? Impressions of child-

---

[1] *The Rural Muse*, 1835, p. 155. *Poems*, 1935, II, p. 112.

hood had so burnt into them that they 'resented the imperti-
nences' of manhood. And both were the first to acknowledge
this as dire weakness in themselves.

But we have far outstepped May, 1822, in London. Just
before Wainewright's dinner on the 27th, Clare spent two days
with Henry Francis Cary at Chiswick. He has left, in his small
gallery of pen-portraits of this rich generation of literary
personalities, 'the best verbal likeness extant' of that translator
of Dante whom Coleridge so actively introduced to John Taylor
(why do we too readily believe those stories about Coleridge's
inactivity?). Cary's translation is not even now superseded.
Tallish, spare, with earnest, heavy-lidded eyes, his authorship
and his priesthood, Clare thought, sat very meekly upon this
'most quiet amiable and unassuming of men'. The two days at
Chiswick were one of Clare's happy spots of time. Cary's house
had belonged to Sir James Thornhill, English exponent of the
late Baroque style in art. From it his daughter had eloped with
Lamb's admired Hogarth of 'Gin Lane'. Clare and his host
made pilgrimage to the grave of James Thomson at Richmond.
No doubt Taylor's inspired ploughman and Cary continued
their discussion on religion. Clare was reported to Mrs.
Emmerson as having at one dinner been 'D—' and 'wished
the Churches were all in ashes and the parsons sent to beg
their bread'. But, Thomas Bennion added, reporting the
reporting back again, 'i told her it was not so you was very
merry' and 'that Mr. C— was on very good terms with you so
i was sure that he was not offended'.

It was Edward Villiers Rippingille (whose paintings Clare
had first seen as a disappointed clerk-prospective wandering
the shops of Wisbech) who might have taken lessons in dis-
cretion from Taylor's diplomatic porter. Hood classed Thomas
Bennion among the *London's* contributors, because of his valiant
struggles with the English language. But Lamb's 'model of a
country parson', Procter's 'mildest and most amiable of men',
was not likely to take offence at a mere forthright opinion.
Clare and Cary corresponded till 1833, when the loss of his
wife and fitful clouds of mental disease obscured the older man
not long before the younger's darkest hour.

Brilliant John Hamilton Reynolds, the *London's* 'Edward
Herbert', was a great favourite of John Taylor. With 'plump

round face', 'nose something puggish', and 'quick knapping sort of eye', Reynolds was the soul of 1822 Waterloo Place dinners. He was Clare's 'three-in-one of fun wit & punning personified'. Tom Hood, the punster on paper, quite often sat silent. A year younger than Clare—if one of his own confessions is to be believed, Reynolds panted for distinction but was conscious of inadequacy; he had not within him 'that immortal power which can command it'; 'I cannot write Aught that may foil the fatal wing of Time'. Twice in his pen-sketches of the Londoners Clare returned, intuitively fascinated—or was the subject *Magazine* table-talk?—to this rock on which any man's scallop-shell of poetry can founder: Reynolds 'is a man of genius & if his talents were properly applied he would do something'. And 'he . . . ought to be a poet of the first order himself is his only hindrance'. Already in *The Fancy: The Poetical Remains of the late Peter Corcoran*, of 1820, Reynolds had made his adieu to poetry, meaning to forsake it for the gain-producing profession of Law. But he was not 'content' to do so. Clare mistook his man there. *Safie*, in 1814, had been praised by Byron; Leigh Hunt, in 1816, had bracketed Reynolds with Keats and Shelley. That trio of young poets was to carry forward the torch of English poetry. In 1819, Reynolds had sent a copy of *The Naiad*, an imitation of an old Scots ballad, to his hero Wordsworth, with a young man's request for criticism. Sara Hutchinson's 'wary' Wordsworth replied in his most solemn manner: the poem would have 'told more' if it had been shorter, without 'the first 57 lines' and 'the last 146'. Severely nettled, the young poet retaliated, seeing the announcement of Wordsworth's *Peter Bell* in 1819, with John Taylor as accessory, in a jest of wider than dinner-table circulation. The ante-natal Peter Bell, a *Lyrical Ballad* affirming 'I am the REAL SIMON PURE' was a parody on the unsuccessful simplicity of *The Idiot Boy*.

Reynolds's impression of Clare was written with a sonnet in a copy of *The Rural Muse*, which Reynolds gave to a niece in 1843:

> I knew Clare well . . . he was a quiet and worthy yet enthusiastic man . . . a guileless yet suspicious man . . . a true observer of nature in her generous earth-work and

water-work, but a man alive to more . . . than town apprehensions. . . .

Another squib of 'Edward Herbert Reynolds' in the *London* was 'The Literary Police Office, Bow Street'. Literary notables of the day were described as appearing before the magistrates, charged with extravagant offences:

> John Clare (a comely country-looking man, in a smock frock and a face to match) appeared to resist an order of filiation, made on the affidavit of one of the Muses with whom he had kept company, and who appeared to have been too liberal of her favours to him. The oath being persisted in, his innocence stood him in no stead; and he was ordered to set apart half-a-crown, out of sixpence a day, to support the child. He pleaded poverty; but the magistrates explained to him that a poor soldier had been known to have managed such an allowance, and therefore they resisted his plea. Clare is said to have a wife, and ten little children all under the age of four years, which makes his case more reprehensible.

The 'rattling' Rippingille, 'a pleasant fellow over the bottle & a strong dealer in puns', whom Clare had met at the Emmersons, took him to playhouses, inns, and boxing-booths, as well as to the Academy. Here the door-keeper came to know him, and allowed him in whenever he wished. When Gilchrist recovered, he joined Clare in London, and took him to see Gifford. The surly Gifford, who was, it must be said, a kindly man in private and fond of children, gave the poet hearty welcome, congratulating him on his last poems, which 'he said were far better than my first'. Gifford bade Clare 'beware of booksellers & repeated it several times'. Next day Gilchrist and Clare called on Murray in Albemarle Street, who pleasantly complimented Clare on what already, in his own words, the poet was tempted to regard as 'the farthing rushlight' of success.

By the 17th of June, Clare was at home again in Helpston. 'He was excellent company while he staid' Taylor wrote to his father: 'such a Fund of Good Sense & besides his Judgement of Books was so very sound, that let what would be the Subject of Conversation he was always well worth listening to'. Lord Radstock sent a gown for Patty, who had borne a daughter on the 16th. The child was called Eliza Louisa, after her god-mother Mrs. Emmerson, who sent a silver cup, and later paid for the little girl's schooling.

Lamb's letter of the 31st of August, which became a treasured family joke, found Clare busy with poems for a new volume of poetry, to be called *The Wilderness*, or *Pastorals, Summer Walks and Sonnets*. Either of these titles would have been better than the one eventually selected by Taylor. Clare was still deeply concerned with Pastoral. But Lamb concluded his letter on Shenstone's excellence in that manner in characteristically lighter vein:

> Since I saw you I have been in France, and have eaten frogs. The nicest little rabbity things you ever tasted. Do look about for them. Make Mrs Clare pick off the hind quarters, boil them plain, with parsley and butter. The fore quarters are not so good. She may let them hop off by themselves.[1]

Hessey wrote in August, that of the six sonnets of Clare's for the *London's* September and October numbers only one was to be signed. His publishers oddly thought it best that Clare's name should not appear too often. Mrs. Emmerson wrote in September of a 'delightful new correspondent' of her own—Derwent Coleridge. By the 4th of January, 1823, Clare was naturally in need of his allowance, which was due on the 1st. On the 17th: 'Here I am . . . expecting & expecting & all to no purpose'. From 1820 onward he kept a careful account of money sent from Taylor and Hessey, but did not find this easy since they did not always state its source. On the 5th of February Hessey wrote: 'The enclosed £10 note has been lying on my desk for you for some time'. . . .

Between then and the end of May Clare was 'scribbling at a cursed risky rate,' sending poems to Taylor for another volume, begging eagerly for criticisms which Taylor was too busy to give:

> I am windbound in my sooty corner now & then a pot of misnamed medly as nigh Ale as shadow is to substance small beers sad reallity or now & then seeking the "Bell" to be cheered with the silence of company who sleep all

---

[1] *Clare Correspondence*, British Museum.

day with their eyes open or only [wake] to howl about the times books & authors are as dark & unknown things as if they inhabited the bottom of the sea.[1]

He had already sent enough for a third book. It was his medium that was troubling him—what Keats would have called the 'true voice' of his feeling. He suggested to Taylor a volume of poems for children; he had tried *The Adventures of a Grasshopper*, but thought it a failure. He could, like Blake, and later he did, beautifully reproduce innocence in poems of childhood. He proposed others—on

> a boy running races with the moon—and another hunting the landrail or landrake . . . you know the bird, its a little thing heard about the grass & wheat in summer & one of the most poetical images in rural nature, 'tis like a spirit you may track it by its noise a whole day & never urge it to take wing.[2]

But there was no one to give the words of vital, equal insight and encouragement, without which poetic potency may wither. To Taylor Clare wrote: 'I am anxious to hear but you take no notice in the world about it men of Business and poets are the worst correspondents that can come together.' The matter was this—about children's poetry: 'when one longs to be simple one is apt to be silly'. He had Wordsworth in mind. Children's poetry *might* have caught the tide: there were the Taylors and Mrs. Barbauld. But by January, 1823, he had finished something quite different: *The Parish*—a satire. Probably on Mrs. Emmerson's advice, he declared he could not send it till Taylor commented on the worth of what he already had. Clare was in one of his exhausted states after a fever of composition, and she condoled with him. Three sonnets over the pen-name 'Percy Green' were in the 1823 *London* besides *Round Oak Spring*, *Antiquity*, and three poems to Mary. H. F. Cary very much admired the 'Percy Green' sonnet for July before he discovered the authorship. Clare proposed a hundred sonnets, knowing one of his faults to lie, not like J. H. Reynolds's in the divided mind, but in diffuseness. He intended the form to window-

---

[1] Cited from *Keats's Publisher*, p. 170.
[2] *Letters*, p. 154.

frame a hundred pastoral descriptions. He could not either, of course, help remembering Charlotte Smith's eleven editions and William Lisle Bowles's feat. But no word came from Taylor: until, in March, Admiral Lord Radstock sailed in for a final attack with a flourish of trumpets and drums:

> We have formed plans in our minds concerning you, but these, unless manfully and steadily pursued by yourself, can avail nothing. . . . You have long known my opinion of T——. The more I hear of him, the more am I convinced that that opinion was well-founded—in a word that it is his determined resolution to keep you in *Bondage* and *Obscurity* so long as he has the power of so doing—— Now if these vile and ignominious chains be not speedily broken the fault will not be mine . . . therefore he shall learn, I trust, to his *cost* that I see clearly through all his . . . duplicity.[1]

The 31st of March brought apologies for delay from Hessey, and a promise of the second edition of *The Village Minstrel*. This, when, in May, it arrived, consisted of the second thousand copies of the first edition, now bound and carrying in the second volume Cowen's engraving of the cottage at Helpston.

Radstock had another score against Taylor. The Rev. W. Allen had written a critique of Clare's poetry in the form of *Four Letters to Lord Radstock*, dated February, 1823. These Taylor had declined either to publish in the *London* or to mention in that magazine's list of new publications. Yet Allen had a wide acquaintance with highways and byways of English poetry, a keen eye for what was new in Clare's tone and treatment, and his critique remains the best and fullest contemporary account of Clare's poetry up to 1821.

Again Taylor won. He held Clare's loyalty—though long silence 'has gone a long way to make us strangers'. He found time for most cheerful encouragement in a letter of the 10th of August:

> I shall be very agreeable to the Publication of another Volume this coming Winter. . . . Talking with Hessey the other day it occurred to me that a good Title for another Book would be The Shepherd's Calendar.[1]

[1] *Clare Correspondence*, British Museum.

H

He ignored, or more likely had entirely forgotten, Clare's own three proposals and his far better title. Well enough Clare knew the age-old creative law of genius that it must make the Form it requires, as well as create the taste by which it is appreciated:

> real excellence [he wrote], must be its own creation it must be the overflowings of its own mind & must *make* its admirers willing converts from its own powerful con- sceptions & not yield to win them by giving way to their opinions of excellence.[1]

But he said no more. Hessey was complaining that the poems he sent were too like what he had already written, and that he did not take sufficient care over the 'mechanical operation of writing'. After the two sonnets to Mary in August, 1823, no poem from Clare's pen was published in the *London* till July, 1824, and the sonnet in that number was the last.

In June, making up his half-yearly accounts, hating the arithmetic that proved the £7 that 'grins at my Folly on the greasy manteltree at the Bell', Clare confessed to Hessey that at the moment Taylor's 'small beer sermons would quite undo' him. We may again warn ourselves that we do not know for certain how long the £7 was for. Country creditors sometimes allow bills to run on for years. We may also remind ourselves of a story that Clare spent whole days in the fields writing, using the Bell ale to save food at the cottage.

In July Octavius Gilchrist died. Soon after that, came news of Robert Bloomfield's death. In 1822 Bloomfield had sent Clare his *Mayday with the Muses*. During August Clare worked at hay and harvest. In September, a rich West Indian, Sir Michael Benignus Clare, sent five guineas for the name's sake. Elizabeth Kent the botanist, Leigh Hunt's sister-in-law, also sent Clare her *Flora Domestica*, in which he was cited and praised as a poet of flowers. But in spite of these gifts, the deaths of friends laid a heavier sense of responsibility and mortality on him, as well as a determination against the Bell ale and any slight alleviation that it might afford.

---

[1] *Prose*, p. 213.

VII

The Parish which, when Taylor did see, he quietly disregarded for *The Shepherd's Calendar,* could certainly not be said to be too like what Clare had so far written. This poem of just over a thousand lines is bitter satire. Words are like knouts. It is unalleviated by what Dryden called 'Wit-writing' and is without that background of cordial understanding good satire needs. Clare finished it in the passion of this period when he was not yet reconciled to his failure to find the public for rural poetry he was convinced still existed. Those Enclosure-precipitated injustices which he was watching at close quarters were to reach a nadir by 1830. His satire is as harsh as Crabbe at his harshest. It is altogether too 'raw'. There are none of those rounded, filled-in characters, those full dramatic circumstances of lives which make the later Crabbe so mellow and human a poet. But perhaps we may first remind ourselves of the Crabbe in *The Borough*:

> Nor war nor wisdom yield our Jews delight;
> They will not study, and they dare not fight.
> These are, with us, a slavish, knavish crew,
> Shame and dishonour to the name of Jew;
> The poorest masters of the meanest arts,
> With cunning heads and cold and cautious hearts;
> They grope their dirty way to petty gains,
> While poorly paid for their nefarious pains.

In *The Parish* Clare presented a tableau of characters- 'farmers of the New & Old School', a 'village politician,' a 'steward', a 'Justice of the Peace', a bailiff, religious enthusiasts of various types, and—the only alleviation in the poem—a Goldsmithian vicar whom he had once known:

> Nature in various moods pursues her plan,
> And moulds by turns the monkey or the man;
> With one she deals out wisdom as a curse,
> To follow fortune with an empty purse;
> The next in opposite extremes is bred—
> O'erflowing pockets and an empty head;

Beggars in merit share a squire's estate,
And squires untitled meet a beggar's fate.
Fortune's great lottery own nor rules nor laws;
Fate holds the wealth, and reason rarely draws;
Blanks are her lot, and merit vainly tries,
While heedless folly blunders on the prize. . . .

. . . Dandy Flint, grown old in youthful shame
By loathed diseases which no words can name
And worn so spare that wit, as passing by,
Swears Nick will thread him through a bodkin's eye;
A sot who spouts short morals o'er his gin,
And when most drunk rails most against the sin;
A dirty hog that on the puddle's brink
Stirs up the mud and quarrels with the stink. . . .

Old Saveall next, whose dirty deeds and fame
Might put a young bard's silken lines to shame;
But my plain homespun verse lets none escape,
Nor passes folly in its rudest shape;
When satire's muse puts on a russet gown,
Tho' vermin start as game, she runs them down
So Saveall shall have place—tho' fortune's smiles,
Unmixed with frowns, have made him known for miles;
Who tries to buy a good name and deceive
With fair pretensions that but few believe . . .
Yet in religion he is made elect
And buys with wine the favours of the sect . . .
Little religion in each bosom dwells,
And that sleeps sound till Sunday's chiming bells. . . .

The Ranter priests, that take the street to teach,
Swear God builds churches wheresoe'er they preach;
While on the other hand protestant people
Will have no church but such as wears a steeple.
Thus creeds all differ; yet each different sect. . .
Each thinks his own as right and others wrong,
And thus keeps up confusion's babel-song,
While half the tribes at bottom are no more
Than saints skin-deep and devils at the core.
Old Ralph, the veriest rake the town possessed,
Felt sins prick deep and all his crimes confessed,
Groaned o'er confessions to his ranting priest,

And prayed and sang and felt his soul released . . .
But hell, untired with everlasting watch
(The fox grows cunning when prey's hard to catch),
Crept into Ralph's new-planted paradise,
And met success in tempting him to vice.
A simpering Eve did in his garden dwell,
And she was fair, and he grew fond—and fell.
'Twas love at first, but e'en when that began
The sinking saint grew more and more the man,
And with his Eve, so treacherously fair,
Could feel more joy than kneeling down to prayer . . .
His fate was evident; it came at last;
His sheep were judge and shepherd Ralph was cast;
Then drink and racket joined their former friends,
And new-born saint in the old sinner ends.

Young Bragg, a Jack of all trades save his own,
From home is little as the farmer known,
Opinions gratis gives in men's affairs,
Fool in his own but wondrous wise in theirs . . .
Hunting for votes some dirty borough town,
'Tis then his genius meets the most renown;
When on the hustings bawling spouters throng,
Who fight and war like women with the tongue . . .
Here shines our orator in all his plumes,
Nor prouder bantam to a dunghill comes
Than he to crow and peck and peck and crow,
And hurl bad English at retorting foe.
He games and drinks and rackets up and down,
A low-lived mocker at high life in town;
And sips his wine in fashionable pride,
And thrusts in scorn the homely ale aside.

Tho' Justice Terror, who the peace preserves,
Meets more of slander than his deed deserves—
A blunt, opinionated, odd, rude man,
Severe and selfish in his every plan—
Tho' pleading want oft meets with harsh replies,
And truth's too often listened to as lies,
Although he reigns with much caprice and whim,
The poor can name worse governors than him.
His gifts at Christmas time are yearly given,
No doubt as toll fees on the road to heaven . . .

Yet still he reigns, whatever faults they find,
A blunt, odd, rude, good picture of his kind;
Who preaches partial for both church and king
And runs reform down as a dangerous thing . . .
But now grown old in reading Sunday's prayers
And keeping village morals in repairs . . .

He seeks a curate to supply his place,
A kinsman of his worship's sacred race,
Who wears his priesthood with a trader's skill. . . .
Perhaps when death-beds might his aid desire,
His horse was sick and might a drink require
Or friends for just necessities might claim
His shooting skill to track the fields for game;
And when they needed partridges or hares
The parish pauper could not look for prayers;
Or if he did indulge the foolish whim,
What cared the priest?—die and be damned for him!
Old Farmer Thrifty reigns from year to year
Their tyrent king, yclept an overseer . . .
From shoe-black vile to valet dignified,
He rose successfully without a fall,
And owned the cunning power to please in all . . .
His nest was feathered ere his fame was old,
And land was bought when farms were cheaply sold . . .
With big round belly and sleek double chin,
He reads the news and smokes and drinks his gin . . .

Fawning a puppy at his master's side
And frowning like a wolf on all beside;
Who fattens best when sorrow worst appears
And feeds on sad misfortune's bitterest tears—
Such is Bumtagg the bailiff, to a hair,
The worshipper and demon of despair . . .[1]

With the portrait of the chief woodman who would not
allow the villagers to gather acorns for their pigs or wood
for their fires, Clare abruptly ends these gall-imbued, one-
dimensional portraits. It was not his true voice, being more
than ever derivative, nor was it any step towards that

[1] *Poems*, 1935, I, p. 542.

excellence he was aiming at, though doubtless the writing of it relieved him.

When he had finished *The Parish* and other poems intended for his third volume, he had been writing almost without remission for close on four years. By November Mrs. Emmerson was sympathising about his 'abiding shadow of misery' and his 'fiery torments'. She enquired about his means. Admiral Lord Radstock wrote again to Lord Milton about a cottage and a piece of ground, but nothing materialised. On the 5th of January, Clare's first son was born and christened Frederick. Soon after, Hessey sent pills from Dr. Darling, who had doctored Keats, Hazlitt, John Scott, Wilkie, and B. R. Haydon, and whom Clare had met at the *London* dinners in 1822. Lady Milton sent her own doctor, Walker of Peterborough, and Walker prescribed good food and assured Clare that he would soon recover. Mrs. Emmerson thought him suffering from 'nervous debility', 'of all diseases the most painful to the poor patient'. Dr. Arnold, who had 'cured' him as a boy, visited him. But all this, as we know from the confusion over Walker's bill, though helpful, meant more accounts for which Clare felt himself responsible.

It was a critical time. One of the most difficult conditions of mental fatigue is its time-lag. At first the mind has become over-active, and all the senses are correspondingly over-acute. Both mind and senses in this state are capable of auditory and visual trickery, as well as of still-brilliant intuition such as attended the creative state. Then the goal when it is won, or the work when it is finished, leaves a void, or may itself not seem worth while because the experience of creation has so deepened or widened vision. This is something of what happened over *The Parish*. Clare did not need John Taylor to tell him that the satire of unevocative hate was not his genre. He did not really need him to tell him now what *was*. It was connected with affirmation as opposed to the negation and renouncement out of which satire springs: the affirmation of rightness and beauty which has been brought to the forefront of poet's minds in each crisis of men's development since the writing of *The Symposium*. The eleventh and twelfth centuries had been one of these periods. The onset of the modern industrial age was another.

The year 1823–4 was thus critical for Clare, both personally
and in relation to his day. The last time he had seen Mary
Joyce was in 1821. Then, in *Farewell to Mary*, he had con-
sciously extinguished hope of the kind of love that could be for
a few years, if not for a lifetime, a 'marriage of true minds', or
'blisse of two hertes'. But he had not held to his intention not
to 'sully' Mary's remembrance further. Poems about her continued. Mrs. Emmerson enquired what 'dear Patty' thought
about 'these loves of your imagination'. If he was faced with
inner emptiness there was little room in it for complaints
against Patty. But *A Daydream in Summer*, of this year or the
next, shows the process of casting love into the alembic of the
mind about to begin:

> . . . The cuckoo sang in soft delight
> Its ditty to departing light,
> And murmuring children far away
> Mocked the music in their play;
> And in the ivied trees the dove
> Breathed its soothing song of love . . .
>
> He thought in rapture's mad extreme
> To hold her though it proved a dream.
> And instant as that thought begun
> Her presence seemed his love to shun,
> And deaf to all he had to say
> Quick turned her tender face away;
> When her small waist he strove to clasp,
> She shrunk like water from his grasp.[1]

That, in spite of the careless repeat-sound instead of rhyme in
the first couplet, is poetry of an essence very far removed from
the rhetorical invective of *The Parish*. It is also much nearer
his true genre. Years later, in 1841, on his return to a liberty
that could be no liberty, after his first exile, the process of
distillation is further illuminated for us in the long vital poem,
Child Harold.[2]

About the time of his son's birth Clare was taken in what he

[1] *Poems*, 1935, I, p. 424. There are at least five drafts: Peterborough Mss.
120, 121, 148 and 24; and Northampton Ms. 7. In the fair copy a Wartonian
echo 'The Enthusiast' preceded Clare's first title.

[2] *Poems*, 1935, II, p. 393. See also *Selected Poems of John Clare*, Ed. Geoffrey
Grigson, p. 194.

called, six months after, in a letter to Thomas Inskip the friend of Bloomfield, 'a sort of apoplectic fit'. This left him with a numbing pain in his head, a sense as of 'being in a dream', and, he said, affected his memory and other faculties.

In this misery of exhaustion in the spring of 1824, he began to draw up his will, with the aid of the London lawyer, Richard Woodhouse, who had been Keats's friend. He left £10 to his sister Sophy, lately married, and living at Newborough, a fen village a few miles from Helpston. Four shillings a week were to go to his parents out of the copyright of his works; and the interest from the Fund money to his wife and family.

His active mind, even when exhausted, and when he could not write, yet could not rest. He began to puzzle about religion, seeking light on the old question 'What is Life?' Momentarily he contemplated joining the Primitive Methodists, the Ranters. They seemed happy—as if they had found at least a satisfying answer. Hessey wrote that 'a broken and contrite heart are much more welcome in the sight of God than undue presumption'.

By the end of April, his health being still unimproved, he decided to take Taylor's advice and consult the 'celebrated Scotch physician' Dr. Darling, in London. He arrived there by the Stamford coach sometime about the end of May.

VIII

In 1824, the *London Magazine*'s brightness had diminished. Its old contributors, for a variety of reasons, were falling away. Taylor was finding new ones, Carlyle, Mary Shelley, and the Irish poet George Darley, and De Quincey had introduced Landor. But Lamb, even by May, 1823, felt that 'I cannot but think the *London* drags heavily'.

After resting for some days at Fleet Street, Clare visited the Emmersons. After that he divided his time between Stratford Place and Taylor's. Under Dr. Darling his bodily health improved, but of course his mental distresses were more stubborn. He had always maintained what he called a 'hardened disbelief' in country superstitions such as ghosts and evil spirits. But with his illness he could not easily control

both an intensely-active fancy and a rationalistic questioning
which had never had sufficient intellectual sustenance of a
kind to satisfy: 'Thin death-like shadows & goblins with
saucer eyes were continually shaping on the darkness from my
haunted imagination.' Chancery Lane between Taylor's and
Stratford Place he particularly disliked having to pass late at
night.

But as he recovered a little, he was able to attend to a few
social encounters. De Quincey was in Town on one of his
elusive and impractical sojourns with pecuniary affairs:

> A little artless simple-seeming body something of a child
> overgrown in a blue coat & black neckerchief for his dress
> is singular with his hat in his hand steals gently among the
> company with a smile turning timidly round the room. It
> is De Quincey the Opium-Eater & that abstruse thinker in
> logic & metaphysic.[1]

Clare admired De Quincey's eloquence. Had he been less ill
he might certainly have been interested to compare notes on
childhood with one who suffered, as Thomas De Quincey
apparently had, from his elder brother's superior will and
delight in strife. In his discursively involuted *London Reminiscences*, the Opium-Eater remembered Clare as throwing 'a
weight of languor at any attempt to draw him out into conversation'. But he recalled also Clare's 'rapturous spirit of
admiration' at mention of Wordsworth. Then he, a little
curiously, concluded that gazing on 'models of colossal excellence' seemed to have the effect of depressing Clare's spirits.
How to remain a poet and yet earn enough to avoid sacrifice
of those dependent on him was certainly at the core of Clare's
self-communing of this time. We know he thought that Wordsworth 'for originality of description' had 'few if any equals',
though he distrusted Wordsworth's 'mysteries'. Yet joy, his
own joy wrested at any cost from grievous experience and without refuge in orthodoxy, was certainly already in the cat's
cradle of invisible threads within Clare's mind during his 1824
London visit.

Hazlitt, married a second time, and perhaps briefly happy,
was in Town about the June of 1824. Clare noted for us

[1] *Prose*, p. 91.

Shelley's 'hooded eagle', too, S. T. Coleridge. The incubation of Coleridge's *Aids to Reflection* was proceeding. Taylor published the *Aids* in 1825:

> There was Coleridge at one of the Parties he was a man with a venerable white head fluent of speech not a "silver-tongued Hamilton" his words hung in their places at a quiet pace from a drawl in good set marching order so that you would suppose he had learnt what he intended to say before he came. . . .[1]

Clare's account, from which the rest of the manuscript page is most unfortunately torn, does not at all convey that greatest talker and most instructive thinker of his age, whose hair had once been 'black and glossy as the raven's'. Perhaps Lamb, Hazlitt, *Anima Poetæ*, and the *Biographia* can best conjure that spirit into bright life again.

But in his ten-week sojourn this time, Clare renewed acquaintance with Lamb, Cary, Cunningham, Reynolds, Bowring, and Elton. He made two new friendships—with George Darley, the *London*'s literary critic, the 'bloody John Lacy', known thus for his 'slashing, pinking, and carbona-doing', and with Harry Stoe Van Dyk. Darley had come from Dublin in 1821 with a volume of poems in his pocket. Beddoes saw Darley in 1824 as 'a tallish, slender, pale, light-eyebrowed, gentle-looking baldpate, in a brown surtout with a duodecimo under his arm—stammering to a most provoking degree'. With the exception of Clare and Hessey, Darley's was the only friendship with John Taylor that outlasted *London* days. But neither Darley's *Errors of Ecstasie* in 1822, nor *Sylvia* in 1826, captured for him the notice of poetry-readers in that distracted decade. Even by 1861, Palgrave knew so little of the Darley behind those one or two glorious lyrics, that he placed *A Ryghte Pythie Songe*—'It is not beautie I demande'—in its spiritual home between poems by Milton and Carew. Taylor published for Darley his text-books on geometry, trigonometry, algebra, and astronomy, which provided Darley with his daily bread in that bustling age about to plunge into its fever of industrial reform and 'progress'. And Darley recognised in Clare's poetry

---

[1] *Prose*, p. 91.

that 'musical singing note' that was, he said, the 'mark of the true poet'.

Harry Stoe Van Dyk, in 1824, was a retiring young man but a 'warm-hearted friend'. Radstock and Mrs. Emmerson were interested in him. He had published a small volume of poems, and he promised to help with the delayed *Shepherd's Calendar*.

When Clare had been in Town a few weeks, on the 14th of July, Byron's funeral cortege crossed London on its way home to Newstead. At the bottom of Oxford Street, George Borrow, amid the crowd, watched the passing of the hearse and the long train of empty coaches, and mused upon the poet and his reputation. Allan Cunningham, also well-posted, moralised on the 'barren pageantry'. Lady Caroline Lamb, as we know, watched too, with less fruitful results. Mary Shelley looked from her window. Clare saw the 'small and rather mean' hearse, the coach carrying the pall-covered embers, the empty gilt carriages, and motley show of the sixty others. He learnt, from the mob of people, whose ashes it was that were on their 'last journey to that place where fame never comes'. Byron had written of Clare, in the Lisle Bowles-Gilchrist controversy over Pope, as a 'deserving poet': a kindly but idle phrase. Beyond magazine verses, it is unlikely that Byron had read any Clare. Yet the impact of Byron on Clare, of Byron's moral and sexual defiance, and most of all, of his fame, was profound: 'wether Byron hath seized on true fame I cannot tell' he wrote for the *Essay on Popularity*; 'my mind is too little to grasp that judgment'. But

> A splendid sun hath set . . .
> The labour of small minds an age may dream,
> And be but shadows on time's running stream;
> While genius, in an hour, makes what shall be,
> The next, a portion of eternity.[1]

Rationally he might conclude that Byron won fame 'less by his sterling merits as a poet than by his oddities as a man': that Byron's exploits in Greece were those of an actor playing at hero. Yet—'these appear to be his infirmitys—& these are but spots in the sun'. Finally,

[1] *Poems*, 1935, p. 105.

It is said that Byron is not to have a monument in West-minster Abbey. To him it is no injury. Time is his monument on whose scroll the name of Byron shall be legible when the walls and tombs of Westminster Abbey shall have mingled with the refuse of ruins & the sun as in scorn be left free again to smile upon the earth so long darkened with the pompous shadows of bigotry & intolerance.[1]

It is the passion behind this strange idea that is arresting: the sun's integrity of light over a Gomorrah-earth of false values betrays how dark a hold the terrible doctrine of judgment and damnation had on this poet's sensibility. It betrays, too, how deeply fame, that 'last infirmity of noble mind' was being reflected upon at this crisis of his career.

E. V. Rippingille came up from Bristol, and Clare 'indulged in some of the town amusements' with his old comrade—the 'smoke, smocks, smirks, smells and smutty doings' of the French Playhouse. Rippingille thought that 'taking all weathers rough & smooth as they came was the best physic for a sick man & a glass of Scotch Ale only served to strengthen his notions'. Here again some of those invisible strands which bind one thing to another become visible for a moment. At the Fives Court, 'Jones the Sailor Boy' took Clare's eye as being the 'finest fellow in the Ring'. Clare caught 'the Fancy' very much from Rip. We shall remember here Clare's admiration of his father: 'I believe we must go into low life to know how very much parents can be beloved by their children', Taylor had noted in his *Visit to John Clare* published in the *London* in 1821. We shall remember, too, Parker Clare's wrestling skill, and in what esteem physical prowess is held in rural communities; what corresponding scorn of physical frailty there is. We may even recall how the physically diminutive Blake's 'visions' of Moses and Dante were always of figures 'more than the common height'. Both Jones the Sailor Boy and the Nonpareil of Reynolds's Corcoran sonnet, 'Good with both hands and only ten stone four', will re-appear out of the mists of frustration of Clare's later years. In 1824, Randall the Nonpareil kept *The Hole in the Wall* in Chancery Lane. And Chancery Lane by night—not for its purse-knappers, of which London had plenty

[1] Peterborough Mss.

in 1824, nor for its body-snatchers, on whom anatomical science was still dependent, but because of its power over his involuntary imaginings—Clare hated to pass alone. All these, like the fascination of Byron, are only strands; but they help to show the way the web of association may weave itself into a mind in a state of exhaustion. If the full odds which that mind took up in its youthful strength are being revealed for the first time, irrational associations may be much more fatally strong.

With Rippingille and Elton, Clare visited Deville, one of the most respected phrenologists of the then-popular craze. From Paris Deville had brought his salon to the Strand. It was Deville whom Harriet Martineau visited incognito, to be told she 'could never accomplish anything, through my remarkable deficiency in both physical and moral energy'. Was it on Clare's head that the 'craneologist' found 'ideality,' 'amorous propensitys', 'benevolence' and 'veneration'? From his amused account we cannot tell which of these belonged to him and which to Rip or Elton:

> "I should say that you had a talent for poetry I don't say that you are a poet but that you have a tallent for it if applied . . . heres veneration very high I shoud say you are religious the head perhaps is worldly minded & remains silent . . . heres combativeness very large I should say you are not slow at avenging an insult, particularly if it be offered to a female for the amorous propensitys are large also I should say you have a love for the fair sex but not so as to make it troublesome . . . heres ideality . . . are you a poet sir (yes) aye aye the systems right" . . . he then in smiling silence waits your decision of his remarkable prophecy & hard & earthlike is that soul who can return an harsh & unbelieving opinion.[1]

With Hessey, Clare met William Etty, who became R.A. this same year, competing for that honour with Constable. Sir Thomas Lawrence, the fashionable portraitist, he found very courteous. He met, too, Francis Freeling, Sole Secretary to the General Post Office for nearly half a century, and the genial and witty T. K. Hervey, later editor of the *Athenaeum*. Rippingille escorted him also to Astley's Theatre, the original of the modern circus. Thomas Bennion took him to the

[1] *Prose*, p. 97.

Exhibition of Mexican Curiosities at the Egyptian Hall.

There was tea with the Lambs at Islington. Bowring, Elton, Taylor, and Hessey were there. John Bowring, master of some fifteen languages, had lately published his successful *Specimens of the Russian Poets*. But it was no good pretending the *London* circle was what it had been. Hazlitt, Procter, Hood, and Wainewright had already parted with Taylor in bitterness. In the preceding January had appeared *Janus Weatherbound, or the Weathercock Steadfast for lack of oil*. Janus took his leave, with addresses to the contributors, particularly Clare, Cary, and Lamb:

> And first, then, for John Clare; for first doth he stand in the sixth volume. 'Princely Clare', as Elia would call thee, some three hours after the cloth was drawn—— Alas! good Clare, never again shall thou and he engage in those high combats, those wit-fights! Never shall his companionable draught cause thee an after-look of anxiety into the tankard!—no more shall he, pleasantly-malicious, make thy ears tingle, and thy cheeks glow, with the sound of that perplexing constrainment! that conventional gagging bill! —that Grammar! ! till in the bitterness of thy heart thou cursest Lindley Murray by all the stars.—Not once again shall thy sweetly simple Doric lay beget the odious *pun*. . . . Little didst thou think that evening would be the last, when thou and I, and two or three more . . . parted with the humanity-loving Elia beneath the chaste beams of the watery moon. . . . There was something solemn in the manner of our clasping palms,—it was first 'hands round', then 'hands across'.—That same party shall never meet again!

There were many reasons, not necessary to recount here, for the falling off. 'Were we too good for the times?' Hessey wondered later. Taylor, as author, editor, and publisher, undoubtedly overworked himself. There were complaints— besides Clare's—about alteration of manuscripts, about claims put forward in copyright, about discussions carried on so long that they made the magazine dull: and, since it was hardly paying its way, about unfair and tardy payment. But Hood posed the still-perplexing question: ' "Arrah, honey, why did you die?" '

Had not you an editor, and elegant prose writers, and beautiful poets, and broths of boys for criticism and classics, and wits and humorists? . . . Hadn't you an Opium-Eater, and a Dwarf, and a Giant, and a Learned Lamb, and a Green Man?

The brief glory of the best of all magazines of its time was, by 1824, done. Lamb, as he himself wrote to Bernard Barton even in 1823, lingered 'among its creaking rafters'. George Darley, Taylor said in disillusion, was the only good that came out of the *London*. There was no longer any hope of its rivalling the *Edinburgh Magazine*, as it had set out to do. At the end of this year or the beginning of the next, Taylor handed its editing over to Henry Southern and raised its price in a last effort at revival. But the virtue had gone out of it. It was 'whip syllabub, thin sown with aught of profit or delight.' Within six months Taylor had sold it to Southern, under whose hand it continued till it was absorbed by the *New Monthly* in 1829. All that remains for us to notice is C. A. Elton's half-prophetic *Idler's epistle to J. Clare* in the August, 1824, *London*:

> . . . What thou hast been the world may see,
> But guess not what thou still may'st be;
> Some in thy lines a Goldsmith see,
>   Or Dyer's tone;
> They praise thy worst; the best of thee
>   Is still unknown.
>
> Some grievously suspect thee, Clare!
> They want to know thy form of prayer;
> Thou dost not cant and so they stare
>   And smell free-thinking;
> They bid thee of the devil beware,
>   And vote thee sinking. . . .

Both Eliza Emmerson and Hessey had written to Patty that Clare was anxious to return home: indeed, nothing but 'the positive orders of his physician', Dr. Darling, who wished to continue treatment with the patient under his eye, kept him in Town. But on the 8th of August, though unrecovered, Clare made up his mind for Helpston.

IV

ISOLATION OF MATURITY 1824-1837

I

WE may be sure, from the vigour of Clare's setting about a Journal and an Autobiography, as well as essays and poems, immediately on reaching home, that he had by this concluded some kind of reckoning with circumstances and with the future. He clearly thought that, given publication, his poems might reach a sufficient number of readers to give him the little profit he needed to make a living. The formidable list of Walter Scott's verse publications before that author decided Byron had beaten him off the poetic field might have daunted him. Talk in London had been of the return to earth of the rocket-burst of poetry which had gone up about the end of the century. But inwardly, where both ambition and humility could be examined and recognised for what they were, Clare in his maturity considered himself an integral part of the age's true poetry: with Keats, Shelley, Coleridge, and even Wordsworth, not among the Richard Wallises and William Goldens; and though he felt he had arrived late and handicapped from his fen backwaters, he was now inwardly certain of his part in the continuance of poetry, a poetry undefiled by 'low creeping language under the pretence of simplicity' or by what he himself called 'affected godliness'.

Already he knew that the whole man is frequently demanded in poetry's service. By 1824 he suspected that nothing less than the whole man might do in his case; and knowing that, he determined to continue. Perhaps he could not help himself. Yet no decision was ever taken less lightly. We know that once he had turned back to writing in this year, 1824, poetry became more than ever 'soul-enchanting' as he said, his 'heart's companion'. But the goblins with saucer eyes and the evil spirits of his fancy that the rational part of him could not exorcise in

London were not so much phantoms of poverty and destitution, as symbols of an actuality which he knew would be his if he failed.

One of his difficulties on his return from London was delay over *The Shepherd's Calendar*. It had not been ready the previous winter as Taylor promised, and it was not ready this winter of 1824. There is little doubt that Taylor had allowed *The Village Minstrel* to take care of itself in order to ascertain whether Clare could find a public. If he could Taylor's generous support would have been forthcoming. But *The Shepherd's Calendar* had already been announced in magazines, and even in the *Times*. By October Van Dyk was regretting for Clare's sake that he had taken the work on, since he was too busy to make quick progress in copying poems. There seems no reason why Clare himself should not from the first have made fair copies of poems for *The Calendar*, as finally he did, and as he also did for his last book under another publisher. In November Hessey again criticised the poems because they abounded in 'description' and lacked 'sentiment and human interest'. By January, 1825, Taylor was engaged in a fierce dispute with Landor, and in his last attempt to revive the dying *London*. On the 10th of February, Van Dyk wrote that all the poems were copied except *January*; Clare should have the first proof, and the book be out within six weeks. A month later the proof arrived, was corrected, and sent back.

No more followed. Van Dyk's next letter, of the 15th of March, was forwarded by the publishers in May. Printing was held up because Taylor had omitted to pass on to Van Dyk some of the poems in his possession. Artis, in London in March, had made several tries to get back some other manuscripts Clare wanted. Clare's Journal for the 17th of April runs:

> I have waited 3 weeks for a new proof of "The Shepherd's Calendar" & nothing has come which was to be in 3 days—I have sent for some rough copys of Poems which I sent up to Taylor when "The Village Minstrel" was in press & I have not got them & never shall I expect— I want them to finish some & correct others. . . . I have never as yet had a settling . . . wrote to Hessey in a manner that I am always very loath to write but I coud keep my patience no longer.

He set forth his grounds of complaint in the rough draft of the letter which has fortunately survived. The letter which Taylor received has disappeared from the Clare letters he so carefully preserved:

> I do not wish to hurt the feelings of anyone nor do I wish they should hurt mine but when delay is carried into a system its cause must grow a substitute for a worse name. I will go no further but I will just ask you to give a moment's reflection to my situation & see how you would like it yourself. . . .

A note to this letter-draft of some years later adds: 'These (the poems he wanted) never were returned nor accounted for.' Taylor replied, in this instance very quickly, about the new book: 'The Fact is my Heart is not in the Business. I could not make up such a Volume from the whole collection, answering to the Title of *The Shepherd's Calendar*, as would surpass the others, or equal them in the Estimation of the Public.' As to certain 'Hints and Cautions' which Clare had received (from Eliza Emmerson), Taylor went on: 'If you or any of your Correspondents think they can put your Poems into the hands of anyone more likely to do you Justice, I will part with them willingly. . . . At all events, it is better to terminate the Connection at once than to continue it in Distrust.'

There is no doubt that Taylor took his responsibility for Clare's finance if not his poetry very seriously, and upheld it under great difficulties. The impractical poet who insisted on paying village boys to spare the birds thought to be too numerous in the new hedges can have been no easy person to feel responsible for, either financially or in any way. He would outbid the overseers' twopence a carcase. He was at this very time teaching 'a poor boy the elements of arithmetic' but refusing to take any payment. He pulled the straw from his cottage thatch so that sparrows might build; he kept hawks, sparrows, and woodpigeons as pets; too tender as a father, he would offer to take the stripes Patty occasionally administered to their children. On this occasion he replied humbly to Taylor:

> . . . I know that my temper is hasty & with that knowledge of myself I always strive to choke it & soften hard opinion

with reasonable interpretations—but put yourself in my
place for a minute & see how you woud have felt & written
yourself. . . .
I have no desire to seek another publisher. . . .[1]

Taylor accepted the olive branch, admitting that he had been
slow. At midsummer he and Hessey were to dissolve partnership, Hessey retaining the retail business and Taylor the publishing. In July, as we know, worn out with his efforts over the
London, Taylor let it go. 'The literary world,' Hessey had
written in May, 'is dulness itself—scarcely a book of any value
published'; and Beddoes had exclaimed in 1824: 'If I were the
literary weather-guesser for 1825 I would safely prognosticate
fog, rain, blight in due succession for its dullard months.'
Prudent and able men, as John Taylor was, restricted their
activities in time; the more reckless or unwary went on to suffer
in the booksellers' crashes of 1826. Yet in September, Taylor
himself went down with brain-fever, and his recovery saw a
dramatically changed man. He no longer sought worthwhile
poetry; no longer was he enthusiastic to discover true poets, or
generously eager to help needy ones. Literary interests came
second; theological and scientific ones first. Under S. T. Coleridge's wizard tongue, he renounced his reputation as a Free
Thinker and was 'converted to Christianity and the Doctrines
of the Church'. De Quincey remembered Taylor's 'enmity of
the Church of England', at a time when, De Quincey thought,
that Church was becoming 'truly pastoral'.

    With characteristic shrewdness Taylor began to look about
for means of linking his new outlook with business. The change
in the taste of the reading public, in its turn part of a much
wider national trend, fitted in. As the potential interest in
poetry declined, the demand for text-books and works of
scientific knowledge rose steadily. With these rose the novel.
Thus the best work of poets like Darley, Hood, and Clare fell
among new poetic toys, the blousily gilt and embellished
Albums and Annuals—Clare's 'tinsel gauds'—which rose in
the 1820s and declined in the 1830s.

    Three months after Taylor's recovery Mrs. Emmerson had a
talk with him about Clare's affairs and *The Shepherd's Calendar*

[1] *Letters*, p. 170

in particular. Again Taylor promised a statement of accounts between them. He thought there was 'about £40 profit on *The Village Minstrel*'. If Clare needed money he had only to ask for it. But when, in January, 1826, Clare evidently wrote himself to remind the publisher of his three-year-old promise to bring out *The Shepherd's Calendar* without delay, Taylor expressed indignation at such 'frank censure', which had relieved him from 'the irksome situation of submission, apology, and self-blame' to which he had submitted. Now he could speak out. Clare and Clare alone was responsible for the delay and present total stoppage of the work. The manuscript for *July*, on which he was now engaged, was almost unreadable. Copyists could do nothing with it.

Clare did not point out, as he might with some justice have done, that delay since Taylor began on the poem was brief compared with the delay before he set about it. He humbly admitted the justice of the criticism and said he would do his utmost at recopying the poem himself. He forwarded a new draft. Professing himself highly delighted, Taylor sent back the remaining manuscripts for recopying.

That behind him, Clare had peace of mind, with confidence enough to have his second son baptised in June, 1826: 'John, son of John Clare, Poet'. Mrs. Emmerson wrote for the occasion:

> Two little girls and two little boys
> Are quite enough for wedded joys.

By September title-page and dedication of *The Calendar* were under discussion. De Wint would do a frontispiece gratis, and Hessey suggested that Clare write the Introduction himself, as there was little to say except to account for the long delay on the score of ill-health. Clare's preface bears his hall-marks of independence and self-suppression. There was no word about 'peasant-poet'. He left the 'poems to speak for themselves', merely hoping that the author's 'low station' would not be held against them. And he slipped in at the end the excuse about his own illness. Toward the end of November he received six copies of the book. De Wint's first drawing had proved unacceptable, and a second was made and engraved. A scene of thirsty harvesters, this has the sincerity that made

De Wint and Clare akin, in this period when gates were opening into luscious and upholstered sentiment. Five months later *The Shepherd's Calendar* was ready for the public. It was within homely grey-blue boards, at six shillings a copy, whereas *Poems Descriptive* in pleasant calf had been four and sixpence.

It contained twelve descriptive pieces, some of which had been written as early as 1822. Nearly all look further back than that to the pre-Enclosure village. Besides these, Taylor had selected four Village Tales; and he reprinted some of Clare's poems from the *London Magazine*, doubtless to save himself manuscript-reading. The Village Tales have a dullish longueur. That kind of thing had been done since the days of Tickell and Mallet. It had been well done by Crabbe; and Clare had no power at all to give the exaggerated sentiment which the new luxury, after about 1824, began to demand. Taylor was discouraging. But not only from Taylor, but from all sides came the cry that there was no demand for poetry. Taylor had no hopes for Darley's *Sylvia*, either, with which he was busy. In future, he said, he intended to publish only works of knowledge, which this 'grand Age of Utility', as Cary called it, wanted.

Reviews of *The Calendar* were few and most of them poor. The *Eclectic Review* again gave praise. The *Literary Gazette* discovered 'fine poetry' in the book, but held out no hopes of a public for it; its poetry was not romantic enough, there being too much 'regular routine of comfort' in the life of the English peasantry for it to be very picturesque. Clare had certainly abetted such a misapprehension about comfort by the happiness audible in some of the *Calendar* poems. At the same time, the further he advanced in his imagistic realism the less was he likely to find either social or poetic understanding in the England approaching the chaotic 1830s.

It did not take long, therefore, for the presage in a dream Clare had recorded for the 9th of March, 1825, to be laid bare:

> . . . I thought I had one of the proofs of the new poems from London & after looking at it awhile it shrank thro my hands like sand & crumbled into dust.

But as if to reconcile himself, Clare had added immediately in his Journal:

the birds were singing in Oxey Wood at six o'clock this
evening as loud & various as at May.[1]

II

Intent on having a quantity of writing behind him, he had
begun, in 1824, besides his Journal and Autobiography, a series
of Natural History Letters, and notes for critical essays on such
subjects as Popularity, Landscape-Painting, Pride, Industry,
Mock-Modesty and Morals, Happiness, Nothing, Affectation,
Honour, and False Appearances. *Popularity in Authorship* was
the only one of the essays to be finished and obtain publication.
Through the good offices of Van Dyk it was printed for
November, 1825, in the *European Magazine*. Its gist is: 'three
centuries will wither every extravagance'. He was laughing at
himself in that age of bookmaking when 'almost everybody
catches the plague'. The other essays remain, repetitive but
illuminating fragments on the absorbing, unending subject,
honesty both inwardly, and outwardly in relation to others. It
is the subject which Coleridge treats so exhaustively in *The
Friend*. Like the questions of freedom, love, and joy, it returns
to men's minds in their crises.

By May, 1826, as we know from a letter to E. V. Rippingille,[1]
he had nearly finished his *Life*. 'I shant dye happy if I leave
any disgraceful remains behind me' he had written to Hessey
in 1823. But the later history of the Autobiography is obscure.
It is uncertain whether it was ever fair-copied or not.

The thirteen Natural History Letters, intended for a *Natural
History of Helpstone*, which J. A. Hessey was to publish, began in
September, 1824, under such titles as *The Sexual System of Plants*
and *The Fungus Tribe*. These might have made a book, and we
might now acknowledge Clare a forerunner of those field-
naturalists who prize 'the fluttering butterflye' above the one
'on a cork board'. But by 1825 the Nature Letters had become
bright but unsystematic accounts of migrating elvers, of bittern
and nightingale, or of adder with providentially 'quick hearing'
and unaggressive retreat: as he walked through 'long grass in a

---

[1] *Prose*, p. 138.
[2] Bodleian Mss.

morning' the adders 'have run away from every step I took &
dropt into the water by scores': but

> botanists . . . merely make collections of dryd specimens
> classing them after Linnaeus into tribes & familys . . . I
> have no wish to do this if my feelings would let me . . . I
> only . . . wish the fluttering butterflye to settle till I can
> come up with it to examine the powderd colours on its
> wings & then it may dance off again from fancyd dangers
> & welcome.

By the end of the year, having abandoned his own aims in this
field, he was writing to Elizabeth Kent, a series of letters unfortunately lost.[1]

In his Journal Clare tells of his garden—though 'never was
there a garden like the meadow'. In it were wild basil, pasque-
flower, bugloss, white horehound, mullein, betony, oxlip, and
black hellebore: all of these he transplanted with some of their
own soil beside his auriculas and chrysanthemums. He was
known among his neighbours as 'a wonderful man with
flowers'. Yarrow and cross-leaved heath he would not trans-
plant:

> on the leas
> Of rough neglected pasture I delight
> More than in gardens thus to stray
> Amid such scenes and mark thy hardy blooms . . .
> Bidding the loneliest russet paths be gay.

He noted '3 fellows' laying out the plans for 'an Iron railway
from Manchester to London'. This, one of the many abortive
rail projects of this decade and the next, would 'despoil a boggy
place that is famous for Orchises at Royce Wood end'.

He set down his reading in his Journal: Chatterton and the
defence of him against Walpole; *Don Juan*, which Henderson
brought from Milton library, roused as little enthusiasm as at
first Wordsworth had: but *The White Doe of Rylstone* had 'some
of the sweetest poetry' though full of Wordsworth's 'mysteries';
Pope's 'uninterrupted flow' had begun to weary his ear—
except the *Essay on Man*; Collins's Odes he thought superior to

---

[1] Miss Kent, of the 'unfeminine' temper which her brother-in-law took her
to task over, and which caused the usually good-natured Hessey some trouble
over the firm's publication of her *Flora Domestica*, was busy with a book on
birds, as well as with *Sylvan Sketches*, which came out in 1825.

Gray's, but Gray's letters he considered the best he had read, written with so much less consciousness of the reader than Burns's; he was reading Milton's shorter poems again and again; he was appraising recently-published poems such as Elton's *The Brothers* and Reynolds's *The Garden of Florence*; he could not appreciate his admired Thomas Tusser's 'taste for Inclosure'; reading from within, he found S. T. Coleridge's sonnets to 'labour after excellence'. Some underlying sense of the elder Coleridge's 'ills past Care and past Complaint' evidently conveyed itself to him. 'Lamb's best poetry is in *Elia*.' Clare felt Hazlitt to be the finest prose-writer of the day—except on political matters; comparing Johnson's Life of Savage with his Life of Gray, he sensed that booby-trap of criticism, unconscious personal prejudice. Worse than this was that Johnson could so lend his wisdom to erecting to pontifical magnitude the tradition of Dryden and Pope: as Clare said: 'beginning at the wrong end' with the *Lives* and 'forgetting there were such poets as Spenser, Drayton, Suckling'. Shakespeare, particularly the Sonnets, *Macbeth*, and *Henry the Fifth* (first read in a sixpenny copy bought when a boy at the fair), he browsed over continually, as well as Izaak Walton's *Compleat Angler*, *Paradise Lost*, and the Bible. Chaucer he seems to have read with surprising ease and understanding.

The bias of Clare's mind, like that of Keats's mind, was anticlerical. This, not abnormal among the genius of their day, may, like the poetic ambitions of these two, have been bound up with sensitiveness about lowly origins. Taylor had at first undoubtedly encouraged it in both of them. But it was also a temperamental refusal, in both Clare and Keats, to accept the causes of life's injustices for what they are said to be. It was a tendency to think forward, rather than back and beyond the universe. In both Clare and Keats this amounted to an integrity of intelligence, that quality strangely independent of culture and of class, which, when sensitive and not arrogant, one trembles to see humbled. Clare did not know in theological detail what he believed. To the end he did not succeed in building any body of belief for himself. He knew better what he did not believe. And he held his 'litany of doubts' within a religion of gratitude for earth's beauty. Hypocrisy in observance—'outward Sundayism', was 'monstrous'. He had no use for theories such as Election and Predestination, and what he saw as condescension of Catholicism toward the common mind seemed to him to abet preservance of false ideas as well as foolish relics in minds common and uncommon. He loathed and feared the Western Church's belief in Force, under whatever creed oppression might be perpetrated. 'War has ever been the watchword of political intriguers and religion'. Only by natural, incredibly slow growth could brutality and stupidity be bettered—'if reason & commonsense cannot convert them . . . she will not oppress them.' Reading Foxe in September, 1824, called forth in his Journal:

> the sum of my opinion is Tyranny & Cruelty appear to be the inseparable companions of Religious Power . . . & the great moral presept of a meek & unoffending teacher was 'Do as ye would be done by' & 'love them that hate you' if religious opinion had done so her history had been praiseworthy.

A re-reading the first chapter of Genesis produced:

> The sacred historian took a great deal upon credit for this world when he imagines that God created the sun moon & stars those mysterious hosts of heaven for no other purpose than its use 'the greater light to rule the day & the lesser light to rule the night' and the stars also 'to give light upon the earth' it is a harmless and universal propensity to magnify consequences that appertain to ourselves & would be a foolish thing to try the test of the scriptures upon these groundless assertions—for it contains the best poetry & the best morality in the world.

The 'brotherly affection & love' of St. John's Epistle delighted him. Supposed references to our Saviour in 'that luscious poem', the Song of Solomon, he thought 'very far-fetched'. Lord Radstock, with excellent intent, supplied him with theological works: Hannah More's *Spirit of Prayer*, the *Maxims of Piety and Christianity* by Thomas Wilson, Bishop of Sodor and Man. The Bishop of Llandaff's answer to Tom Paine, though Clare had heard Paine called a 'low blackguard', did not blind him to Bishop Richard Watson's attitude to 'ignorant peasants and mechanics', which attitude Wordsworth more publicly answered. In Thomas Erskine's *Remarks on the Internal Evidence of Revealed Religion*, Clare found 'some of the best reasoning in favour of its object' he had ever read. After reading that, a reasoning Deist might 'loose doubts sufficient to be half a Christian'. Further than this he could not go, and the following fragment from a commonplace book of probably a year or two later than this sums up the irrefragable humility and idealism of a mind too ready to renounce the complex and devious intolerances among human cultures:

> A religion that teaches us to act justly to speak truth & love mercy ought to be held sacred in every country & whatever the differences of creeds may be in lighter matters they ought to be overturned & the grand principles respected.[1]

Such insistence on tolerance and oneness in the Kingdom was held in those days in the same suspicion as Free Thinking, as Elton had warned him in his farewell Epistle. Clare's religious outlook was a little like that 'negative capability' when, as Keats wrote, 'a man is capable of being in uncertainties, mysteries, doubts, without any irritable searching after reason'. Such an outlook is difficult to support and suffering soon tests it. During 1824 and 1825, Clare could not prevent his mind pondering over 'a future existence'; it overweighted him with its 'upbraidings and miseries' when his children were ill, as, short of good food, they frequently were. A sense of over-responsibility that arose from the rejection of traditional ideas, made him dismally dream time after time he was in hell. But through all, and in spite of Taylor's paternal influence, which was great, and of Taylor's example in conversion, his down-to-earth mind never accepted the doctrines of Original Sin, of personal immortality, nor of Judgment. At most, his perception of earth's beauty convinced him, though even this only at times, of the 'sacred design of an Almighty Power'.

Reading that winter of 1824 Bishop Percy's *Reliques of Ancient English Poetry*, as well as Ellis's *Specimens of the Early English Poets*, and Ritson's *English Songs*, influenced by thoughts of Chatterton, 'Elia', 'Corcoran', 'Barry Cornwall', and 'Guy Penseval', and still thinking to work for poetry unhampered by patten and

---

[1] *Prose*, p. 227.

smock, Clare hit on the idea of a group of poems in the manner
of the older poets between Tottel and *The Hesperides*. Despite
some 'foolish follys', presumably at *The Blue Bell* about Christmas
of 1824, he wrote on the 5th of January, 1825, to James Montgomery, the editor of the Sheffield *Iris*. He said he had 'copied
the following verses from a Ms. on the Flye-leaves of an old
book entitled The World's Best Wealth a Collection of choice
Counsils in Verse & Prose printed for A. Bettesworth at the
Red Lion in Paternoster Row 1720'. Montgomery printed the
nineteen stanzas entitled *The Vanitys of Life*, cautiously repeat-
ing the story of their supposed origin. Hungry for a little
unqualified praise, Clare found Montgomery's letter on the
poem's 'condensed thought' and 'felicity of language' 'heart-
stirring' enough to tempt him further. In June William Hone
published some verses on *Death*, fathered on Andrew Marvell,
and purporting to have been found by one James Gilderoy.
The name of the old romantic robber might have warned Hone,
but there was nothing in either of these poems to have given
Clare away. *Death* has a word or two reminiscent of Shirley as
well as of Marvell, and its theme is death's levelling of injustices. Clare thought of Marvell as 'a great advocate for
liberty'. Shirley he would find next to Izaak Walton in Ellis.
He was careful to cover his tracks. But a prose piece, *Excursion
with the Angler*, of about this date, makes it clear that Walton,
Cotton, and Wotton, with their sincere love of the country, and
their individualistic outlook, Donne and 'Ignoto' Raleigh with
their realism, as well as Shirley's metrical freedoms, were all
attractive to him. So were Browne of Tavistock and South-
well. In August, under the name of Frederic Roberts of Milton,
and in a disguised handwriting, saying he preferred 'Shake-
spear to Byron Spenser to Sir Walter Scott Sir John Suckling
to Moor & every other of the Elizabethan Bards to the rest of
the Moderns', he sent Hone *A Farewell and Defiance to Love* from
'an old Copy of *Reliquiæ Wottonianæ*'.[1]

   This is, but very faintly, reminiscent of Raleigh's *Defiance to
Disdainful Love*. Clare was steeped in these poets, capable of
expanding and vivifying them from across the dividing
centuries, but not able, as Keats with Dryden and Burton,

---

[1] In a letter of May 8th, 1826, he told Montgomery he fathered it on Sir
John Harrington.

of making the newness and complex precision of great poetry from them. Hone did not accept this poem, but it appeared later in the *European Magazine*, as did *Thoughts in a Churchyard* fathered on Sir Henry Wotton, *The Gipsy's Song* on Tom Davies'[1] and *Go with your tauntings go* on Suckling. Montgomery suspected the authenticity of *The Vanities of Life* all along, and by the next year had extracted a confession from Clare, but he printed *To John Milton, from his honoured Friend, William Davenant,* knowing its origin. This poem is Clare's insight into the irrelevance of recognition or neglect for a poet's work, as well as into the intrepid D'Avenant's admiration for Milton.

> The bard his glory ne'er receives
> Where summer's common flowers are seen,
> But winter finds it when she leaves
>   The laurel only green;
> And time from that eternal tree
> Shall weave a wreath to honour thee.

In 1846, J. H. Dixon included *The Vanities of Life* in *Ancient Poems, Ballads, and Songs of the Peasantry of England*. Dixon did not believe Montgomery ever had any doubts about it as a genuine old poem: because of its lack of 'any little slip that detects the forger', he was convinced that Clare's claim to it merely 'betrayed mental aberration'. It went into other anthologies, and it was not until 1873 that J. L. Cherry put an end to the discussion by giving proof of Clare's authorship.

Clare continued these imitations till after the publication of *The Shepherd's Calendar*, when he had a small collection. He wished to publish them anonymously. Taylor persuaded him that they might better appear as *Visits of the Earlier Muses*. H. F. Cary, when asked, was also against 'literary forgery'. Most important of these ten poems and six songs is *The Triumph of Time*, a daylight vision, a snapping of his fingers at the old dark myth of a Judgment day, an acceptance of Time's possible world without man, and a surprisingly realistic statement of human limitation:

[1] Did he mean Frank Davison, of *A Poetical Rapsodie*, whom he mentions in *Excursion with the Angler* as singing 'Play, beggars, play'? *That* song is anonymous. Or did he mean Sir John Davies? Tom Davies was an eighteenth century bookseller.

A mighty poet thou, and every line
Thy grand conception traces is sublime:
No language doth thy godlike works confine;
Thy voice is earth's grand polyglot, O Time!
Known in all tongues, and read in every clime,
Changes of language make no change in thee:
Thy works have worsted centuries of their prime,
Yet new editions every day we see—
Ruin thy moral theme, its end eternity. . . .

Mighty survivor! Thou shalt see the hour
When all the grandeur that the earth contains,
Its pomp, its splendour, and its hollow power,
Shall waste like water from its weakened veins,
And not a shadow of a myth remain—
When names and fames of which the earth is full,
And books, with all their knowledge urged in vain—
When dead and living shall be void and null,
And nature's pillow be at last a human skull. . . .[1]

He wrote that in his search for folk ballads he found few
complete ones among the peasantry of Helpston. They had
become, he noted in 1828, the 'senseless balderdash that is
brawled and sung over at Country Feasts, Statutes, and Fairs'.
He contrived only about a score from the scraps which 'I heard
my father and mother hum over'. Among them is the *Maid of
Ocram*, the *Lord Gregory* which Burns gives in three baldish
stanzas. This ballad had been many times reprinted in the cheap
garlands of songs, the last we have found being in 1799. The
delicacy within directness of Clare's version places it in an
altogether different category from the garland reprint:

Gay was the Maid of Ocram
As lady e'er might be
When she did venture past a maid
To love Lord Gregory.
Fair was the Maid of Ocram
And shining like the sun
Ere her bower key was turned on two
Where bride-bed lay for none.

And late at night she sought her love—
The snow slept on her skin—

[1] *Poems*, 1935, II, p. 198, 199.

'Get up', she cried, 'thou false young man,
And let thy true love in.'
And fain would he have loosed the key
All for his true love's sake,
But Lord Gregory then was fast asleep,
His mother wide awake.

And up she threw the window sash,
And out her head put she:
'And who is that which knocks so late
And taunts so loud to me?'
'It is the Maid of Ocram,
Your own heart's next akin;
For so you've sworn, Lord Gregory,
To come and let me in.

O pause not thus, you know me well,
Haste down my way to win.
The wind disturbs my yellow locks,
The snow sleeps on my skin—'
'If you be the Maid of Ocram,
As much I doubt you be,
Then tell me of three tokens
That passed twixt you and me—' . . .

The Maid tells the three tokens, and the mother finally spurns
her in the voice of the son:

'Begone, you lying creature, then,
This instant from my hall . . .
For I have none on earth as yet
That may me father call.'

Among Clare's best are also *The Banks of Ivory; Betrayed;* two
versions, both expanded, of *My Luv is like a red red Rose;* the
happy *Love's Riddle;* and the amusing *O silly Love! O cunning
Love!*

His sonnet-collection continued far beyond the hundred he
had planned for a book. These form an apparently endless
series of verse-paragraphs of captured country moments; they
have such titles as *Hares at Play, Pleasant Places, The Foddering
Boy, The Woodland Stiles, The Breath of Morning,* and *The
Shepherd's Tree:*

> Huge elm, with rifted trunk all notched and scarred
>   Like to a warrior's destiny, I love
> To stretch me often on thy shadowed sward,
>   And hear the laugh of summer leaves above;
> Or on thy buttressed roots to sit, and lean
>   In careless attitude, and there reflect
> On times and deeds and darings that have been—
>   Old castaways, now swallowed in neglect,
> While thou art towering in thy strength of heart,
>   Stirring the soul to vain imaginings
> In which life's sordid being hath no part.
>   The wind of that eternal ditty sings
> Humming of future things, that burn the mind
> To leave some fragment of itself behind.

About this time Clare had written for his Essay on False Appearances: 'mind alone is the sun of the earth—it lives on when the clouds & paraphenalia of pretensions are forgotten'. In the sonnet *Mystery*, he ventures his homespun weave of what he further saw as a pattern of reality running through abstract ideas:

> Books are penned
> Mere guesses into truth, and at the last
> Mere guesses only, going where they came
> To that exhaustless blank that swallows all. . . .

But for the most part, the sonnet-collection contains simple evocative statement. Dylan Thomas put it forward as Clare's finest achievement.

Lastly, in this period of middle-thirty maturity, he produced a group of poems, chiefly about birds. The idea may have come to him from Grahame's *Birds of Scotland*. These are rough drafts, in a separate notebook, meant, no doubt when time had withered extravagances, for publication, but shown to nobody at the time. They are clearly dated, 1825–30: they are short poems of varying lengths, in which, free from *Calendar* impositions, he could carry out his own experiment. The group contains *The Blackcap*, *The Pettichap's Nest*, *The Redcap is a painted bird*, *The Green Woodpecker and the Wryneck*, *The Sedgebird's Nest*, *The Thrush's Nest*, *The Snipe* from the solitudes of Whittlesey Mere, and *The Nightingale's Nest*. This last cannot fail to remind us of other poems on the same subject. Like

Coleridge, Clare heard little melancholy in the bird's song, nor
did he echo the worn conceit. He had already given an extra-
ordinarily exact onomatopoeic translation of the bird's song in
The Progress of Rhyme. There is, in his Nightingale poem, none
of the 'sentiment' Hessey felt so desirable, nothing such as
Keats's infusion of a sense of limitless human desire within
human limitation into the rise, change, and often abrupt
ceasing of the bird's song; there is none of that contrast between
nature's 'permanence' and man's individual extinction, such
as Keats has in the seventh stanza of his poem.[1] *The Nightin-*
gale's Nest is pure statement of experience among 'the incident
and secrecy of wild life'—not comparable with Coleridge's
famous conclusion in 'Frost at Midnight', but live and good, at
a moment when poetry was only just maintaining itself:

> Up this green woodland-ride let's softly rove,
> And list the nightingale—she dwells just here.
> Hush! let the wood-gate softly clap, for fear
> The noise might drive her from her home of love;
> For here I've heard her many a merry year—
> At morn, at eve, nay, all the livelong day,
> As though she lived on song. This very spot,
> Just where that old man's beard all wildly trails
> Rude arbours o'er the road and stops the way—
> And where that child its bluebell flowers hath got,
> Laughing and creeping through the mossy rails—
> There have I hunted like a very boy,
> Creeping on hands and knees through matted thorn
> And vainly did I many hours employ:
> All seemed as hidden as a thought unborn. . . .
>
> Her joys are evergreen, her world is wide—
> Hark! there she is as usual—let's be hush—
> For in this blackthorn-clump, if rightly guessed,
> Her curious house is hidden. Part aside
> These hazel branches in a gentle way
> And stoop right cautious 'neath the rustling boughs,
> For we will have another search today
> And hunt this fern-strewn thorn-clump round and round:
> And where this reeded wood-grass idly bows,

[1] This idea is in Clare's *Triumphs of Time*, in *The Eternity of Nature*, in
Earth's Eternity, and in the later *Song's Eternity*. *Song's Eternity* represents
his acceptance of man's mortality within a possible 'immortality' of the truth
of poetry.

K

We'll wade right through, it is a likely nook:
In such-like spots and often on the ground,
They'll build, where rude boys never think to look.
Ay, as I live! her secret nest is here,
Upon this whitethorn[1] stump! I've searched about
For hours in vain. There! put that bramble by—
Nay, trample on its branches and get near.
How subtle is the bird! she started out,
And raised a plaintive note of danger nigh,
Ere we were past the brambles; and now, near
Her nest, she sudden stops—as choking fear
That might betray her home. So even now
We'll leave it as we found it: safety's guard
Of pathless solitudes shall keep it still.
See there! she's sitting on the old oak bough,
Mute in her fears; our presence doth retard
Her joys, and doubt turns every rapture chill.
Sing on, sweet bird! may no worse hap befall
Thy visions than the fear that now deceives.
We will not plunder music of its dower,
Nor turn this spot of happiness to thrall;
For melody seems hid in every flower
That blossoms near thy home. These harebells all
Seem bowing with the beautiful in song;
And gaping orchis, with its spotted leaves,
Seems blushing with the singing it has heard.
How curious is the nest! no other bird
Uses such loose materials, or weaves
Its dwelling in such spots; dead oaken leaves
Are placed without and velvet moss within,
And little scraps of grass, and—scant and spare,
Of what seem scarce materials—down and hair;
For from men's haunts she nothing seems to win . . .
                    Deep adown
The nest is made, a hermit's mossy cell.
Snug lie her[2] curious eggs in number five,
Of deadened green, or rather olive-brown;
And the old prickly thorn-bush guards them well.
So here we'll leave them, still unknown to wrong,
As the old woodland's legacy of song.

---

[1] He usually used 'whitethorn' for 'hawthorn'. In this poem he uses both 'blackthorn' and 'whitethorn' for sloe. Countrymen do.

[2] Following Chaucer and Shakespeare, Clare makes no mention of the male bird, though he discussed the matter of which bird sang in a prose note.

Self-suppression for the sake of delicate observation, and clear, faithful, emotion-suffused imagery were what he had been aiming at since 1820:

> True poesy is not in words
> But images that thoughts express,
> By which the simplest hearts are stirred
> To elevated happiness.

The Nightingale is not a great deal better than others of this group. The suspense of search for both watcher and bird, the watcher's triumph in his difficult find, and the relief of the bird communicated to the reader when the watcher turns away, are all conveyed in an attempt to use the most ordinary but vital speech-rhythms. The ten-syllabled line is sprinkled with occasional, seemingly-artless rhyme. The speech-rhythms are not perfect, being marred now and then by inversions and worn phrases. The whole poem is imperfect. But its immanent impulse has beauty and truth, springing from a successful attempt to keep a poetic gift whole.

Whilst waiting for *The Calendar*, he had begun contributing to the Annuals. This might have been thought an advance for him; the vulgar little books were on most of the tables of the rich. Van Dyk scolded him for 'giving away' poems to Montgomery, Hone, and others—'a dangerous precedent'. But Scott might demand his £5 a page for the sake of advertisement: if a rusticated Clare would accept a copy in lieu of payment, many of the editors had no scruples about offering it. The *Literary Souvenir* for 1826, edited by Alaric Watts, published two poems. Clare was represented in the 1827 and 1828 volumes. In the next few years he had ten poems in S. C. Hall's *Amulet*, and others appeared in Ackermann's *Forget Me Not* and Mrs. S. C. Hall's *Juvenile Forget Me Not*. Marshall, publisher of *A Pledge of Friendship*, was another of those from whom, despite promises and professions of good will, Clare had difficulty in extracting payment. A full list of the newspapers and magazines in which, in these years, his poems were to be found, would include the *New Monthly*, the *Literary Magnet*, the *Spirit and Manners of the Age*, the *Morning Post*, and Moxon's *Englishman's Magazine*. He also supplied a number of songs to the composers, Power, Barnett, and Hodgson. There is no complete bibliography of his fugitive poems, and the payment he managed to obtain, at this time when he needed money badly, was very little indeed.

III

During the years 1824 to 1837, there is, as it were, a veil over the cottage at Helpston. In it shelves of carefully bound and re-bound cheap volumes of poetry, side by side with gift books 'flashed about with golden letters', gave a deceptively leisured and luxurious air. Information outside Clare's writing is scanty. The intense pride of certain of the rural poor is partly responsible for this veil, as well as for some misconceptions of contemporaries. Clare tended to write letters, particularly to Eliza Emmerson and Taylor, out of need to break through mental isolation; but almost all his letters to Mrs. Emmerson have been lost. Yet whereas Lamb the many-friended could survive the bitterness of Coleridge's inability to compass his mystery, in Clare reconciliation to years of solitude grew in the end out of partial alienation from himself.

In September, 1825, soon after Lord Radstock's death, Clare spent three days with the Emmersons at Deeping. In January, 1826, Eliza Emmerson wrote begging him by every 'reasonable entreaty' to give up his acquaintance with ——, about which he had evidently told her in his previous letter. In March, 1826, she again pleaded with him to rid himself of 'domestic discontents'. There is no word in Clare's half-dozen letters to Taylor of February and March either about Patty or any other woman. Only: 'I shall be very glad to hear from you directly as my mind is very unquiet & life has more causes than one to torment us——' He was writing a tragedy, the subject being 'Jealousy' or 'Conscience'. Taylor was, rightly, quite sure he was incapable of drama, but the manuscript of this, among the Peterborough papers, is probably the most relevant evidence we have of the incident in question. There are only about four hundred lines of this completely undramatic fragment. The scene is midnight in a thick and lonely wood. A robber, who has just killed his love, is smitten by both fears of betrayal and doubts whether his supposed evidence for her faithlessness is any more than suspicion:

Curse on this villainous trembling!
If I can't wear a better face in crowds
This ague will betray me. Conscience' shame!
Art thou a man's? I would thou wert a woman's,
For then dissembling might make good excuse
For this frail dastardry!

Oh that my eyes could drink in this black night
So that the daylight could not enter there
To show me what I've done!
But soft misgivings grow not on this ground:
The index to a murder should be writ
With pens of steel & not a lover's pen:
So conscience' work be clean as are these hands—
I'll snap my fingers at thy dismal tales,
& muster all the courage that I can;
Mixing with monsters to appear a man.
There's not a cloud-rift through the darkness
To let a star's eye peep. Escaping tales—
Impeachments—all are hidden as the grave. . . .

Then the scene apparently alters back to the last encounter of
the lovers, when the robber, hearing voices, came upon her in
the wood:

> . . . I was only gathering blossoms, Hubert,
> & talking to them as I cropt them—

> What were thou saying?

> Nay love I cannot tell you—

> I think thou liest!

> Here are the poor flowers
> Which have caused me thy displeasure:
> They wrong my purpose—for I cropt them
> To be Love's heralds—& to have reminded thee
> Of that I gave thee on our bridal day. . . .

The title gives Clare away. A mind, or a pen, of steel had
never been his, though youthful aggression, need for recognition, and subsequent frustration would compensate by desir-
ing both. Fidelity seems to have been important to him, either

from upbringing, temperament, or both. There are further
indications from the group of songs written between 1824 and
1826 of a debate in his mind about passionate love and marriage
—those two states so often thought to be irreconcilable:

> For fair as spring, as summer warm,
>   Her young blood it did seem to flow;
> And yet her heart did prove so cold
>   Love's bud died there and could not blow.
>
> Her face looks open as the day,
>   And on her lips and in her eyes
> Smiles and goodwill do seem to play,
>   That are love's deaths in green disguise;
> Her breasts peep from her kerchief folds
>   Like sunshine through a parting cloud,
> And yet love finds within that bed
>   Nought but a dead and wintry shroud.

And again:

> Upbraiding I can offer none,
>   Nor scorn for scorn allow;
> I had not loved as I have done
>   If I could hate thee now.

If Patty accused him on this occasion in 1826, it made him
remember the lilies of Casterton in the spring of hope. His own
share in the disappearance of love seems to have been what
shocked him. And the image of the ideal remained in the Patty
who 'never knew what the headache was' but who yet was 'of
much comfort to me both in illness & health'.[1] It remained,
too, in Patty's eyes, hair, bosom. So it was he who was murder-
ing love rather than any lack in the Patty then pregnant of her
fourth child.

In May of 1826 a disturbing rumour reached Clare that
Taylor had gone bankrupt. June brought a brusque letter from
Edward Drury at Lincoln, demanding settlement of a bill of
over £40. Taylor, still engaged in settling the affairs of the
firm of Taylor and Hessey, had sent Drury a claim for £100
which he said had been advanced years previously in the form
of books to booksellers to whom Drury owed money. Drury

---

[1] *Letters*, p. 250.

had countered this with a claim for money and goods supplied to Clare during the writing of *The Village Minstrel*, procuring medical advice for his mother, and binding books. Taylor ambiguously assured Clare that Drury had no right to charge anything; his account had been received and allowed by the firm long before. But when Drury threatened legal proceedings, this matter was eventually settled by Hessey's curiously placing a balance of £30 on the debit side of Clare's account with the firm.

Writing after a visit to Helpston in July of this year, Henry Behnes the sculptor urged Clare, for the sake of Patty and the children, to make known his situation to people who thought poets could live on imagination. Taylor and Darley were to have visited Helpston at Christmas, but Darley had recently offered himself for the chair of English literature in the new University of London. Though Lamb and Cary gave him handsome recommendations, it is not surprising that Darley of the 'silent grots and caves'—in conversation 'dull as a signpost', as he himself expressed it to Clare—did not get the appointment. In that same month John Taylor succeeded in becoming publisher and bookseller to the University, which new appointment assured him freedom from business worries, and some leisure to pursue his own researches.

In February, 1828, Mrs. Emmerson urged Clare to visit London himself, see Dr. Darling, and at the same time discuss his affairs with Taylor. His fourth visit to the capital began in the latter part of February and lasted five weeks.

Of the goodly company that had once gathered round Taylor's dinner-table, only Darley had kept in any close touch with the publisher. Clare hesitated even to call on H. F. Cary, now installed in the British Museum as Assistant Keeper of Printed Books, his curacy at Chiswick given up. On Taylor's persuasion, however, Clare did call, and though our British collection at Montague House could not then compare with great Continental libraries, Clare was delighted and awed when Cary showed him all the books. The Lambs had moved from Islington to Enfield the previous September, and Mary Lamb had been ill all the winter. Rippingille was not in London. De Wint was in Normandy. The only other 'Londoner' whom Clare met again was Allan Cunningham, to whom he gave the poem *Autumn*. Cunningham printed it in the *Anniversary*, an Annual he was editing for John Sharpe, in an effort to outshine the popular *Keepsake*.

Resting quietly at the Emmersons' at Stratford Place, Clare met a few of the editors of Annuals to which he was contributing; Alaric Watts offered to help in procuring a new publisher for any further volume of Clare's poems; but records do not show Watts eager either to pay debts or to implement his promise. S. C. Hall was also either unable or disinclined to pay for poems he took. Hall's *Book of Gems*, of 1838, contains a belated appeal about Clare to others, with a pen-sketch of the poet as Hall saw him in this year, 1828: he recalled the 'gentle and unassuming manners' of the 'simple rustic', the 'forehead broad and high almost to deformity', the 'dreamy expression', and the 'peculiarly winning smile'. Thomas Pringle, editor of *Friendship's Offering*, and the friend of Cunningham and Hogg and secretary of the Anti-Slavery Society, took, between 1824 and 1834, ten poems for his Annual—and saw Clare paid.

Far better than Hall's pen-portrait is the bronze bust which the sculptor Henry Behnes made on this fourth London visit. It is our only likeness of Clare in these middle years. For some time, too, Behnes (who took the name Burlowe to avoid confusion with his more gifted but degenerate brother) worked determinedly on Clare's behalf in practical matters, extracting money from editors and offering poems round.

The chief outcome of Clare's contact with Taylor was a plan that Clare should buy back, at a reduced price, unsold copies of his three books, and try to 'peddle' them at home. At the end of a month Clare wrote to Patty telling her of the books he had bought for the children and announcing his return. He was anxious to be home, and soon after his return his third son was born, to be baptised William Parker on the 4th of May. But the visit to London had heartened him. In April he was writing to Taylor asking for the unsold books to be sent. By July he had sold two copies and been paid for one. One could have wished for him, long before this, a little of Coleridge's 'aspheterism'. Even in small matters, as he wrote to Taylor about some Roman coins he had failed to procure for his publisher, 'I hate to be less than my word'. He pressed Taylor at the same time for a settlement of the long-overdue accounts, no doubt recalling the £40 which the publisher had declared to be outstanding on *The Minstrel* in 1826. Though Hessey sent £5, there was no reply from Taylor; Mrs. Emmerson could extract nothing more substantial than promises; and a letter from Lord Milton, whom Henderson enlisted on Clare's behalf, brought no immediate answer.

Some possible aftermath to those domestic disharmonies of 1826 was also causing him disquiet about this time. Hessey, about to set up as a publisher of religious books, felt he had better humble himself before the God of Purity, in that he had committed the 'double crime of adultery and murder'. But 'it has pleased God to frustrate your rash designs upon your own life'. We cannot find the rash designs to have been more than wishing himself well out of the world when under the stress of melancholy, and he could report by Christmas that his other fears had been groundless.

In September he was invited to Boston, where the Mayoral hospitality at a supper in his honour was a trial such as going into the 'wicked city' became for Lamb: 'A lady at the table talked so ladily of the Poets that I drank off my glass very often without knowing it & he as quickly filled it'. He sold six copies of his complete poems, and obtained orders for more. The whole family suffered from a 'fen fever', either typhus or malignant influenza. Taylor thought it surely caused by 'excesses' at Boston.

Heartened by Cary's 'what you most excel in is the description of such natural objects as . . . none before you have noticed', Clare was, during the winter of 1828, engaged on a long poem *The Pleasures of Spring*.[1] These five hundred lines in ten-syllabled couplets have only their name reminiscent of Campbell's, Rogers's, or Akenside's *Pleasures*. Their altitudo is 'How beautiful thou art, mysterious world!'. Clare does not attempt to explain how 'substances are circumfused . . . with light divine'; he states the substances themselves as accurately as perception knew how—of a part of earth that was no more than the hard old fen on a most ordinary spring day. He made at least six copies of the poem, but had still so little espied that 'tyrannous judgment, that æsthetic economy' that he could only keep adding, 'the cole black bee', the slug that 'clumb the

[1] See Kenneth Richmond: *Poetry and the People*.

tottering-grass', 'the meanest thing that lives to crawl or flye'.
People come in, though he had countered Darley's argument
that literature should be 'garnished with live-bait' by saying
that poets often bring in humanity 'at the expense of nature'.
Clare's perception of all round him must have been as if he ate
daily of the sacred peyotl. Yet *The Pleasures of Spring* is little
better poetry than what he had written twenty years before.
It was a concession to Taylor's choice of poems for *The
Shepherd's Calendar* and to the kind of verse Annual editors were
accepting from Clare. It was a halt, an imitating of himself
which, as poet, he could not afford.

Spring and summer of 1829 were an oasis of good health and
freedom from complications. In February Clare visited
Northampton at the invitation of George Baker, author of a
monumental but unfinished history of the country, and brother
of Anne Elizabeth Baker, whose *Glossary of Northamptonshire
Words and Phrases* was to be published in 1854. Clare helped
with both these works. In summer, the cottage shelves now
full of unpublished manuscripts, he turned to field-work; and
at the end of August he received from John Taylor the long-
delayed statement of accounts. Clare had been secretly hoping,
ever since 1820, that this would show at least a few pounds
profit. On the contrary, it held an adverse balance of about
£140. There were discrepancies and omissions which Clare's
own memoranda help to reveal. The £36 for *London Magazine*
work were not shown, and the £100 which had stood as a gift
from Taylor and Hessey in the subscription list for *Poems
Descriptive* was repaid to the firm. £20 was shown as having
been paid to Drury for the copyright, which Drury declared
Clare had made over to him by written agreement. £28 from
The Village Minstrel was the only profit shown to Clare on any
of his three books. And, obstinate as we know he could be
with Lamb, Moxon, Landor, and others, over a Copyright Law
over a century old, Taylor claimed rights on all the poems.
These rights, though he had allowed them to be Clare's in 1824
at the time Clare made his will, Taylor sold in 1864—though
probably even then with intention to safeguard Patty. Another
memorandum of Clare's shows money credited to him in odd-
ments between 1821 and 1829 from Taylor or Hessey to be
£85, which tallies with Taylor's list. Taylor made no demand

for the apparent debt of £140. The statement of accounts was meant to imply that poet and publisher, in 1829, had no score against each other.

Clare saw all this, and felt it fair. But he could not help seeing too that his sole recompence for ten years of labour at poetry was a debt for £140: and his sole profit on a successful book in 1820 worked out at a charge of £20 for his own poems —'a damnable luxury'.

He had four attempts at the uncongenial task of writing to Taylor about the accounts before a letter finally went in November; and even then what might have been statements were couched in the form of 'enquireys':

> & you must excuse me . . . if I make them where none are nessesary for my ignorance in such matters must be my innocence of any impertinence that may appear to be so— as every wish in making the enquirey is to be satisfied of things I do not understand & not one utterd with the intention to offend——[1]

Taylor replied with the cheerless news that if the present Government carried out its intention of lowering interest rates, Clare's income would be further reduced, and that Hessey, having failed in his religious-book-publishing, was to set up as a book and print auctioneer. The publisher agreed that some of Clare's points should be conceded. He was 'much pleased with the manner in which you have stated them'. But even when *London Magazine* omissions, error over peddled copies, and portrait matter were rectified, and Drury apportioned the easy blame of the absent, the injustice of the copyright was left to rankle in Clare's mind; and he still owed Taylor a considerable sum he would never be able to pay.

In the spring of 1830, after reading of Gurney's steam-traction and a recent balloon ascent, he wrote a long letter to Allan Cunningham, but for some reason did not send it:

> . . . You will have communications with all nations by & by & steam will be boiling from one end of the world to the other . . . me thinks with a long pole you'll be shaking hands with Africa & with some patent ear-trumpet be

[1] *Letters*, p. 235.

bidding good night and good morning to all the
world. . . .[1]

After a short cessation of writing in 1828 and 9, on Cunningham's suggestion, he tried two prose tales: *The Stage Coach*, and
The Two Soldiers. In the first, the hero rescues three ladies from
the unwelcome attentions of two fops, and holds a far-too-long
discussion on the follies of the day, the arrogance of riches, and
the prevalence of bad novels. The second is of two soldiers
returning from service abroad, who, seeking help late at night
from a large house, are turned away with customary civilian
ingratitude as suspicious characters.

He was reading Montesquieu and *Humphry Clinker*; at the
same time he was attempting a tale in dialect. It began as *The
Adventures of Uncle Barnaby*, with amusing characters like Mr.
Slinkum the schoolmaster, and Mr. Snip; it continued a little
further as *The Bone and Cleaver Club*. Its fragments tantalise.
Still watching that malfaisance in progress we today find so
difficult to comprehend—all that which, as the young Coleridge
had cried fiercely, worked against the poor, but 'so slowly that
none call it murder'—Clare had an insight into hypocrisy and
moments of realistic humour that might have served him well
if he could have wrought these novel-fragments into anything
approaching a whole. In one fragment principles of conduct
are being formulated from speeches at *The Butcher's Arms*:

'Practicality Mr President that's religion—cheat as cheat
can—that's the plan for hard times Mr P. To live in the
world we must live by the world that's fact—to be moral
and virtuous is to be books not men—it will take a wise
man to bind me in calfskin Mr P.—we cannot act as we
read. Demure our matters as we will Life's a rudish plant
& we cannot become a bunch of lavender pressed into a
lady's bandbox or a rose folded into a novel—this is
romance Mr P.—and deals with enchantment & I don't
want to be reckoned a wizzard Mr P.—& as to religion
why we cannot be folded into a sermon or lie in a parson's
pocket'—(cheering) 'we must do as others do or where's
the living?' (tremendous cheering) 'we must cheat to be
cheated, that's fair' (thunders of applause). . . .
'And now for a song!'[1]

[1] Peterborough Mss.

In June Clare was invited to the Palace at Peterborough to dinner and to a performance at the theatre. There was some feeling in the town for and against theatricals, and Clare and Mrs. Marsh were allies in that both were wholehearted lovers of the play. *The Merchant of Venice* was on in July, and Clare was again invited, when—in the midst of the trial scene, he rose precipitately to his feet and vigorously cursed Shylock.

No sooner did the story become known than Frank Simpson wrote: no doubt it was 'frailty and not viciousness', but 'you should write at once to your offended patroness and apologise'. Other letters, from Hessey, Mrs. Emmerson, and Behnes Burlowe, are full of reference to this 'serious illness'. Taylor compared it with his own of 1825. He had not the 'imagination of unreal sights and sounds', but he had had the 'same suspicion of those around'. He had also had a 'conviction of the indestructible nature of my own soul' Mrs. Marsh herself begged Clare to obliterate the incident from his memory, and sent books, grapes, and gingerbread. She and the Bishop had a son of their own who suffered with mental difficulties, and it was common knowledge how Byron had been thrown into a convulsion at Kean's presentation of Sir Giles Overreach.

This loss of control at the theatre was followed by physical ills—inflammation, indigestion, violent pains in the head; and then the old enemy attacked—acute melancholia. A prescription from Dr. Darling included leeches to the temples, a seton on the neck, cold cloths about the head, and poultices for the body. He was to eat and drink only water. For two months he was too weak to write a letter. But by late September he managed one to Taylor, needing more copies of his poems. This letter illustrates the difficulty, for us, of distinguishing symptoms from remedial effects:

> —my fancies & feelings vary very often but I now feel a great numbness in my right shoulder—& the seaton tho I cannot bear it to be dressed for 3 or 4 mornings together discharges so much that I fear I shall fall into a Decline at last—but thank god my head is now relieved tho it stings now & then as if nettled.[1]

In a few months, however, he could soothe Hessey's concern for

[1] *Letters*, p. 247.

his further welfare by telling him that he believed the Bible's promise of eternal bliss; 'if I did not I should be ever miserable'; but it was its 'poetry in perfection' that supplied 'soul and body with happiness'; Yet from this point onward there is an ominous echo somewhere, like distant warfare on a still, sunless day, and he seems to have been aware of his own most deadly peril:

> last night . . . the pain in my stomach was more frequent in its attacks & I awoke in dreadful irritation thinking that the Italian liberators were kicking my head about for a football—my future prospects seem to be no sleep—a stupid & stunning apathy or lingering madness.[1]

By the end of 1831 two years' rent was owing, editors of Annuals owed him £20, and he wrote to Behnes Burlowe:

> I am at the world's end Harry & if you can get Mr Hall to pay me ever so little of what he promised me I shall be set up & satisfied.[2]

But he did not send this letter. He was forming a habit of writing letters and not sending them. It may have begun in order to avoid further debts for answers. The recipient still paid his 1/4 or more unless a frank were obtained.

But as he said, the statement of account had at least 'cleared the prospect to see a little farther'. His great desire since 1829 had been to take a smallholding and achieve independence that way. Ryde, the estate-agent of Burghley, had long been assuring Mrs. Emmerson about a cottage he could get for Clare at Milton. Smallholdings held in spade-husbandry were not in any great favour in those days of big and bigger estates; but, though they were precarious to run, Patty had the qualities needed. At last there was a chance of a small piece of land in the straggling, orcharded, fen-village of Northborough, three miles from Helpston. The cottage was being built, and Henderson urged Clare to disregard Jeremiahs and apply for it. Lord Milton agreed to accept him as tenant at a rent of £15 a year, and the house was to be ready by April.

[1] *Letters*, p. 253.
[2] Peterborough Mss.

To stock the place and 'start upon a new leaf' obviously would need capital. Clare wrote to Taylor for some of the Fund-money. Adamant as ever on that matter, Taylor, perhaps wisely, made no reply. Arrangements for Northborough were held up. A pasture for a cow is of little use if there is no cow to put in it. Again Clare tried to write to Taylor—'in the paralysing suspence your silence completely stultifyes my intentions'—and again, he neither sent, nor even finished the letter. In the end the kindly parson of Helpston, Charles Mossop, wrote; but when, in January, Taylor replied, nothing apparently could be done till Richard Woodhouse, who was now dying of the disease which had carried Keats off, and who had drawn up the Deed of Trust with Taylor, returned from Italy in May. Woodhouse did not return. The Emmersons inquired, and it was then clear that the principal could be used only to provide income during Clare's lifetime.

Lord Milton naturally wondered why Clare was hesitating. Patty and Henderson, perhaps parson Mossop, urged him to the plunge. Finally the Emmersons raised a subscription. They themselves gave £10, to be laid out in a cow to be called Blossom or Rose or May; Taylor promised £5 for two pigs; and another £5 were to be found for tools. Grateful, but unable to hide his regrets that his difficulties could only be solved by another 'begging list', Clare left his old cottage and the woods and fields of forty years' associations in May, 1832. It was a joyful day. Hope for his practical plans and for a new literary venture was unquenched. Yet he followed behind Patty's cart, in which were their six children, his books, his host of unpublished manuscripts, and their joint possessions— head bent, reluctant to depart.

IV

The thatched cottage, built on a two-acre piece at North-borough, was much more roomy and comfortable than the one Clare had left. It had six rooms, a sitting-room he could use as a study, a good kitchen, a large cool back-kitchen, and three bedrooms. It had been made, at his request, to face away from the road, so that he stepped from his only door straight into his secluded garden, and hence to his orchard and his small pasture bounded by fen pollards. He could, and did, escape unwelcome visitors that way.

It was the very place for writing, and already change, as change will, was deepening experience. Affirmation of his poetry had always been stubborn, even incontinent. He had never been able to regulate his bursts of creative labour and joy. Although Taylor, flourishing again, obviously could not touch completely unsaleable poetry, Clare's new venture was almost complete. Burlowe, Pringle, and the Emmersons had been trying since 1830 to find a London publisher who would take the book. At last Clare had been his own copyist, Eliza Emmerson patiently answering queries about punctuation. It was the fashion, she finally told him, hardly to 'point' at all. So he did not 'point', as the careful manuscript shows. The Midsummer Cushion, in neat and vigorous handwriting, with its ten years' exploration in the fruitful accuracy of image and emotion, he now determined to publish by subscription.

On the 1st of September, a hundred copies of his proposals for printing were ready. 'Midsummer Cushions', he explained— title at last his own and to his liking—were 'patches of green- sward full of field flowers placed, according to age-old custom, by cottagers in their windows on Midsummer eve'. The book was to be printed on fine paper and cost no more than seven and sixpence. By the end of October, with the help of the Emmersons, the Simpsons, the Mossops, the Marshes, and Henderson, two hundred subscribers had been collected. Then, never very happy over a local printing, on the advice of the Emmersons, Clare changed his plans. Through J. How, relative of the Peterborough printer, and connected with the London firm of Whittaker, he could sell the volume outright and thus relieve himself of anxiety over publication.

About three hundred poems had been copied up from thirty- five rough manuscripts. There were only a few more poems to be fair-copied, important ones belonging to this very summer since he had left Helpston. These include *The Flitting*, and, in Reynolds's 'Shrewsbury' metre, *Remembrances*. He wrote a letter to Henry Francis Cary—and sent it: . . . If you laugh at my ambitions . . .

Drawn & Eng'd by C. Marr

THE POET'S COTTAGE

THE NORTHBOROUGH COTTAGE IN 1832

Where trees & hedges & astonished bushes
are filled with music as if music grew
From happy blackbirds & delighted thrushes
Who daub their nests & love in happy cue
Where little blackcaps in their early song
Do calm the marchwinds with their merry throats
& cuckoo singeth blythe ere it be long
A full toned anthem with two simple notes

There trim a little garden at ones leisure
To watch the flowers to bud & so to bloom
To reap from pleasant labour added pleasure
& have an hour for talk when friends do come
Hoeing up weeds that bed & path deforms
& smoothing grassplots with a roll & scythe
While tiney Robin poppeth down for worms
Then strokes his little bill & singeth blythe

Spending an hour with quiet now & then
By floodwashed river & sedge flounced pool
Musing like hermit from the haunts of men
Indulging idless like a child from school
To find on leaningtree an easy chair
Where one can sit & bid the minutes pass
& mark the dodging float sink speedy there
Then land the large bream bouncing on the grass

Or seek out spots where nature doth disport
In curious phantasy her whims to please
Where the minds eye may shape a princely court
Without its cares from intertwining trees
Or muse in grottos by rock hidden spring
Where fairey folk from summers noon retires
There feel the place a throne oneself a king
With nought to govern but ones own desires

Safe are such antidotes such means supply
For what decayed ambition aye endures
& hearts grown sick of show may meet therebye
Coy pleasures long pursued & speedy cures
Tis but vain fashions tinsel gauds to shun
& speed where health & happiness employs
The simple swain to labour in the sun
Tending his toils therebye to share his joys

Peterborough Museum
Photograph: Peterborough Citizen and Advertiser

A PAGE IN THE MANUSCRIPT OF
'THE MIDSUMMER CUSHION'

I am ready to laugh with you at my own vanity for I sit
sometimes & wonder over the little noise I have made in
the world untill I think I have written nothing as yet to
deserve any praise at all so the spirit of fame of living a
little after life like a name on a conspicuous place urges my
blood upward into unconscious melodys & striding down
my orchard & homestead I hum & sing inwardly those
little madrigals & then go in & pen them down thinking
them much better things than they are until I look over
them again & then the charm vanishes into the vanity that
I shall do something ere I die & so in spite of myself I
rhyme on & write nothing but little things at last.[1]

Hope of the modest, unconfused success he hungered for was
stirring again; no 'burning blaze'; merely 'a theme remembered long'—and for poetry's proper reasons; with money to
pay his creditors and buy food for his children:

> E'en now my heart leaps out from grief,
> And all the gloom thrown round by care's o'ershading
>   wing:
> E'en now those sunny visions to recall,
> Like to a bird I quit dull earth and sing:
> Life's tempests swoon to calms on every string.
> Ah! sweet enchantress, if I do but dream,
> If earthly visions have been only mine,
> My weakness in thy service woos esteem,
> And proves my truth as almost worthy thine:
> Surely true worship makes the meanest theme divine. . .

> Is poesy dwelling in a nice-culled sound,
> Or soft smooth words that trifle on the ear,
> Unmeaning music? Is it to be found
> In rhymes run mad, that paint to startled fear
> Monsters that are not and that never were?
> Is it in declamations frothing high,
> Worked like machinery to its mad career?
> No, poetry lives in its simplicity,
> And speaks from its own heart, to which all hearts reply.

> Fame's hopes with me are faint to look upon;
> The cloud of doubt with gloom her skies defiles;

[1] Letters, p. 268.

L

Though fluttering pulse and burning thrills urge on
And hope at intervals the way beguiles,
The flowers she plucks me wear precarious smiles,
Yet do I follow with unwearied eyes
The shadowy recompence for real toils:
Ah would the heart cease aching and be wise,
And think life vainly spent, staked for a doubtful prize![1]

About this time he noted a recurrent dream: 'That Guardian spirit in the shape of a soul-stirring beauty again appeared to me.' On the first occasion of the dream, before the publication of his first poems, she had led him through a press of people: 'you are only one of the crowd now', she had said, and then had led him into a bookseller's shop. There on the dim shelf, she pointed to 'three volumes lettered with my name'. The second dream had also been of a concourse of people, as at a Judgment Day. Uneasy, he had heard his name called, and the Guardian spirit had appeared again, 'in white garments beautifully disordered but sorrowful in her countenance.' Yet she had smiled at him: 'all was well'. The substance of these recurrent dreams betrays at least two conflicts in Clare: one was between what he felt as the selfishness of his ambition and his deep need for recognition of his poetry; the other was between the affirmative trust in people he found so hard to deny and his sense of inadequacy over its results. Years before this he had written:

> Every friendship I made grew into a warm attachment I was in earnest or I was nothing & I believed everything that was uttered came from the heart as mine did. . . . On the other hand I have a fault that often hurts me though I cannot master it I am apt to mistake some foibles that all men are subject to as breaches of friendship & thereby grow dissatisfied.[2]

But as he himself added concerning the recurrent dreams, they gave 'the sublimest conceptions of beauty to my imagination'.

His adequacy with people and in practical matters was certainly under renewed test. The small publicity over The Midsummer Cushion had brought visitors again. This was 'no

[1] *Poems*, 1935, I, pp. 453, 454.
[2] *Life*, p. 377, Peterborough Mss.

common man' the reviewer from the *Druids' Magazine*, coming
with Clark of the *Stamford Bee or Herald and County Chronicle*,
saw at first glance: his eyes 'flashed with the fire of genius'; his
conversation was 'animated, striking, and full of imagination'.
News that the cottage had been bestowed on Clare free for life
spread to the *Athenaeum*. Not knowing who was responsible, he
wrote to his friends to have it corrected. But both Behnes
Burlowe and Cunningham were convinced that he should make
his wants known, and such a crop of errors sprouted, that the
political hotbed of the *Bee* and the *Alfred* produced statements
that he had been cheated out of all profits by his publishers,
and that he had £15 a year on which to maintain a wife and
six children. As near to anger as he ever seems to have been
in these earlier years, Clare wrote to the editor of the *Athenaeum*:

> I wish not to have my difficulties trumpeted by everyone
> who chooses to pen his spleen in my favour . . . I never
> solicited praise or profit from any individual in my life . . .
> I am not seeking charity but independence.[1]

But the notices had reached the eye of John Taylor. He
reminded the poet that he too had been out of pocket by the
poems; that he did not carry on business merely to have the
opportunity of giving away what he did not get. By January,
1833, he was threatening litigation against the proprietors of
the papers concerned in aspersions on his character.

Matters were not flourishing on the small-holding. Patty's
seventh child had been born, and fresh doctors' bills were
accumulating. The important last poems were not copied into
The Midsummer Cushion; he was driven to ask whether How
would advance money on the abundance already there. Eliza
Emmerson urged him to exert himself: no publisher would
countenance such advance: "Good heavens, Johnny," she
pleaded, "how can you sink down to such apathy?"

Clare wrote to Taylor, assuring him of friendship and trust.
Gratified with such 'expression of friendly Regard', Taylor
agreed to forget gossip, withdrew his threatened libel action,
and offered his name as a subscriber to the new poems. August,
1834, saw the manuscript of The Midsummer Cushion in Mrs.
Emmerson's hands, and the following January Thomas Emmer-

[1] *Life*, p. 359.

son obtained How's solemn promise to bring out the book that spring.

But it did not appear that spring, whilst at Northborough Clare's £20 debt from Helpston days had become £35. He was being pressed—in spite of one or two kindlier creditors like bookseller Wilson of Stamford, who refused to harass, he declared, 'a son of the Genius of Poetry'. March brought the much needed financial relief, Taylor agreed to read the proofs, and both these events produced improvement in Clare's spirits and consequently in his health. The copyright of his fourth book—title changed by Mrs. Emmerson to an unpromising echo of the eighteenth century—yielded £40, and in December, 1834, he received £50 from the Literary Fund.

The Rural Muse, 'one of the richest and most melodious collections ever published by an English poet',[1] and less than half the manuscript of The Midsummer Cushion, appeared in 1835. No one in his own day, except perhaps Henry Francis Cary, saw what Clare was aiming at, yet the poem *Summer Images* shows very clearly the way he had travelled. The first draft of *Summer Images* is written in the non-rhyme stanza which belonged to the spell of Collins's *Autumn*. Every versifier of any sensitiveness since Collins had longed to write his unrhymed ode. What interested Clare was not classical non-rhymed poetry so much as freedom from rhyme's possible artificiality. The second draft of *Summer Images*, in *The Rural Muse*, is in a seven-line rhymed stanza. This is one of the many rhythmic innovations he was to try from this time onward. A particularly happy poem, it had been the fruit of the critical period in 1824, as the richly perceptive and almost equally happy *Autumn* had been the fruit of the depressed winter of 1827–8. The 1820 first draft of *Summer Images* has

> Jet-black and shining, from the dripping hedge
> Slow peeps the fearful snail
>   And from each tiny bent
>   Withdraws his timid horn.

> The yellow frog from underneath the swath
> Leaps startling as the dog with heavy feet
>   Brushes across the path
>   And runs the timid hare.

[1] Edmund Blunden: Introduction to *Madrigals and Chronicles*.

This becomes in the 1824 version:

> I love at early morn, from new-mown swath
>   To see the startled frog his route pursue,
> And mark, while, leaping o'er the dripping path,
>   His bright sides scatter dew;
>   And early lark that from its bustle flies
>   To hail his matin new;
>   And watch him to the skies:
>
> And note, on hedgerow baulks, in moisture sprent,
>   The jetty snail creep from the mossy thorn,
> With earnest heed and tremulous intent,
>   Frail brother of the morn,
>   That from the tiny bents and misted leaves
>   Withdraws his timid horn,
>   And fearful vision weaves:

A better poetic economy has been achieved, not through spareness and selection but through greater richness in precision. The 'jet-black and shining' snail has become the 'jetty' snail; that second homely word of living speech leaves us to deduce blackness and shiningness from it for ourselves. The image of the timid hare, too like that of the snail, has been suppressed to allow frog, lark, and more importantly, snail, to be more vividly seen. The image of the lark contrastingly adds to the image of the earth-bound frog. Lark and frog are symbols: positiveness and aspiration are set above frustration and fear; and the richly filled-out snail verse contains within it a submerged metaphor of human life—a snail's tentative silver track. All this is done so unassumingly, so without 'palpable design' that we are almost beguiled into thinking Clare's art so instinctive that he intended nothing. Denuded of the faintest hint of complacency, 'frail brother of the morn' betrays how deeply he, by heritage and temperament so attuned to earth and to poetry, had, even by 1824, begun to see a relationship between the two.

Unity of form in *Summer Images* and *Autumn*, other than the inexhaustible abundance he claimed as an aspect of poetry, was not yet within his power. 'The poet . . . loves variety better than order'[1] he had written round about that critical year 1824.

[1] Peterborough Mss.

All his longer descriptive pieces have this fault: they might end anywhere else than where they do. His shorter pieces end as if by instinct in the right places. But sense of form may be bound up in the 'wrestle with experience'; and of this greater unity he had, in 1835, much more to achieve.

By the end of the year *The Rural Muse* had not sold its first edition. A few friends looked up from their pre-occupations to applaud, James Montgomery, Rippingille, Charles Elton, John Bowring, Sherwill, and Derwent Coleridge. Wilson of *Blackwood's* exhorted the public to buy a book so full of beauty and merit. He thought Clare's popularity might be increased if he confined himself, as Bloomfield had, to describing the feelings and manners of the lower orders, and he commented on Clare's comfort beside Bloomfield's and Burns's deaths in poverty. There were appreciative enough reviews in the *Literary Gazette* and the *Druids' Magazine*, and the *Athenaeum* and the *New Monthly* commended the book.

v

There is no doubt that the removal to Northborough had brought him deeper experience, though there was still none to glimpse with him the excellence that, as he had written round about the critical 1824, 'must be its own creation'. The time was past when he could relieve emotional frustration, as he could up to 1827, with poems of jovial carousal such as *The Cellar Door*, in which a tinker, a toper, a miller, a ploughman, and the host, all a-thirst, were unable to move the heavy barrel from the street where the drayman had dropped it:

> Says the host, 'We shall burn out with thirst, he's so big!
> There's a cag of small swipes half as sour as a wig.
> In such-like extremes, why, extremes will come pat;
> So let's go and wet all our whistles with that.'
> Says the gipsy, 'May I never bottom a chair
> If I drink of small swipes while Sir John's lying there!'
> And the blacksmith he threw off his apron and swore
> Small swipes should bemoisten his gullet no more:
> 'Let it out on the floor for the dry cock-a-roach'—
> And he held up his hammer. . . .

But approach toward poetic unity may be observed in *Song's Eternity* in *The Rural Muse*, though we do not know the final form he intended for this poem. The first perfect achievement of unity may be more clearly observed in *With Garments Flowing*. Both these poems belong to the last period of hope for happiness through independence, the important summer of 1832. There is no need to conjecture that he saw Mary Joyce again in 1832. Northborough is nearer Glinton than is Helpston. Its scenery was that of his schooldays. Without any conjecture, we may perceive the further recession into poetry that Patty's activism and his own impracticality under the difficulties facing them at Northborough made.

Some time between 1832 and 1837, he wrote a hundred and fifty poems of a stark objectivity. These could never have found publication in their own day. Many of them have a deceptively calm recording of cruelty and violence. This, though accurate and impersonal, must also be regarded as a means of release from loneliness and need for recognition. Among these are *Wild Duck's Nest*, *Vixen*, *Hedgehog*, *Marten*, and *Badger*:

> When midnight comes a host of dogs and men
> Go out and track the badger to his den,
> And put a sack within the hole, and lie
> Till the old grunting badger passes by.
> He comes and hears—they let the strongest loose.
> The old fox hears the noise and drops the goose.
> The poacher shoots and hurries from the cry,
> And the old hare half wounded buzzes by.
> They get a forked stick to bear him down
> And clap the dogs and take him to the town,
> And bait him all the day with many dogs,
> And laugh and shout and fright the scampering hogs.
> He runs along and bites at all he meets:
> They shout and halloo down the noisy streets. . . .
>
> Though scarcely half as big, demure and small,
> He fights with dogs for hours and beats them all.
> The heavy mastiff, savage in the fray,
> Lies down and licks his feet and turns away.
> The bulldog knows his match and waxes cold,
> The badger grins and never leaves his hold.
> He drives the crowd and follows at their heels
> And bites them through—the drunkard swears and reels.

The frighted women take the boys away,
The blackguard laughs and hurries on the fray.
He tries to reach the woods, an awkward race,
But sticks and cudgels quickly stop the chase.
He turns agen and drives the noisy crowd
And beats the many dogs in noises loud.
He drives away and beats them every one,
And then they loose them all and set them on.
He falls as dead and, kicked by boys and men,
Then starts and grins and drives the crowd agen;
Till kicked and torn and beaten out he lies
And leaves his hold and cackles, groans, and dies.[1]

Through these stark poems Clare was accepting his own torment. Others worthy of note in this group are *The Braggart*, *Scandal*, *The Lout*, and *The Outcast*. The manuscript is in a home-made ink of bruised 'nut galls', 'Green Coppurs', and 'Stone blue'. This burnt its way into the paper as the desire for his poetry to be remembered was burning its way into the poet's mind. Yet even among this group, airy conjurings of complete happiness occur, like *Break of Day*. In this unpolished poem we may note the packed adjective 'guessing', to convey the watchless ploughman's knowledge of the hour by the feel of it. Note, too, the felicitous use of the short line:

The lark he rises early,
    And the ploughman goes away
Before it's morning fairly,
    At the guessing break of day;
The fields lie in the dawning,
    And the valley's hid in gold,
At the pleasant time of morning
    When the shepherd goes to fold.

The maiden laughs and hollos
    When she sees the feeding cows;
They switch their tails and follow
    When she can't get over sloughs;
I love the gentle dawning,
    And the valleys hid in gold,
At the pleasant time of morning
    When the shepherd goes to fold.

---

[1] *Poems*, 1935, II, pp. 333, 334.

VI

In 1836 the Bread Tax was at its height. There were, as Elliot the Corn Law rhymer said, 'ten dogs to one bone'. By the end of 1830 the southern counties of England had been ablaze with the last attempt of the peasantry to call attention to their wrongs of the previous forty or fifty years. There had been rick-burnings in Northamptonshire, and risings of labourers round Peterborough and Oundle. But the Government had seen the cause of freedom become in France a tool for tyrants. The Archbishop of Canterbury prepared a special prayer to the Almighty to 'defeat and frustrate the malice of wicked and turbulent men'. The prisons of Winchester, Salisbury, and Dorchester overflowed with these 'wicked and turbulent'. Many of those whom the *Times* for December of that year describes as 'industrious, kind-hearted, but broken-hearted beings, exasperated into madness by insufficient food and clothing, by utter want of necessaries for themselves and their unfortunate families', were condemned to capital punishment or transportation.

Clare had seen beneath the banner of village politicians the forces of self-interest and tyranny arrayed. He was under few illusions about possibilities of violence and excess from any party: 'With the mob freedom and plunder are synonymous' he had written among his Essay notes;[1] and to Mrs. Marsh in 1830, concerning 'the reform of parties where the benefit of one is the destruction of the other', could there possibly be a reform that 'would do good and hurt none'? Writing, a little later, for the new local paper the *Bee*, to which Frank Simpson and Eliza Emmerson contributed, he was soon glad to dissociate himself from its 'violent and high' politics, since, as Simpson said, he received none of its sweets, and it had attempted to make use of its knowledge of his affairs. 'I hate party feuds,' he wrote,

> . . . in fact you would laugh at my idea in that branch of art for I consider it nothing more or less than a game at hide & seek for self interest & the terms Whig & Tory are nothing more in my mind than the left & right hand of that

[1] *Prose*, p. 225.

monster the only difference being that the latter lies nearer the windfalls of success.[1]

He would have liked to see the effect of schools established in every village:

> I think they would put human life & common sense into the dull & obstinate class from whence I struggled into light like one struggling from the nightmare in his sleep.[2]

He was still struggling 'up the steep road'. Forbidden, as he was in 1833, by his physicians, to read or write, he was beset by hallucinations of 'evil spirits'. These are obviously a sense of ill-luck dogging his steps. He could not rest. His brain seemed 'boiling up'. Since 1827 Mrs. Emmerson's letters had referred to his distress of mind and pains in the head. Pains in the head were not, of course, unusual among writers. Burns, Goldsmith, Collins, Swift, and Johnson, all had them. Dr. Darling's letters mention irruptions on the body which he thought were due to Clare's working less and eating more. Darley, puzzled, thought he should be like 'a sturdy elm' that groaned in the storm, but 'only for pleasure'. 'Poetry', Darley added, 'I mean the composition of it, does not always sweeten the mind as much as the reading of it.' Yet if only, Clare thought in 1834, he could get to London, he could recover. But Eliza Emmerson was going on a visit to a country retreat they had just purchased, 'a sweet enchanting place' near Bath, and Taylor had no room that summer.

VII

The way forward had been chosen as far back as 1824. Clare had supported his decision then as we all support our most vital decisions made after conflict has seemed temporarily overwhelming—by a process of dissociation. The mind rejects the most refractory obstacles. Then the associative processes jump them. For a time they may disappear out of sight as into

[1] Letter fragment without recipient's name. Peterborough Mss.
[2] *Prose*, p. 225. Peterborough Mss.

ditches. But when obstacles project themselves again, either the original ones or new ones, the mind is liable to make quite a new way round, even averting reason's scansion. The obstacles, originally accepted, may then be seen as unwarrantable persecutions. Or the mind may substitute fantastic comforts to allay the unease of a responsibility that seems too heavy to be borne.

Clare's mother died in December, 1835, having stoutly resisted both poverty and dropsy till the age of seventy-eight. His father went to live with them at Northborough. Though there was little hope of publication after the failure of *The Rural Muse*, Clare went obstinately on preparing yet another volume. We may call this an 'obsessive compulsion', or we may see it as a remnant of richest sanity. But he was exhausted and he could not control his mind. Letter after letter was written and not sent. There is a series of letter-beginnings when his struggle to hold on to his mind is transparently clear. Only one or two of these appeals reached their destination: to Henderson of Milton for 'something my wife calls everlasting' and a 'red japonica'; to Dr. Darling—'sounds affect me very much & things evil as well [as] good thoughts are continually rising in my mind . . . a sort of nightmare awake . . . and . . . a sinking'; to John Taylor, his literary father.

There is no given point, of course, at which a person is, or is suddenly seen to be, the prey of delusions. Irrational prejudices, incurable blind-spots, and incapabilities and susceptibilities of many kinds, are so often the brown-penny reverse-sides of successful traits. Clare made no mention either to Darling or Taylor that he had an almost settled conviction that Mary Joyce was his first wife by whom he had a set of dream-children; or that Patty was only his second wife.

In December, 1836, Taylor visited Northborough. He found Clare sitting in the chimney corner 'looking much as usual'. He talked 'properly', knew all the people of whom Taylor spoke, and smiled in remembrance of past days. But Taylor heard him muttering 'God bless them all', 'Keep them from evil', and 'Doctors', 'Doctors', 'Doctors'. Patty, whom Taylor found 'a very clever, active woman', evidently confessed that she could not cope with her husband's occasional fierce outbursts of anger.

Dr. Darling wrote suggesting paraphrasing the Psalms and the Book of Job to quiet the mind. Eliza Emmerson, ill herself, besought: 'Up, up brave spirit'. But in June, 1837, Taylor's messenger presented himself at the cottage. He would take Clare to Town, where the medical aid near would cure him effectually. The poet went willingly; but the penalty of exile had begun.

V

HIGH BEECH, ST. ANDREW'S, AND THE
LATE LYRICISM 1837–1864

I

THE man John Taylor found to look after Clare was Dr. Matthew Allen; and Matthew Allen played a pious yet lively part in humanising the treatment of the insane in England in the early nineteenth century.

Plato's *Republic* had recommended that relatives should watch over the mentally errant at home; 'and if they are negligent let them pay a fine'. The mentally afflicted were also taken to the temple of Æsculapius, for incantations to purify the mind. But the Greeks also used methods such as flogging, chaining, tying to stakes, hungering, fomentations, and bleeding. Cælius Aurelianus seems to have been an exception. Cælius Aurelianus placed his patients under conditions of quiet, with light diet, tactful attendance, and the most limited use of physical restraint. Theatricals, entertainments, walking, and work were all encouraged, and starvation, bleeding, and excessive use of drugs were all denounced by him.

From the Greek period to the early nineteenth century, stories of cruelty to the insane shock our ears. Duckings, ligations, and whips, were all used in England in the Middle Ages to exhaust the fury of maniacs and instil into them that sense of terror that can temporarily cow a wild beast. Till well into the seventeenth century Sydenham's Venice treacle, containing the flesh and blood of vipers and sixty-one other witches' ingredients, was used with bleeding and purging. Willis's treatment of George the Third roused indignation in the country, and the exertions of Tuke and Lindley Murray resulted in the opening of York Retreat in 1796. Matthew Allen was at the York Lunatic Asylum (now Bootham Hospital) from 1819–1824.

It was not until 1828 that a Commission was appointed to look into conditions in Homes of Detention such as London's

'Bedlam', where bleedings, vomits, and chains were the current treatment for violent behaviour. It was not far from Bethlehem Hospital that Matthew Allen, on leaving York, fixed upon a place to try out his Cælian theories of domestic peace and comfort, 'diversity of occupation and amusements, pure air and sweet scenery for walks without restraint, and judicious moral and medical management'. At High Beech, on the south-west of Epping Forest, Allen rented three separate houses, Fair Mead, Leopard's Hill, and Springfield; and to Leopard's, or Leppit's, Hill Clare was brought in June, 1837.

Allen had already published his theory in *Cases of Insanity*, 1831, and *Essay on the Classification of the Insane*, 1837. He held it of 'first importance that truth should never be violated'. He carried out a system of rewards with his patients whereby good behaviour promoted them to life with his own family in Fair Mead House. His 'classification' was, by any later standard, scientifically superficial, and he obviously over-simplified the problems. But he was capable of such insight as: 'one part of society, as well as one part of the mind, is at war with another': or 'science, intelligence, wisdom, and religion, are all one, and woe to the man who separates them'. A profoundly religious man, he felt that the 'doctrine of Reprobation' was 'blasphemous'; he thought, too, that whipping or punishment, however universal, were entirely unproven panaceas for mischievous conduct. Fear of many kinds lay at the root of punishment, and for a long time to come, he held, fear would make men confuse gentleness with weakness. Most often, he stated, it was the sensitive, amiable, and lovable characters which were soonest overthrown into what we call madness.

Thus, perhaps nowhere in England could Clare have found a more understanding physician than Dr. Matthew Allen. Emphasising the need for early diagnosis and expert handling, believing in judicious mental as well as bodily exercise—the prevailing idea then was against mental exercise for the insane —Allan encouraged Clare to go on writing what he called Clare's 'beautiful poetic effusions'. By 1839 he could report to John Taylor's partner, Walton, that 'our friend' is 'improving and improving'. He was 'stout and rosy', and in spirits 'all life and fun'. By 1840 Clare was physically well and his mind was 'not worse'. Allen could contrast his improvement with his condition soon after he reached High Beech: Clare's mind then, Allen wrote, 'did not so much appear lost and deranged as suspended in its movements by the oppressive and permanent state of anxiety . . . extreme poverty, and over-exertion of body and mind'. Proposing, in that year, an appeal for £500, sufficient to raise the poet's income to £60 a year and so place his family beyond want, Allen was not entirely unheard. The Queen Dowager sent twenty guineas. Lord Fitzwilliam sent a further subscription. The Marquis of Northampton promised £5 a year. As a result of Cyrus Redding's challenging account, and his publication of a group of Clare's poems in his *English Journal*, there were a few more offers of help.

Redding and two friends visited Clare twice in the spring of 1841. They found him in the fields hoeing and smoking. Redding noted the 'complexion clear and forehead high, a nose somewhat aquiline', 'long full chin', and 'that indescribable something which lifts men of genius above the herd'. Clare was then forty-eight, but he 'looked younger'. He talked freely, as he always did when he liked people. He was in need of books, he said. The visitors promised, and Redding sent, a Byron. The 'only symptom of aberration' in Clare's 'correct and fluent language' and 'perfect good taste' in talking of *Childe Harold* and Byron, was a mention of prize-fighting introduced—as if, Redding said, 'a note had got into a piece of music which had no business there'. Appealing for the extra £20 a year for Clare, against the 'parasites of luxury, the panders to bad morals, gaming table, racecourse, and dog-kennel, with all their brutal adjuncts', Redding added that 'a finer organism', 'if more easily put out of order than that of a more obtuse character, is in all probability more likely to retune itself, the evil cause (anxiety about poverty) being removed'. Allen had told Redding that Clare's mind was 'so little affected' that he might have been better at home.

It is possible that one of Clare's other visitors with Redding was William Henry Hunt, painter in both water and oils of the living bloom on rural things. Hunt's 'A Self-taught Genius' of 1841 may be a hitherto unknown portrait of Clare. If so, it is a grateful glimpse for us of him in this year—an impending crisis surely visible in the tension of the features.

The final sum of money from Redding's and Allen's appeal,

which appeal was publicised by the *Athenaeum* and other papers, fell far short of £500. The money was merely used to help pay for Clare's upkeep at High Beech. Mrs. Emmerson, De Wint, Lord Fitzwilliam, Taylor, Walton, Darling, and two others unknown to us, had up to then contributed the full amount.

In his fourth year of exile, conscious of renewed interest from the outside world, of spring, and of returned vigour, Clare's restlessness increased, even in so loose a captivity as Allen's. We may see his mind reflected in the notebooks he was using at this time. In March he wrote to Patty not so very eccentric a letter except that every word begins with a capital. He does not know why 'They Keep Me Here'. He had never been 'Very Ill Only Harrassed By Perpetual Bother'. His Affection was Unaltered, and he would 'Soon Be In Northamptonshire'. Yet he would rather 'Wear Life's Troubles Away Single Handed Than Share Them With Others'. A short letter draft to Mary is in his pocket-book: 'As This Will Be My Last Letter To You Or Any One Else—Let My Stay Here Be As Long Or As Short As It May—I Will Write To You & My Dear Patty In The Same Letter.' He made notes in one of his notebooks that on Easter Sunday he had seen a boy come out of Buck-hurst Church 'in a slopfrock like a ploughboy & seemingly about nine years of age He was just like my son Bill . . . He had a serious interesting face . . . I am sorry I did not give him the last halfpenny I had . . .' And on Easter Monday at the hunt he had seen 'a stout tall young woman dressed in darkish fox red cotton gown as a milkmaid'. Between these two entries, in seemingly stark irrelevance, but evidently after-wards crossed through, as if it had been thought better of, is

> Boxer Byron
> Made of Iron, alias
> Boxiron
> at Springfield.

And Springfield's was Allen's house for women patients. In the same notebook there are verses

> Nigh Leopard's Hill stands All-n's hell
> The public know the same . . .

A man there is in prison there
Locked up from week to week
He's very fond they do declare
To play at hide & seek. . . .

Again:

Madhouses they must shut up shop
& tramp to fairs & races
Master & men us madmen stop
Life lives by changing places.

There is also

Jack Randall's challenge to All the World.

And Jack Randall the Nonpareil, we shall remember, in 1824 kept *The Hole in the Wall* in Chancery Lane which, in conflict between the choice of giving his life to poetry, or of returning to inarticulateness, Clare had hated to pass alone and at night because of his difficulty in combating its influence on his thoughts.

There is a letter draft, from 'this Hell of a Madhouse', to Eliza Phillips, either an imaginary girl, or someone of his High Beech acquaintance. A second letter he evidently wrote on 'Fern Hill at the back of the chapel a beautiful retreat from a madhouse'. This was to 'My dear Wife Mary'. In these two letters he spoke of poems he was writing. The small notebook has more information:

Speedily will be published
The Sale of Old Wigs & Sundries a Poem by Lord Byron

This is followed by a stanza which became in the fair copy he made later at home stanza six. A second 'advertisement' reads

In a short time will be Published a New Vol of Poems
By Lord Byron Not Yet Collected in his Works Containing
Songs New Cantos of Child Harold Additional Hebrew
Melodies Fragments &c.

Redding's visits and gift of Byron had no doubt spurred him to attempt what eventually became 'a new Canto of Don Juan' and 'a new Canto of Child Harold'. To Mary he wrote:

M

I might have said my first wife first love & first everything —but I shall never forget my second wife & second love for I loved her once as dearly as yourself & almost do so now so I determined to keep you both for ever—& when I write to you I am writing to her at the same time & in the same letter. God bless you both for ever & both your families also I still keep writing though you do not write to me. . . .

Wives ought to be allowed to see their husbands anywhere religion forbids them being parted but I have not even religion on my side. . . .

What is the use of shutting me up from women in a petty paltry place as this merely because I am a married man & I daresay though I have two wives if I got away I should soon have a third & I think I should serve you both right in the bargain by doing so for I dont care a damn about coming home now—so you need not flatter yourselves with many expectations . . . (a change in the colour of the ink suggests that the letter was finished on another occasion).

My dear Mary take all the good wishes from me as heart can feel for your own husband & kiss all your dear family for their abscent father & Pattys children & tell Patty that her husband is the same man as he was when she married him 20 years ago in heart & good intentions. . . .

He finished the 'Don Juan' canto, and some twenty-two or more scattered stanzas of the 'Child Harold'. To July the 15th belong the verses, clearly dated, *Written in a Thunderstorm*:

> The heavens are wroth; the thunder's rattling peal
>   Rolls like a vast volcano in the sky:
> Yet nothing starts the apathy I feel,
>   Nor chills with fear eternal destiny.
>
> My soul is apathy, a ruin vast;
>   Time cannot clear the ruined mass away;
> My life is hell, the hopeless die is cast,
>   And manhood's prime is premature decay.
>
> Roll on ye wrath of thunders, peal on peal,
>   Till worlds are ruins, and myself alone;
> Melt heart and soul, cased in obdurate steel,
>   Till I can feel that nature is my throne.

I live in love, sun of undying light,
  And fathom my own heart for ways of good;
In its pure atmosphere, day without night
  Smiles on the plains, the forest and the flood.

Smile on, ye elements of earth and sky,
  Or frown in thunders as ye frown on me;
Bid earth and its delusions pass away,
  But leave the mind, as its creator, free.

Within five days of this identification of life's relentless forces
with the thunderstorm, and of this first tentative reaching
towards final regenerative capacity, Clare had collected his
notebooks. Successfully he evaded those 'servants styled
keepers'—'who assumed as much authority over me as if I had
been their prisoner'. Outwitting all Allen's supposedly unob-
trusive watchers, he was tramping northward toward home
and Mary. In three days he walked the eighty miles, with
neither a penny in his pocket, nor food and drink beyond half
a pint of beer and a little tobacco which he chewed, till he
reached Peterborough. He slept under the hedges of the Great
North Road, with his head toward the 'steering point' for the
morning, dreaming his 'first wife' lay on his left arm, but 'someone came & took her away from my side'. A note in his
pocket-book reads:

> The man whose daughter is the queen of England is now
> sitting on a stone heap on the high way to Buckden without
> a farthing in his pocket . . . but if I put a little fresh speed
> on hopes may speed tomorrow—O Mary Mary if you
> knew how anxious I was to see you & dear Patty with the
> children I think you would come & meet me.

On the third day he satisfied his hunger 'by eating the grass by
the roadside which seemed to taste something like bread'. At
Peterborough someone passed who knew him, and went to
warn Patty. She brought a cart to meet him. But alas he knew
neither Patty nor his family, and would only get into the cart
when 'they told me it was my second wife'.

The day after his arrival at Northborough, he confided to his
notebook:

> Returned home out of Essex & found no Mary—& how
> can I forget?

For three days he occupied himself writing in prose the moving account of his journey, to which, when finished, he added a letter to 'Mary Clare, Glinton'. He told Mary he was 'homeless at home': but not quite so lonely as in Essex, since he could see Glinton spire. 'Give my love to your dear beautiful family & to your Mother', he ended, and 'believe me as I ever have been & ever shall be, My Dearest Mary, Your affectionate Husband, John Clare'.

Neither Allen nor Taylor did anything directly. They got in touch with Patty, who, apparently thinking him much better, wished to 'try' him a while at home. At the end of August Clare himself wrote to Allen. He told the doctor about his need for 'freedom', his disappointment at not finding his 'poetical fancy' at Northborough, his desire to be a 'hermit for a few years', and his present opinion on women:

> . . . the man who possesses a woman possesses losses without gain. The worst is the road to ruin & the best is nothing like a good cow. Man I never did like & woman has long sickened me.

Allen's exemplary reply was perhaps purposely delayed till November. He then invited Clare back to High Beech, with 'liberty to come and go as you choose, provided you do nothing to make yourself unpleasant as a Visitor. You might lead the life of a Hermit as much as you choose and I would contrive to give you some place for the purpose'.

One must suspect that Allen had not seen the New Canto of Don Juan. If he had peered into those craters of Clare's mind, would he still have felt able, as he undoubtedly did feel able, to dispel such obstinate mists of delusion? By 1841, despite his better command of himself and his improved physical health, Clare had three fixed delusions. They did not appear if he was talking of nature, and rarely if he was talking of poetry. But they were there below the surface. In this his malady seems to have differed from Cowper's. Except for a conviction of his own damnation, Cowper apparently recovered between his earlier attacks. Christopher Smart, as Johnson tells us, showed the disturbance of his mind by 'saying his prayers in the street, or in any other unusual place'; 'rationally speaking' Johnson continues, 'it is greater madness not to pray at all', and, as Herman Melville also reminds us, man's insanity has often in it à quality of 'heaven's sense'. A man is counted mad, not so much on account of aberrations from reason, but from the form those aberrations take. Majority irrationalities, prejudices, and ideas that are not based on any kind of true reasoning, are not yet accepted as delusory—which they of course frequently are. Allen's optimistic accounts, as well as Clare's late output of poetry, have given rise to the idea that he was not really mad; but three of his delusions were that Byron and he were one and the same, that he had two wives, and that he was one of the old bruisers, Randall, or Jones the Sailor Boy, or one of the boxers, Ben Caunt or Tom Spring.

In the Don Juan Canto he clearly enjoys imitating Byron's unusual rhymes and exploring the possibilities of those justly admired octave stanzas and colloquial rhythms. He had seen, from within a madhouse, what Byron's popularity might be worth. And in this oddly modern poem, he seems to be re-taliating for imposed sense of guilt, particularly in sexual matters: 'Poets are born—and so are whores.' Then he in-veighs against marriage, confesses he 'left' his wife, but not until he found her 'false and faulty'; he laments how we 'lose the honey' of love after marriage. There is among the stanzas about High Beech one revealing a slant on madhouse life of which Allen was either not sufficiently aware, or against which he deliberately closed his eyes and lips. In this stanza Allen is given as 'Doctor Bottle-Imp who deals in urine'. Clare repeats the delusion that he is Byron; but, in the stanza following so lucently does he state the reason for it[1] that it is clear he at that moment knew himself to be using words figuratively about the mantle of the poet. Architecturally the poem has a certain coherence. It is full of Hamlet-crazy statement, con-fession, and naked candour, which present anew a warning about how close the metaphor of wit is to that of madness, how fine the line between sanity and insanity.

Sense of the essential loveliness of life as a whole, and of man's own share in innocence as part of that whole, go back, as De la Mare has said, far beyond early nineteenth-century romanticism, beyond Rousseau, Christian myth, or Platonic

---

[1] This kind of awareness is common in certain kinds of dementia.

idealism. Nature is, of course, no more peaceful than warring man. But realist-romantic temperaments such as Clare's seem to seek, outside metaphysical authority, by their own values, arrogantly perhaps, yet in another way humbly, to keep the sense of life's good untainted by the sense of human failure to hold on to that good.

Sceptical as ever of remunerative happiness for the individual after death, he could not, even now, guard himself against terror by a steady faith. He had long felt that knowledge was 'mere guesses into truth': now—'no plummet ever sounds the soul's affairs'. He was attempting, in his Cantos of Child Harold, a small saga of the spirit lost among tensions. In this poem he has plainly forgotten any intention to imitate Byron.

'Love is the mainspring of existence'. Then 'My life hath been one love—no, blot it out'. 'I have had many loves and seek no more'. The 'solitudes of the leaf-hid forest'—where violence is not only decently hid, but accepted as man's self-consciousness can never accept violence in the human world—give his mind a sense, but now only a sense, of liberty. Freedom is still far off:

> Cares gather round; I snap their chains in two
>   And smile in agony and laugh in tears,
> Like playing with a deadly serpent, who
>   Stings to the death—there is no room for fears
>   Where death would bring me happiness. His shears
> Kill cares that hiss to poison many a vein.
>   The thought to be extinct my fate endears.
> Pale death, the grand physician, cures all pain:
> The dead rest well—who lived for joys in vain. . . .
>
> Life is to me a dream that never wakes:
>   Night finds me on this lengthening road alone.
> Love is to me a thought that ever aches,
>   A frost-bound thought that freezes life to stone.
>   Mary, in truth and nature still my own,
> That warms the winter of my aching breast,
>   Thy name is joy, nor will I life bemoan.
> Midnight, when sleep takes charge of nature's rest,
> Finds me awake and friendless—not distrest. . . .[1]

[1] This and other poems quoted in the rest of this chapter may (unless otherwise noted) be found in *Poems*, 1935, Vol. II, in *Poems of John Clare's Madness*, or in James Reeves's Selection. Geoffrey Grigson's volume contains his valuable contribution to the chronology of the Asylum poems.

He may have projected two cantos, or a seasonal four—spring, summer, autumn, winter. The poem is unfinished. The cantos are not clear. The first is of spring, and its scenery is Epping. He tells of the difficulties of holding on to love and happiness, and his unflinching sense of the rightness of young, natural love is first invested in both Mary Joyce and Patty, and then in Mary as a girl. Mary then becomes the symbol of nature, of poetry, and of love, to which we must all, in our different ways, so deeply cling:

> At dusky eve or sober silent morn,
> For such delights 'twere happy Man were born.

But that happiness is lost again. Even nature is not enough. He is back in the fens, where 'Melancholy autumn comes anew'. Conflict has returned, too, tempting him to forget: worse than that—to hate. Although he persistently reached out into matters far beyond his intellectual equipment, intelligence in him did not so much 'meddle' with his feelings as combine and unite with them. Marriage had to be lived at close quarters again, renewed, incessant poverty kept at bay only by the sharp, battling practicality of a Patty. The spirit of Mary is eternally lost:

>   like the dove
> I mourn her absence. Fate that would deter
> My hate of all things, strengthens love for her.

Temporarily nature's beauty may solace, the imaging of her in poetry still satisfy:

> What mellowness these harvest days unfold
>   In the strong glances of the midday sun!
> The homestead's very grass seems changed to gold
>   The light in golden shadows seems to run,
>   And tinges every spray it rests upon
> With that rich autumn hue of sunny joy;
>   Nature life's sweet companion cheers alone.
> The hare starts up before the shepherd boy
> And partridge coveys whirr on russet wings of joy. . . .[1]

[1] Northampton Mss.

But this golden autumn canto dwindles into a winter one of bare fields and frozen ponds. He is no nearer solution:

> The strangest, bitterest thing that life can prove
> Is woman's undisguise of hate and love.

The cantos break off. He can only struggle blindly on, striving to reconcile in his own mind the ambivalence that troubled so many poetic consciousnesses—Rousseau, Blake, Shelley, Keats, Pushkin, Clough, and Arnold. Clare strove, not through shedding of feeling, but by accepting life's conflicting responses, while rigidly he held on to what he thought he perceived beyond the conflict.

It is either a profound mysticism or a so-called neurosis, to let the imagination dally with any kind of perfection, certainly with the perfection of freedom, joy, honesty, or love. But mystics and so-called neurotics are among those who push back the frontiers of life for us. The need to seek beyond the confusion, loneliness, and commonplace of his life, and to continue his search after the 'vast shipwreck' of madness, seems to have involved Clare's reflective capacity more and more deeply. In this he differs from Smart, who in his realm of Praise was singularly untroubled by either reflection or conscience.

Clare still held the dominion over his poetry that Lamb declared was genius's true sanity. But Lamb could never save Bridget Elia her violent phases, however much her 'rambling chat', when quiet, was better to him than the talk of the great. Mary Unwin could care for, but not save, Cowper, Clare had five months' 'freedom'. Then we must conclude that Patty, finding the situation beyond her, consented to his certification. The fair-copying of the Don Juan and Child Harold Cantos prove his mental health had improved since 1837. In his occasional fits of violent anger, if one of his elder children could but lead him into the fields, it was said that he became even during these difficult months at once quiet.

Certification required the signatures of two doctors. Fenwick Skrimshire of the Peterborough Infirmary, who had intermittently attended Clare since 1824—and at least once reduced his bill—filled in the application for Clare's admission to what was called, on its foundation in 1836, the Northampton General Lunatic Asylum—now St. Andrew's Hospital for Mental Diseases. William Page also signed the certificate. St. Andrew's could then accommodate fifty 'pauper' patients and thirty private ones, and it stood in wooded grounds that slope to the valley of the Nen. Skrimshire entered the statement usual for those days that the supposed causes of insanity were 'hereditary'. He gave no evidence, and no insanity in the family has yet been disclosed. Skrimshire stated that the 'existing attack' in Clare had begun four years ago. He underlined information that the patient had 'escaped' from High Beech, but stated that he had never attempted violence to himself or others and that he was not 'idiotic, mischievous, or dirty'. To the question whether insanity had been preceded by 'any severe or long-continued mental emotion or exertion', this naïve author of *The Village Pastor's Surgical and Medical Guide in Letters from an Old Physician*, did not mention poverty, loneliness or sensitivity. He gave his now-notorious reply: 'After years addicted to Poetical prosings'. On the 29th of December, 1841, Clare was taken from his home a second time.

II

A second time he was lucky in the people who cared for him. Dr. Thomas Prichard was among the earlier alienists to continue improving the harsh, ignorant old methods of treating the insane. Tall, handsome, and athletic, he did not scruple to use his mesmeric temperament and his interest in mesmerism to influence his patients. Earl Fitzwilliam paid for Clare at the eleven shillings a week rate for poor patients, but he also paid for boots and clothing. Thus Clare was respectably dressed. He was known as 'Mr. Clare', classed among the harmless and the 'gentlemen patients', and allowed, at least for the first ten years, to go into Northampton town as he wished.

Spencer T. Hall, the mesmerist, saw him in May, 1843. Instead of the 'spare, sensitive person' of Hilton's portrait, Hall found a 'burly and florid' Clare, but 'clean and neat as if he had been fresh brushed up for market or fair'. Clare told Hall that 'they' were 'feeding him up for a fight'. Poetry? He had 'once had something to do with poetry, a long while ago; but it was no good'. On another of Hall's three visits, Clare had just returned from a long ramble, which he described 'in beautiful language, and then broke off into talk it would be wrong to repeat'. Dr. Prichard reported to Charles Mossop in November, 1843, that his patient's physical health was good, but his mind was becoming 'more and more impaired'. He was 'writing little' and in 'a coarse style', whereas he had once written 'many and very good little pieces'. Prichard much feared that the disease would 'gradually terminate in dementia'.

In 1845, W. F. Knight became house steward at St. Andrew's. On the instigation of Thomas Inskip, former friend of Bloom-field, Knight encouraged Clare, as Allen had done, to con-tinue writing, and at the same time Knight collected and transcribed all the poems which Clare gave him.

Clare had other visitors. The Howitts, William and Mary, saw him in July, 1844, and Mary received from him the poem *The Sleep of Spring*. They were struck by Clare's narrative of the execution of Charles the First, 'most graphic and minute,' with great accuracy of detail.[1] J. F. Nisbet, in *The Insanity of Genius*, records of these early years of Clare's second confine-ment, his astonishing memory:

> He seemed to assimilate everything that he read or heard, picturing events so vividly in his mind that he related them afterwards as if he had seen or taken part in them . . . and he was accustomed to tell most graphically his pre-tended experiences of the battle of the Nile and of the death of Nelson.

There was, of course, nothing clairvoyant about this, as Mary Russell Mitford was convinced there was, to whom he also gave the 'narrative of the execution of Charles the First, recounted . . . as a transaction that occurred yesterday, and of which he was an eyewitness'.[2] From the first Clare had trained his mind to remember poems by heart when he 'found' them in the fields and had no paper on which to write them down. Recall,

---

[1] Talfourd recorded of the vagaries of Mary Lamb's 'fine brain', that she, too, 'would fancy herself in the days of Queen Anne or George the First, and describe the brocaded dames and courtly manners, as though she had been bred among them.'

[2] *Recollections of a Literary Life*, 1852.

too, the eager-eyed boy who could repeat whole chapters of Job by heart and was rewarded by his schoolmaster. The pattern was still the same, its tenacity the astonishing thing.

'J. N.' from Worcester recorded a visit. He learned that Clare was 'on most subjects tolerably rational', but that his productions were often 'coarse and vulgar'. These, whatever they were, must have been judiciously destroyed. Cyrus Redding thought, as we know, that Clare's feelings toward 'the sex', though they 'appear always strong', were 'pure and delicate'. Allen, too, not having seen the Don Juan Canto, thought the same. 'J. N.' attested as to Clare's 'unlimited' supply of books, although we know him to have been dependent on loans, and then pronounced his delusions to be 'protean'. J. H. Wiffen saw Clare and lent him books, and Eliza Cook and John Dalby visited him. N. P. Willis, one of the first of the American cultural tourists in Europe, who gratuitously apprised Leigh Hunt of Dickens's 'offensive cryptography', has also recorded a visit, but without valuable information. The ageing John Taylor went at least once. But half-curious, half-bene-volent visits from strangers could not allay loneliness, and most of the other friends of Clare's youth and famous days were themselves dead or dying: Lamb, Cunningham, and Cary already gone, Darley and Hood ill, soon to follow. Eliza Emmerson's letters to her 'dear suffering friend' ceased in 1837, and she was by this time a permanent invalid. Except for Thomas Inskip, Clare's visitors were usually unknown to him.

In November, 1844, he watched the Queen and Prince Albert make their Royal Progress through Northampton, on their way to Burghley: and from another point in the town, Wordsworth watched, too. Claridge Druce, author of *The Flora of Northamptonshire* in which he set down his admiration of Clare's 'close and accurate' information, records seeing him in his favourite seat in the portico of All Saints' church. He would sit for hours, 'musing, watching the children at play, jotting down passing thoughts in his pocket-notebook', or 'a little, pathetic, distraught figure gazing into the sky'. His portrait was painted in this year, 1844, by a local artist, Thomas Grimshawe. G. J. De Wilde, editor of the *Northampton Mercury*, often met him about the town, and has memorised for us the sad yet still eager eyes, the towering Shakespearean forehead, 'oppressive with its mind', and the expression as of habitual contemplation. On one occasion, before De Wilde knew who Clare was, on their walking together along the Kingsthorpe Road, Clare startled his companion by claiming quotations from Byron's *Childe Harold* and from Shakespeare as his own. When De Wilde remonstrated, Clare replied: 'It's all the same. I'm John Clare now. I was Byron and Shakespeare formerly.' 'And then he went on to identify himself with a most miscellaneous and unselect lot of celebrities.'[1] De Wilde saw him frequently after that, and found him sometimes 'taciturn', giving to questions the 'briefest answers possible'.

De Wilde also tells of a conspiracy among some of the St. Andrew's patients to escape. This Clare steadily refused to join, fearing, De Wilde says, Dr. Prichard's 'far-seeing eye and his mysterious knowledge of their whereabouts when beyond his ken': 'I told you how it would be, you fools,' he said when the two escapers were brought back.

From a letter in the *Times Literary Supplement*,[2] Mrs. Townshend Mayer quotes another sidelight of De Wilde's. He

> did not think Clare ever doubted who he really was. [He was] only amusing himself with the art of mystification . . . I believe, further, that this mystification had its beginning in his hero-worship of Charles Lamb. Clare well knew that to impersonate Marvell would mean nothing to the general, but that to pose as Tom Spring or T. G. Wainwright (sic) would probably produce considerable effect . . . unsocial he was—but this was the lesson of experience. . . . Secrecy played a further part in his attitude toward his poetry. . . . As in the town it did not signify to the recipient whether the verse was doggerel or not (Clare received his tobacco in exchange in either case) he scribbled as idly as he could. But meanwhile he kept his private memorandum-book, and doggerel found little room there.

It is quite certain, of course, that Clare had delusions about his identity. The writer above is confusing the gaps allowed in rational thought which is the way delusions may begin. Prichard could only report in November, 1845, to Charles

---

[1] *Rambles Round About.*
[2] *Times Literary Supplement*, June 30th, 1921.

Mossop: Clare's mind 'is becoming more and more obscured by his distressing malady—He enjoys perfect liberty here, and passes all his time out of door in the fields or the Town returning only for his meals and bed'. A letter-draft in the poet's pocket-notebook for this year, to Patty, reveals a different angle on 'perfect liberty' . Remembering Frederick, their eldest son, as a child: 'I see him now', Clare wrote: 'his little face round as an apple & as red as a rose . . and now a stout Man both strangers to each other . . . the father a prisoner under a Bad Government . . . so bad in fact that its no government at all but prison Discipline where every person is forced to act contrary to their own wishes . . . the English Bastile a goverment prison where harmless people are trapped & tortured till they die—English priestcraft & English bondage more severe than the slavery of Egypt & Africa'. Clare then apologised for a letter that had turned into a sermon. Frederick, an intelligent boy, never strong, had already died in 1843. In a letter-draft in the same pocket-book, Clare wrote to his children: 'I should hope you think of & behave well to your poor Mother for I myself am rendered incapable of assisting or behaving well to anyone'.

1846 and 1847 continued with the same outward monotony. In March, 1846, old Parker Clare died, aged eighty-one. Anna, Clare's eldest child, had died in 1844. In June, 1847, Clare wrote to his youngest son, Charles, with a philosophic comment on the old man's departure. He also warned Frederick and John against coming to that 'Bastile of Hell' to see him. But by the next letter, February, 1848, he has forgotten that his father is not still alive. In this letter he wrote very sanely on books about angling—Walton, Harry Phillips, 'Piscator', and Humphrey Davy. He advised Charles to study—Mathematics —and what he himself had been as a boy astounded over— Astronomy. He had always had difficulty in buying the books to make his children 'scholars'. But:

> in my boyhood Solitude was the most talkative vision I met with Birds bees trees flowers all talked to me incessantly louder than the busy hum of men.

Charles, a promising boy, articled to a solicitor at Deeping, in his usual soothing replies to his father's letters—before his own death in 1852—made no reminders. Clare wrote to Patty in July, 1848, from 'the land of Sodom where all the peoples brains are turned the wrong way'. He was glad 'to see John yesterday & should like to have gone back with him'. He thought it 'about two years since I was first shut up in this Hell & not allowed to go out of the gates'. The young John, a strong and capable person who became a railway bridge-inspector in Wales, visited his father on one or two occasions. Patty, 'Widow Clare' as she was called at Northborough, still struggling to make a livelihood, did not make the then-arduous and probably profoundly useless journey to Northampton. She was the same sharp, lively chatterer she had always been, retaining her black hair and rich colouring till her death: good-natured her neighbours found her—with sweets in her pockets for children; talkative—but she did not mention her husband's lost wits or their poverty outside the cottage. Among the family letters which have survived for these years, there is one from Taylor to someone about Patty's having 'insolently demanded' the principal from the Fund money, in order to 'pay her own rent'. There is one from Charles to some creditor, offering to take on one of his mother's debts. Charles proposed to pay by instalment, from his salary of £4 a year. William, who ran the holding, had at that moment no extra work. He kept a seed-drill, hiring himself and his machine out among their neighbours. William visited his father once at Northampton. Eliza Louisa, who best understood his poetry and him, made the £4 journey at least once.

In April, 1849, a letter from Clare to Charles complains:

> I am now quite lost in reveries & false hums . . . in the ninth year of my captivity among the Babylonians. . . . When I was a day Labourer at Bridge Casterton & courted your Mother I knew nine Languages & could talk of them to Parsons & Gentlemen & Foreigners but never opened my Mouth about them to the Vulgar—for I always lived to myself . . . never act Hypocrisy for Deception is the most odious Knavery in the World. . . . Learning is your only wealth. . . .

The 'reveries & false hums' denote yet one more project for publication—by Knight—one more hope to be surmounted and destroyed. This letter is the most interesting of all Clare's known letters from St. Andrew's.[1] Unlike his other letters, it has the years of his 'captivity' right. He is evidently answering something Knight has told him of Charles's reply to Knight's request for unpublished manuscripts lying at Northborough: 'Three or four Volumes of Mss Poems that have not been published': 'I know nothing but of one Vol which I partly filled the last five months I was at Home & I think I reccolect something of the others which I brought home with me'. He then goes on: 'but cant you send the "Three or Four Volumes" of Mss as they are & let him see what he wanted for himself'. Knight had written for all there was at Northborough, and Patty was refusing to part with anything without first being paid. The interesting thing is—how accurately Clare remembers the important poems of his High Beech period and of his five months' freedom, about which there had been so far no publishing plan and hence no conflict arising from frustration. But he cannot remember about The Midsummer Cushion and the earlier manuscripts of poems, which he had struggled so long to get published. He had always attempted to avoid the dwindling of hope toward bitterness. The second revealing thing is that, ready to trust Knight completely, Clare was still wanting the practical Patty to trust too. Aware of what began to happen the moment commercial operations between two people were in hand, he longed for trust on both sides, proclaimed his trust in both; but, knowing the abysm of this business of man's honesty with himself and with others, he disclaims the fact that he is troubled by it, lest he should seem to be doubting anybody, when what he wants above all to do is trust: 'do just as you please & you will do right enough'. But he adds the caution to Charles about 'Hypocrisy', 'Deception', and Knavery'. It was among these rocks of Hypocrisy, Deception, and Knavery that his own Identity had seemed to founder. Dreams and imagination, though truth, seemed to make him weak. We may recall how other people's 'identity' pressed on the 'chameleon' Keats. Clare found himself unable to discover, once practical complications began to pile themselves up, what was the truth of any matter. His mind then tricked itself into letting slip some of the links between certain groups

[1] His letters to Inskip are still lost.

of ideas. These links, once dropped, could never be recovered. The seeming irrelevance in some of his talk is often only there because we have not all the clues to this 'thought-unceasing mind'. Clare's own awareness of the process of loss is apparent in a prose fragment about Self-identity, belonging to about 1841, whilst he was still struggling to hold on to the wholeness of his own; by identity he meant his ability to make workaday decisions and act quickly, without bothering too much about that integrity he never seemed able to lose sight of. We all know the interminable process of polite petty falsities which can sum up everyday living. 'Self-Identity' Clare wrote,

> is one of the finest principles in everybody's life & fills up the outline of honest truth in the decision of character.

Thus the picture we have of him in these first nine years at St. Andrew's is that he retained his candid charm and ingenuousness of conversation for those with whom he felt anything in common. Toward those to whom he was not drawn, or if he were thinking or writing at the time, he was but briefly responsive. In spite of his love of 'the wildness, the stillness, the sweetness', Clare had never deliberately cut himself off from his fellows, as did Hölderlin with whom he has been compared. On the contrary, he was continually facing outward, toward trust and friendship. His 'I hate the very noise of troubling man' can always be matched against 'I love good company and wit and punning'. These years between 1841 and 1850 and the letters which belong to them would seem to give additional proof to the view that solitude with him had always been chiefly a necessity for writing, in that it constituted his only quiet refuge from a crowded cottage.

One of the happiest of poets, he was concerned with unending expression of the evidences of beauty and joy as he saw them all round him. From melancholy he could always be 'elevated' to happiness by contemplation of small flowers that 'pat agen the shoe', by 'the soft inside of the shell of the bean', and by 'those tiny loiterers in the barley's beard'. His occasional and uncharacteristic evocation of the forces of cataract, mountain gulph, and sea which he never saw, is symbolic of his life's catastrophic descent. Where Clare seems to have differed from Cowper, Smart, and Collins is in his far more persistent working

JOHN CLARE ABOUT 1841 (?)
From the water-colour by William Henry Hunt

Northampton Library

DR. THOMAS PRICHARD

Photograph: Cooper

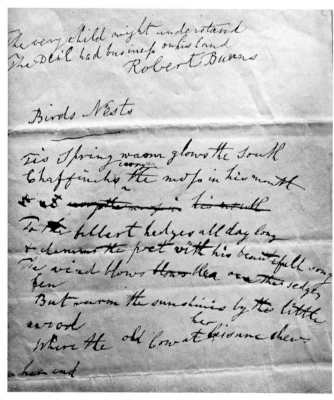

THE LAST POEM, 1863

out of ideas during his madness, involving a much more sus-
tained attempt at union between the perceptions of his senses
and his experience, and between his experience and his thought.[1]

III

Knight's transcripts up to 1850 hold nearly eight hundred
and fifty poems. Of these a little less than half have been
printed. Most of the others need never be. There is Gay-
Shenstone jingle, and odd Byronic rhyme; sea-songs and
drinking-songs in metres such as he had early used in *Helpstone
Statute* and *The Toper's Rant*:

> Away with your proud thimble-glasses
>   Of wines foreign nations supply;
> A toper ne'er drinks to the lasses
>   O'er a draught scarce enough for a fly.

There are imitation love-songs, dashed off in a moment, the
'Ha'penny Ballads' De Wilde spoke of, for which Clare received
a little tobacco or a pot of ale. These are to innumerable
Marys, Mary o' the Plough, Mary Featherstone, Mary Collingwood, as well as to other girls, Lucy, Jane, and Kate. They
remind us a little of John Cunningham's ditties to damsels.
They are described as Ha'penny Ballads in his pocket-book, and
the book is headed, like his others of this period, 'John Clare,
Northborough'. De Wilde states that there were vast quantities
of Clare's ballad-scraps current among the townspeople, many
of whom had become interested in the quiet onlooker who day
after day watched from his niche near the busiest part of the
town. These are not to be confused with the carefully composed ballads such as *I would not feign a single sigh*, nor with the
one he has in an early title-list of his father's ballads, but had
apparently not filled out till now, *My old Love left me I knew not
for why*. Nor must they be confused with songs like *Adieu*, and
I peeled bits o' straw, and the one beginning

> She tied up her few things,
> And laced up her shoe-strings,
> And put on her bonnet worn through at the crown. . . .

[1] See appendix for further note on his madness.

Thirdly, they are distinct from such a serious, rebellious pene-
tration into the mystery of human love as:

> Oh had we ne'er loved one anither
> We had ne'er been curs'd togither;
> Never shunned and never hated
> Had we never been created.
>
> Woman in her own true nature
> Is a fair and lovely creature;
> Man a savage from the wild,
> But when loved a very child.
>
> Had they ne'er been put togither
> They'd ne'er slighted one anither;
> Rift and scarred like clouds o' thunder,
> Now they're lost and torn asunder.
>
> Lost in crowds and lone togither
> Love says love ye one anither;
> Love's anither name for sorrow
> Which from hate we often borrow. . . .[1]

There are many that, in their sensuous candour, continue
poetry's story from Burns and Blake to the Swinburne of the
1866 *Poems and Ballads*. As long ago as 1821, Clare had written
poems like *Winter winds cold and blea*—not printed, incidentally,
till 1950. Though minor, such poetry yet has its importance.
This was what Clare had been after as early as 1821; this was
what he was still after—keeping words in keen, honest, un-
alloyed contact with the reality of the senses. This was part of
his share in the struggle against verbal dissociation, a struggle
not specifically begun or lost in the seventeenth century, but
which belongs to civilisation and time itself;

> . . . How sweet can courting prove,
> How can I kiss my love,
> Muffled in hat and glove
>   From the chill air?
> Quaking beneath the grove,
>   What love is there?

[1] Knight's Transcripts, Northampton Mss.

Wait in thy cushioned chair
Wi' thy white bosom bare;
Kisses are sweetest there;
   Leave it for me.
Free from the chilly air
   I will meet thee.

Lay by thy woollen vest,
Wrap no cloak o'er thy breast
Where my hand oft hath pressed
   Pin nothing there;
Where my head drops to rest
   Leave its bed bare.

Now he wrote one after another with this simplicity of directness, such as *My Minnie told all*:

. . . The linnet sang o'er us a pleasant gay tune
As ever I heard him before;
While there we lay down by the light of the moon,
And he kissed me quite home to the door.
My Minnie said nay and my Daddie forbade,
But they could do nothing with him,
A whisper by dark is not lost in the shade,
And to kiss one we love is no sin.

The peas are in blossom and sweet the beans smell,
And the grass where we sat wavers green,
And love in that place not a secret will tell
Where we were not listened or seen.
My Minnie said nay and my Daddie forbade,
But forbidden my lover won't be;
We meet there at e'en when he's put by the spade,
And will while a leaf's on the tree.[1]

Greater delicacy which Allen and Redding would have
approved is in such unpublished gleanings as the late

O come to me i' the evening
   And let us walk together,
When talking is believing,
   And beautiful the weather.

[1] Knight's Transcripts, Northampton Mss.

> There's a siller bleb in the golden-eye,[1]
>   A daisy's by the thorn,
> On the wilding[2] purest diamonds lie,
>   The souls o' summer morn.
> But come to me i' the even, love,
>   When the lark drops in the corn.[3]

But the best of the poems written between 1841 and 1850 are connected with certain ideas which had absorbed him, sensuously and intellectually, since his entry into the realm of poetry as a boy. The utmost claim of a poet who failed to stay the normal mental course and in madness wrote some of his best poetry, they have, besides an emotional refreshment to offer, a wisdom of our common humanity to communicate.

Our conception of him during these nine years is not that his malady was characterised by any particularly deep troughs and alternate rises, but that he wrote, as he had written for the previous twenty-five years, fairly continuously if fitfully, and particularly under stimulus from Inskip's letters and visits, and of Knight's interest. As far back as 1831 he had written how encouragement 'refreshed the heart like a summer shower'. His moods varied, as visitors testified, from day to day. It is not possible to put anything like precise dates to the poems either of these nine years, or of the years just after 1849, Knight's last date. Even if Knight's occasional dating is for when he received the manuscripts from Clare, or when Clare said he wrote the poems, we know his sense of time was already fallible, and he might still have written the poems some time previously. Prichard's statement to Charles Mossop in November, 1843, that Clare was then writing 'little', though he used 'at one time to write many and very good little pieces', looks as though Prichard were referring to the first year or two as a fertile period. Either these poems did not survive, or they are the ones which Knight copied first. Thus the poems dated 1844, Knights' first date, may have been written in 1844, or between 1841 and 1844. One, we know, *The Autumn Wind*, dated for 1845, crept in a second time, in less good form, among the dateless later poems. Reading through Knight's transcripts, one is tempted

---

[1] Corn-marigold.
[2] Wild rose.
[3] Knight's Transcripts, Northampton Mss.

to try to count years by recurrent poems on spring. But that will not do. What does emerge is a unity among the best of the poems. To 1844 or earlier belong *Love is Life's Spring, The Sleep of Spring, Love's Pains,* and *A Vision. The Pale Sun,* missed by Knight, is in its rough draft dated for 1845. *I Am* and *Invite to Eternity* were perhaps not later than 1844; so with *Sorrow is my Joy* and *Hesperus.* About 1848 we may place *Clock-a-clay. The Invitation, Little Trotty Wagtail,* and *Love Lives Beyond* were 1849. *Secret Love* may have been later than 1844, and *Love cannot Die* is among the dateless post-1849 transcripts but may not belong there. To 1850, just before, or just after, may be assigned the longest poem among all these Asylum poems—*A Rhapsody.* And here it is observable that music and stanza-architecture are both beginning to falter.

To recapitulate a moment: Clare's earliest apprentice verse, with its growing point in the eighteenth century and in his eighteenth-century reading, but with his strong emotional and visual perception of the life around him, had aimed at leaving as full a picture as possible of a vanished village life. This verse kept an acute eye on its object. It was based in realism which was determined to owe nothing to the Thomsonian and Shenstonian Picturesque which had followed the cult of Pastoral. Using what he often called 'the critic's prerogative of fault-finding with as light a hand as possible', Clare was yet never able wholly to sympathise with Wordsworth's romanticism. The romantic elements in his own composition held more in common with Byron and Blake than with Wordsworth. Flowing and almost inexhaustible, this early verse of Clare's was often, through his inability to compress, formless, though it was successfully individual in tone. In his first mature period, provincial ballads, imitations of older lyrics, and study of Percy, Ellis, and Ritson, all helped to give him a sense of poetic structure. Rejecting bitter social satire, although the misfortunes of those closely identified with him almost forced it on him, and still searching for his 'real excellence that must be its own creation', he produced instead two large collections of poems chiefly in sonnet-frame. These had great feeling and particularity, but in them form was still organic rather than composed. Words and word-order in them approached closer to living speech and speech rhythms, further receding from what might be tainted with artificiality of any kind. After the onset of his madness and his removal to Northborough, the group of starkly impersonal poems about cruelty and vulgarity were of this instinctive, artifice-refusing form. But during this period he also contrived for the first time lyrics of metrical perfection and of highly original metre. At High Beech the lyric intensity deepened, the sensitive intelligence narrowed over the gaps that had appeared in the mind. Envy of Byron which he had striven too hard to overcome helped produce the Don Juan Canto, at which mixture of wisdom and insanity we cannot fail to find ourselves smiling as we do occasionally over Smart's *Jubilate Agno*. But there is also the fragmentarily beautiful *Child Harold*. At St. Andrew's, deepening, narrowing, and reconciliation went further still. And strangely the mad mind was capable of poetic truth as well as of metrical originality.

In this group we are now to examine, there are innovations which, in a period of over-lush rhyme and crowded poetical imagery, point forward to Matthew Arnold and modern Provençal poets rather than backward to Southey and Shelley's un-rhymed experiments. That Clare was interested in the possibility of 'prose-poetry' is clear from *Dewdrops, House or Window flies*, and *Pleasant Sounds*, though this last, so easily printable in lines, is written as prose in the manuscript. In *The Pale Sun*, the vivid hope of a young spring day breaks through spare imagery and rhymeless wintry lines:

> Pale sunbeams gleam
> That nurture a few flowers,
> Pilewort and daisy and a sprig of green
> On whitethorn bushes
> In the leafless hedge.
>
> These harbingers
> Tell spring is coming fast,
> And these the schoolboy marks
> And wastes an hour from school
> Agen the old pasture hedge,
>
> Cropping the daisy
> And the pilewort flowers,

Pleased with the spring and all he looks upon,
He opes his spelling book
And hides her blossoms there.

Shadows fall dark
Like black in the pale sun,
And lie the bleak day long,
Like black stock under hedges
And bare wind-rocked trees.

'Tis chill but pleasant.
In the hedge-bottom lined
With brown sear leaves
The last year littered there and left
Mopes the hedge-sparrow

With trembling wings, and cheeps
Its welcome to pale sunbeams
Creeping through; and further on
Made of green moss
The nest and green-blue eggs are seen.

All token spring; and every day,
Green and more green, hedges and close
And everywhere appears.
Still, 'tis but March,
But still, that March is spring.

Another metrical experiment that may yet give its author place as a qualified representative of his age's poetry is a lyric which Lascelles Abercrombie praised in *The Theory of Poetry* for 'poignancy of expressiveness in metre'. Clare might have agreed in theory with both Aristotle and Sidney that 'it is not riming and versing that maketh a poet, any more than a long gown maketh an advocate'. But he himself, whose gift was not gotten solely 'by labour and learning', could never avoid the greater expressiveness that Sidney heard in rhyme and metre:

Come hither, my dear one, my choice one, and rare one,
    And let us be walking the meadows so fair,
Where pilewort and daisies in light and gold blazes,[1]
    And the wind plays so sweet on thy bonny brown hair.

[1] See note for p. 188.

Come with thy maiden eye, lay silks and satins by;
　　Come in thy russet or green cotton gown;
Come to the meads, dear, where flags, sedge, and reeds
　　appear
　　Rustling to soft winds and bow up and down.[1]

Come with thy parted hair, bright eyes, and forehead bare;
　　Come to the whitethorn that grows in the lane;
To banks of primroses, where sweetness reposes,
　　Come love, and let us be happy again.

Forthright refusal of imposed guilt over physical love is in *I saw
her crop a rose*. With its effective short lines followed by final
couplets with six variant stresses, this poem is also one of his late
metrical successes:

> . . . There is a small green place
> 　　Where cowslips early curled,
> Which on sabbath day I trace,
> 　　The dearest in the world.
> A little oak spreads o'er it,
> 　　And throws a shadow round,
> A green sward close before it,
> 　　The greenest ever found;
> There is not a woodland nigh nor is there a green grove,
> Yet stood the fair maid by me and told me all her love.

The Dying Child may be compared with Coleridge's *Something
Childish but very Natural* and with Blake's *Schoolboy*:

> He could not die when trees were green,
> 　　For he loved the time too well.
> His little hands, when flowers were seen,
> 　　Were held for the bluebell,
> 　　As he was carried o'er the green.

> His eye glanced at the white-nosed bee;
> 　　He knew those children of the spring;
> When he was well and on the lea
> 　　He held one in his hands to sing,
> 　　Which filled his heart with glee.

---

[1] We have given Knight's reading rather than Cherry's pencilled corrections,
though in both lines at sacrifice of strict grammar.

Infants, those children of the spring!
   How can an infant die
When butterflies are on the wing,
   Green grass and such a sky?
   How can they die at spring? . . .

And then he shut his little eyes,
   And flowers would notice not;
Birds' nests and eggs made no surprise,
   He now no blossoms got:
   They met with plaintive sighs.

When winter came and blasts did sigh,
   And bare was plain and tree,
As he for ease in bed did lie,
   His soul seemed with the free,
   He died so quietly.

We now come to the group of poems on joy, freedom, and greater love: love, that is, beyond the individual. If we exclude the well-anthologised and therefore also well known *I am*, because of a disturbing hint of self-pity, the others are: *Love is Life's Spring, Love's Pains, Love Lives Beyond the Tomb, Love's Story, Love Cannot Die, Secret Love, Sorrow is my Joy, Invite to Eternity*, and *The Vision*. Our estimate of a poet is often based finally on no more than a handful of his best poems. If we leave out much of Clare's early work, we should not miss the collection of poems on country delights and cruelty, nor these last reflective poems.

He had now passed far beyond the limits of normal experience. Long ago, he had aimed at more compression, and at what seemed most important of all to him, directness and honesty for poetry. These had been granted through having sincerity thrust upon him by failure and intensity by the narrowness of prison. 'Love is the mainspring of existence', he had written at High Beech. He concluded *Love's Story* with a statement of the difficulty of realistic affirmation. Affirmation— love as he called it—he well knew was not only akin to, but easily confused with, the weakness that is justly abhorrent in this life:

      I cannot hate thee,
        Yet my love seems debtor

> To love thee more,
>   So hating—love thee better.[1]

Again, in *Love is Life's Spring*:

> Care keeps her cash-book where none like to borrow;
> Tears are as lonely as the lonely dove;
>   Procrastinated falsehood is hell's horror;
> Hope is its fire that kindles from above;
> Hate burns hell-deep in chronicles of love![1]

There are, among the poems for these years 1841 to 1849, plenty to Mary Joyce as a girl, like *It is the Evening hour*, and *I sleep with thee and wake with thee*, as well as a few, like *Maid of Walkherd* of the High Beech period, to Patty. It was not any simple attraction to female beauty, however much that obviously played its part, he meant in this group of important poems. We may recall a fruitful discussion on the theme, twenty-five centuries old: 'As the son of Resource and Poverty, love is . . . ever poor, and far from tender or beautiful as most suppose him, rather is he hard and parched, shoeless and homeless . . . true to his mother's nature he ever dwells with want. But he takes after his father in scheming for all that is beautiful and good . . . throughout life ensuing the truth'. What Clare is saying, surely, is that individual trust, friendship, and love can survive their own betrayal; that while hope is of heaven, hell may be much nearer earth. It may be no more than the gap between what we say and what we mean or do. These are the questions in the more important of the St. Andrew's lyrics, written while their author was taciturn to the curious. Besides transmuting the anguish of his personal predicament, he was stating what he felt as a universal dilemma.

It is with immemorially-endowed words that Clare makes his last experiment among old ideas, but the words have acquired a new sharp edge. *Love's Pains* is simple and clear in the way Blake's *Songs of Innocence* are:

> This love, wrong understood,
>   Oft turned my joy to pain;
> I tried to throw away the bud,
>   But the blossom would remain.

Poems of John Clare's Madness, Ed. Geoffrey Grigson.

Or

> Love lives beyond
> The tomb, the earth, the flowers, and dew.
> I love the fond,
> The faithful, young, and true.

Nothing could be plainer, more straightforward—or more profound—than

> Love lives with nature, not with lust
> Go seek it in the flowers.

In the late lines, *Borne upon an Angel's Breast*,

> In crime and enmity they lie
> Who sin and tell us love can die,
> Who say to us in slander's breath
> That love belongs to sin and death,

'they' are obviously the priests of the doctrine of Original Sin, as well as the disillusioned romantic, the negative, and the despairing. *Secret Love* is another of those statements under which Clare felt that the poet's soul lay, as he said in a later fragment still, 'buried in the Ink' with which he wrote. Its import is how 'secret' in essence love's very communication may be. Glib, overt, noisy—it is likelier to be tainted with apathy or other falsities. Love is the prime riddle we have been given to solve. And nature offers here no help at all:

> I hid my love when young till I
> Couldn't bear the buzzing of a fly;
> I hid my love to my despite
> Till I could not bear to look at light;
> I dare not gaze upon her face
> But left her memory in every place:
> Whene'er I saw a wild flower lie
> I kissed and bade my love good-bye.

> I met her in the greenest dells,
> Where dewdrops pearl the wood bluebells;
> The lost breeze kissed her bright blue eye,
> The bee kissed and went singing by.
> A sunbeam found a passage there,

> A gold chain round her neck so fair;
> As secret as the wild bee's song
> She lay there all the summer long.
>
> I hid my love in field and town
> Till e'en the breeze would knock me down;
> The bees seemed singing ballads o'er,
> The fly's buzz turned a lion's roar;
> And even silence found a tongue,
> To haunt me all the summer long;
> The riddle nature could not prove
> Was nothing else but secret love.

Invite to Eternity asks some woman—but it no longer matters whom—to accompany him to the eternity that, besides being a compensation for his present neglect and isolation, is yet something other than the orthodox 'better world' of happiness beyond the grave. It is psychologically true that there is a sense in which the pursuit of 'truth does lead us, though slowly and painfully, to the only happiness of which we are capable'. Clare meant in this poem, by 'eternity', the eternity of poetry he had spoken of in *Triumphs of Time* and *Song's Eternity*. He could no longer care about personal life after death. What he did care about was poetry's truth. The path to that truth was but a continuation of the way he had come—through the 'living intense moment in the waste of time'; that was the only way —though it often caused friends and lovers to avert their faces— that joined living and dead:

> Say, wilt thou go with me sweet maid,
> Say, maiden, wilt thou go with me
> Through the valley depths of shade,
> Of night and dark obscurity;
> Where the path has lost its way,
> Where the sun forgets the day,
> Where there's neither light nor life to see,
> Sweet maiden, wilt thou go with me?
>
> Where stones will turn to flooding streams,
> Where plains will rise like ocean's waves,
> Where life will fade like visioned dreams
> And mountains darken into caves,

Say, maiden, wilt thou go with me
Through this sad non-identity,
Where parents live and are forgot,
And sisters live and know us not. . . .

This land of shadows wilt thou trace,
Nor look to know each other's face;
The present marred with reason gone
And past and present both as one?
Say, maiden, can thy life be led
To join the living and the dead?
Then trace thy footsteps on with me;
We're wed to one eternity.

Though slightly rhetorical, this poem conveys how the poet's sense of non-identity helped him to understand personal dissolution.

The Vision, another statement of escape from the quicksands that can threaten the human mind, completes, with the *Invite*, what we may call his regeneration. It is the last of this group:

I lost the love of heaven above,
    I spurned the lust of earth below,
I felt the sweets of fancied love,
    And hell itself my only foe.

I lost earth's joys, but felt the glow
    Of heaven's flame abound in me,
Till loveliness and I did grow
    The bard of immortality.

I loved but woman fell away,
    I hid me from her faded flame.
I snatched the sun's eternal ray
    And wrote till earth was but a name,

In every language upon earth,
    On every shore, o'er every sea,
I gave my name immortal birth
    And kept my spirit with the free.

The 'love of heaven' which he could not gain is clear enough. There was also a strained etherealism which both temperament and experience had taught him to distrust; 'fancied love'—the possible pretension in conventionalised emotion—he had experi-

enced in early days with his 'dearest Emma'. Other booby-
traps are a self-righteous acceptance of supposed wrong, a
reducing of the spirit of joy such acceptance can be—if it does
not turn to hate, cynicism, or any other of the possible hells.
Beauty and joy, in the naturalistic common-sense to which he
had always clung, are love's cause and its most bountiful result.
It is this positive attitude to life Clare felt to be both freedom
and deep necessity, man's undeniable heritage. Like *Invite to
Eternity*, *The Vision* is another of his submerged metaphors. The
illogicality in its last stanza drives home the poem's final truth.
For poets, as for most artists of all kinds, there are fewer barriers
of race, creed, learning, and land, than there are for most of us.

It would be uncritical to say that the joy celebrated in this
poem has much in common with the 'intellectual joy' of *The
Excursion*. Clare has more in common with the Blake of 'The
wild winds weep/And the night is a-cold,/Come hither Sleep/
And my joys unfold,/and with the young Keats, than with the
Wordsworth of 'confirmed tranquillity'. But his ideas are, as
far as ideas ever can belong to one man, his own.

Freedom, he saw at last, was different from liberty. Liberty
receded further as life went on:

> Gather on mountain and on plain!
> Make gossamer the paper chain!
> Make prison walls as paper screen,
> That tyrant maskers may be seen!
> Let earth as well as heaven be free!
> So on, ye brave, for liberty!

But it could never be more than a longing, a struggling towards
—certainly not in a madhouse:

> I make earth's home my dwelling place,
> Love liberty and think I'm free.

Insensitivity and blunting, through materialism, had curtailed
liberty among those who had once been equalised by communal
work and common interests. That had not altered:

> Hypocrisy the highest holds her head
>   In pulpit placed with fair and smiling face,
>   With tongues new-oiled and hearts as cold as lead. . . .[1]

[1] Part of unpublished stanza probably intended for one of the Cantos of
Child Harold.

Apathy over that most complex thing, simple honesty, a kind of moral cowardice among place-holders, cut for ever at the liberties of the unguarded and the undefeated. To guard oneself was in one sense to betray. Further than that he could not see. But mental freedom, the triumph of *The Vision*, was a personal thing of which nobody could be deprived.

IV

Secretly he still yearned for another book of his poetry to find its way among what Redding had called the 'puling, wordy, sentimental effusions' of mid-century popular poetry. But in November, 1849, Inskip, already an old man, after a lingering illness, died. By early February, 1850, Knight had left St. Andrew's to take up another post at Birmingham, and nothing came of his intention to publish the poems. With Inskip and Knight went the prisoner's last links with the outside world and the kinship in poetry. Small wonder that, in December of 1848, the year in which he had been painted by a local artist[1] and copies of the portrait sold about the town, we find a hopeless pencil-scrawled letter-draft:

> My dear Mary but there is no faith here so I hold my tongue & wait the end out without attention or intention— I am that I am—& done nothing yet

or that in July of 1849 he repeated his words of dreary frustration from his April letter to Charles: 'I have nothing to write about for I see Nothing and hear nothing'. After 1850 there are no extant letters in his own hand till 1860. In that year he wrote to Patty, resuscitated his father and mother and all his children except Charles, asked to be remembered to enquiring friends and signed himself yet once more 'Your loving husband till Death—John Clare'.

There are few good poems in Knight's second and dateless Volume of apparently after 1849. And even these, chiefly Ha'penny Ballads, may have been sent to Knight but belong to before 1849. The elemental music had lost its eerie power of

---

[1] G. Maine, not Marne, as given in *John Clare: A Life*.

nervous language and was beginning to die away. A notebook
entry for 1850 runs:

> Lord Byron was 16 years when he began to write Childe
> Harold & finished it in 1818 when he was 25. When he
> wrote the 4th Canto he was courting one Martha Turner
> the daughter of Mr. Willm Turner, Walk Lodge. He began
> it on Sunday afternoon & finished it in three or four hours
> under an Ash Tree in her Father's Home Close.[1]

Beneath that tree—it is an oak in the poem—was the spot, with
its 'cowslips early curled', where the Maid 'told her love'. This
is still another of those hidden associations—some link between
what he rigidly saw as a natural morality and his poetic aims,
covering a crater in the mind now thirty years deep. An unpublished *Crazy Jane* rhyme in the same pocket-book runs:

> O Love is so deceiving
> Like bees it wears a sting;
> I thought it true believing
> But it's no such a thing.
> They smile but to deceive you;
> They kiss and then they leave you;
> Speak truth—they won't believe you:
> Their honey wears a sting.
>
> What's the use o' pretty faces?
> Ruby lips and cheeks so red?
> Flowers grow in pleasant places;
> So does a maidenhead.
> The fairest won't believe you,
> The foulest still deceive you;
> The many laugh and grieve you
> Until you're coffin-dead.[1]

And the same notebook, as well as identifying him with Nelson,
announces his poetic death after Knight's going:

> John Clare
> Fell on the Deck of the Belerophon
> Where his brains were knocked out
> With a Crowbar by the Crew
> Horatio Nelson

[1] Northampton Mss.

Jerom, a fellow-patient, recalled Clare's nightly refrains as a captain under Nelson:

> Fight on my boys, he said
> Till I die, till I die.

Jerom recalled, too, his 'witticisms and crank sayings', his moral courage, and his fiery blue eye. His notebook dated for 1849 contains a letter to some 'Hellen', and a second one to Mary Collingwood (the 1848 draft has only her name at the top mixed with Mary Ann Averey's), in a consonant code. He warns Mary Collingwood against coming to this 'mnstrs bd plc' where all were 'trnd Frnchmn', and added: 'flsh ppl tll m hv gt n hm n ths wrld'.

When Dr. Prichard left St. Andrew's in 1854 to found an institution of his own at Abington Abbey, Dr. Edwin Wing and Dr. Nesbitt took his place. Under the new doctors' regime Clare's liberty was further restricted to the Asylum grounds. Dr. Nesbitt in the statement he left wrote that he had 'always understood Clare's affliction to have had its origin in dissipation'. That evil spirit was still pursuing. But Nesbitt was also the doctor who described Clare as 'essentially a kind-hearted, good-feeling man with an unusually large cerebral development, possessing great breadth and altitude of forehead, such as we are in the habit of associating with men of the highest order of intellect'.

About this time a belated plan for the publication of the complete poems was mooted. John Taylor, jealous perhaps of Knight's intentions, had purchased the copyright of *The Rural Muse* from How for £10. But the scheme fell to earth, and, fortunately, the poet did not hear of it. For the moment he was occupied. He was helping Anne Elizabeth Baker, one of the best of the provincial glossarists, with her *Northamptonshire Words and Phrases*. He furnished one-half of the strictly Northamptonshire words.

But it is likely that closer confinement helped darken the clouds over his mind. We hear of him in 1856, when the Rev. Thomas James, lecturing on Dryden and Clare, left the homiletic account on which J. L. Cherry drew in 1873 for his *Life and Remains of John Clare*. In 1857 the *London Journal* had

o

verses to him, and the *Quarterly* a short appreciation. Unfortunately the Asylum case-books up to 1862 are lost. In February,
1860, Dr. Wing's report was that his patient's bodily health
was still good, though mentally he was incoherent.

But in the spring of this year the gentle, yet most determined
of poets, gathered his forces yet once more. In March, the day
after his last letter to Patty, Dr. Wing persuaded him to answer
the inquiry of an unknown, a Mr. Hipkins. Clare wrote;

> Dear Sir
>   I am in a Madhouse & quite forget your name or who
> you are. You must excuse me for I have nothing to com-
> municate or tell of & why I am shut up I dont know.

Robert Walton, overcoming his own 'insuperable objections
. . . of being an eye-witness of the punishments or afflictions to
which our less fortunate brethren are subjected' visited St.
Andrew's, and repeated as incontroversial the story of dis-
sipation as being the cause of Clare's 'downfall'. He remarked
Clare's 'appropriativeness': 'I know Gray. I know him well,'
Clare had said, when asked if he recalled some lines from *The
Elegy*, a remark you or I might surely make.

That spring of 1860 he wrote, but probably under persuasion,
The Daisy, Early Spring, and *The Green Lane* or *A Lane in Spring*.
In *Early Spring* he listed crocus, polyanthus, and hepatica—
which last he called by its country name, a pun on Patty's.
The dog sitting out-of-doors completed the picture of spring
seen from a house. In *The Green Lane* he noted spangles on the
brook, gliding fish, pingle and wood, pilewort, and grass-green
linnets; and as so often among his plethora, like the point of
balance in a picture, his last image, the bottle-green fly on the
arum leaf in this small poem, gathers the rest together and con-
centrates the very feel of season, scene, or time of day.

He answered in the same months a letter to his 'dear daughter'
Sophia, and sometime this year, but protesting that he had forgotten how to write, and producing first a sheet of grotesque
heads no two alike',[1] he wrote the *Address to John Clare*; 'Well
honest John how fare you now at home?/The Spring is come,
and birds are building nests.' These four poems still bear

---

[1] Godfrey's Notes, Peterborough Papers.

echoes of his music 'easy as breathing', and hints of the rich 'eye-on-weed' particularity that had been his first gift to poetry. For some years, knowing his vision failing, one of his minor delusions had been that his eyes had no pupils.[1]

To Agnes Strickland, the documentary historian, in August, 1860, he gave a manuscript of *The Daisy*, and some rather startling answers to her questions. When she asked what he meant by 'they pick my brains out' he replied:

> Why, they have cut off my head, and picked out all the letters of the alphabet—all the vowels and consonants— and brought them out through my ears; and then they want me to write poetry! I can't do it.

Asked which he liked best, 'literature or your former avocation', he answered

> I liked hard work best; I was happy then. Literature has destroyed my head and brought me here.

There were a few other visitors. John Plummer, a verse-writer from Kettering, in either 1860 or 1861 found him reading in a comfortable sitting-room with a warm fire, commented on his large forehead and benevolent-looking features, was informed that he was 'very frequently blithe and talkative', but thought him on that occasion 'taciturn'—perhaps not even then an attitude of the insane. Paxton Hood called on him and recorded his visit in *The Peerage of Poverty*, and among John Ascham's *Sonnets on the Months*, 1861, there is one to Clare, revealing him after he could no longer walk into the garden.

For he was now seventy, and his physical strength declining. The case-books for these last years record that in February, 1863, he was put to bed through inability to use his legs after 'one of his many apoplectic seizures'. Wing commented on his bad memory and his ingrained delusions of being Byron and a sea-captain under Nelson. Though by October he was stronger and was wheeled into the garden, it could give no pleasure. He was still haunted by creatures and spirits of his 'own disordered fancy', at which he would 'often swear most coarsely'. Occasionally, like Swift in his last decline, he became 'excited, noisy and

---

[1] See Inskip's letters to Clare, Northampton Papers.

abusive'.[1] But yet, sometime, in the very early spring of 1864, he seems to have collected himself sufficiently to write his last poem, *Birds' Nests*, heading it with a quotation from *Tam o' Shanter*—from memory, most likely, since it is not quite correct.

On Good Friday, 'very helpless and quite childish', he was taken out for the last time. On the 10th of May—the month was notable for its excessive heat—he had another seizure, and Patty was notified. For Friday, the 20th of May, 1864, the case-books record again, and finally, he 'died quietly late in the afternoon'.

The Bellars, once of Woodcroft, hearing the news, took steps to ensure that he should be buried at Helpston. Years before, he had made a sketch for his own gravestone. He desired 'no date thereon'. 'I wish it to live or die with my poems . . . which if they have merit with posterity it will & if they have not it will not be worth preserving'. His coffin, arriving home unexpectedly, had to be housed at *The Blue Bell*. Local hearsay declared that his remains were not in the coffin, since none of the family from Northborough came to look at the dead. But his dates are on his gravestone; and the evening sun lingers, as he had wished, lighting the now-mossed inscription over the place where his dust mingles with the earth he loved and understood.

CLARE'S SKETCH FOR
HIS GRAVESTONE

[1] Case-books, St. Andrew's Hospital.

APPENDIX

NOTE ON CLARE'S MADNESS

IN spite of the great advance in medical science and psychological knowledge of mental disease during the last century, not enough examination and comparison has yet been made of the madness of poets. The difference between the psychoanalytic viewing of life and the artistic, though both are necessary and valuable, is in other ways a handicap to the understanding of artistic, and particularly of literary, madness. Symptomatology is still very confused. The term insanity itself is still used to denote a heterogeneous group of phenomena in disease having but little in common.

Clare was most likely of manic-depressive temperament. His bursts of creative work were followed by periods of exhaustion, and these were often prolonged by pecuniary worry and undernourishment. His energy has an astonishing continuity, and its alternations with exhaustion should not be confused with schizoid elation and despair. The view that his temperament and hence his disease were manic-depressive and not schizophrenic is supported, not only by the slow progress of his disease, but by his capacity for rhythmic originality and poetic unity during the first ten years of his second incarceration. The other term given to the manic-depressive temperament and group of mental diseases is 'cyclothymic'. See *Reflections of Genius*, by Thomas Tennant, Physician Superintendent of St. Andrew's Hospital, in *The Journal of Medical Science*, Vol. XCIX, No. 414; see also James Reeves's Introduction to *Selected Poems. John Clare*. Ernst Kris in *Psychoanalytic Explorations in Art* offers the view that Clare was schizophrenic, as does Geoffrey Grigson in Introduction to *Poems of John Clare's Madness*.

BIBLIOGRAPHY

WORKS

Poems Descriptive of Rural Life and Scenery. London: Printed for Taylor and Hessey, and E. Drury, 1820. Second and third editions, 1820. Fourth edition, 1821.

The Village Minstrel, and Other Poems. London: Printed for Taylor and Hessey, and E. Drury. Two Volumes, 1821. Second issue 1823.

The Shepherd's Calendar; with Village Stories, and Other Poems. London: Published for John Taylor, by James Duncan, 1827.

The Rural Muse. London: Whittaker & Co., 1835.

The Poems of John Clare. Edited with an Introduction by J. W. Tibble. Dent, 1935.

The Letters of John Clare. Edited by J. W. and Anne Tibble. Routledge and Kegan Paul, 1951.

The Prose of John Clare. Edited by J. W. and Anne Tibble. Routledge and Kegan Paul, 1951.

SELECTIONS, BIOGRAPHIES, AND IMPORTANT MISCELLANEA

Four Letters from the Rev. W. Allen to the Right Honourable Lord Radstock, G.C.B., on the Poems of John Clare, the Northamptonshire Peasant. Hatchards', 1823.

Three Very Interesting Letters (two in curious rhyme). By the celebrated poets Clare, Cowper, and Bird. With an Appendix (Clare's 'Familiar Epistle to a Friend'). Charles Clarke's private press, Great Totham, 1837.

The Life of John Clare. By Frederick Martin. London and Cambridge: Macmillan & Co., 1865.

Life and Remains of John Clare. By J. L. Cherry. London: Frederick Warne & Co., Northampton: J. Taylor & Son, 1873. Issued in *Chandos Classic*, 1873–77.

The John Clare Centenary Exhibition Catalogue. Introduction by C. Dack. Peterborough Natural History, Scientific, and Archæological Society, 1893.

Poems by John Clare. Selected and introduced by Norman Gale. With a Bibliography by C. Ernest Smith. Rugby: George E. Over, 1901.

Poems by John Clare. Edited, with an Introduction by Arthur Symons. London: Henry Frowde, 1908.

Northamptonshire Botanologia: John Clare. By G. Claridge Druce, 1912. (Includes a memoir and a classification of the flowers described in Clare's poems.)

John Clare: Poems Chiefly from Manuscript. Edited by Edmund Blunden and Alan Porter. With an Introduction by Edmund Blunden. London: Richard Cobden-Sanderson, 1920.

Madrigals and Chronicles. Being newly-found poems written by John Clare. Edited, with a Preface and Commentary, by Edmund Blunden. London: The Beaumont Press, 1924.

More Footnotes to Literary History. By Edmund Blunden. Tokyo: Kenkyusha, 1926.

The 'Godfrey' papers from St. Andrew's Hospital. Peterborough Mss.

John Clare's Library. By Reginald W. Brown. Northamptonshire Natural History Society and Field Club, 1929.

Sketches in the Life of John Clare. By Himself. With an Introduction, Notes, and Additions by Edmund Blunden. London: R. Cobden-Sanderson, 1931.

John Clare: a Life. By J. W. and Anne Tibble. London: R. Cobden-Sanderson, 1932.

Poems of John Clare's Madness. Edited with an Introduction by Geoffrey Grigson. London: Routledge and Kegan Paul, 1950.

John Clare and Other Studies. By John Middleton Murry. London: Peter Nevill, 1950.

Green Shadows. The Life of John Clare, by June Wilson. London: Hodder and Stoughton, 1951.

Selected Poems of John Clare. Edited with an Introduction by Geoffrey Grigson. Routledge and Kegan Paul, 1950.

John Clare: Selected Poems. Edited with an Introduction by James Reeves. Heinemann, 1954.

INCIDENTAL REFERENCE VOLUMES

ABBOTT, Claude Colleer. *Life and Letters of George Darley*, 1928.

ABERCROMBIE, Lascelles. *The Theory of Poetry*, 1924.

ANON. *Pen and Ink Sketches of Authors and Authoresses*, undated.

BAKER, A. E. *Glossary of Northamptonshire Words and Phrases*, 1854.

BLEULER, E. *Dementia Præcox* (or the Group of Schizophrenias) 1950.

BLUNDEN, Edmund. *Nature in English Literature*, 1929. *Charles Lamb and his Contemporaries*, 1933. *Keats's Publisher*, 1936.

CARRITT, E. F. *A Calendar of British Taste* from 1600 to 1800, 1949.

CARY, H. *Memoirs of H. F. Cary*, 1847.

CECIL, David. *The Stricken Deer*, 1929.

CHAMBERS, R. *Cyclopædia of English Literature*, 1861.

COLERIDGE, S. T. *Biographia Literaria* ('Rustic Life and Human Diction'), 1817.

DAICHES, David. *Robert Burns*, 1952.

DENNIS, J. *Studies in English Literature*, 1876.

DE QUINCEY, T. *Works: London Reminiscences*, 1890.

DE WILDE, G. J. *Rambles Round About*, 1872.

DOBELL, B. *Sidelights on Charles Lamb*, 1903.

ELTON, Oliver. *Survey of English Literature, 1780–1831*, 1912.

EMPSON, William. *Some Versions of Pastoral*, 1936.

FERGUSSON, Robert. *Scots Poems* (Selected and edited by Alexander Law, M.A.), 1947.

FORSTER, —. *Life of Charles Dickens, Vol. III*, 1874.

GALIGNANI, A. and W. *Living Poets of England*, 1827.

GRIERSON, Herbert J. C. *Lyrical Poetry from Blake to Hardy*, 1928.

GRIGSON, Geoffrey (Ed.). *The Poet's Eye*, 1945.

GOSSE, Edmund. *Silhouettes*, 1925.

HALL, S. C. *Book of Gems*, 1838.

HALL, S. T. *Biographical Sketches*, 1873.

HAMMOND, J. L. and Barbara. *The Village Labourer, 1760–1832*, 1927.

HASBACH, W. *A History of the English Agricultural Labourer*, 1908.

HEATH, R. *The English Peasant*, 1893.

HEATH-STUBBS, John. *The Darkling Plain*, 1950.

HEWLETT, Maurice. *Last Essays* ('Peasant Poems'), 1924.

Hone, William. *Every-Day Book*, 1832.

Hood, E. Paxton. *The Literature of Labour*, 1851. *The Peerage of Poverty*, 1870.

Hood, Thomas. *Hood's Own, No.* 12, 1839.

James, T. *MS. Lecture on Dryden and Clare.*

Kent, Elizabeth. *Flora Domestica*, 1823. *Sylvan Sketches*, 1825.

Kermode, Frank (Ed.). *English Pastoral Poetry from the Beginnings to Marvell*, 1952.

King, R. W. *The Translator of Dante*, 1925.

Kris, Ernst. *Psychoanalytic Explorations in Art*, 1953.

Lamb, Charles. *Letters, Essays.*

Lucas, E. V. *Life of Charles Lamb*, 1935.

Lynd, Robert. *Books and Authors*, 1922.

Marsh, G. L. *John Hamilton Reynolds*, 1928.

Middleton Murry, John. *Countries of the Mind*, 1931.

Mitford, Mary Russell. *Recollections of a Literary Life*, 1852.

Nicholes, E. *The Shadowed Mind* (unpublished), 1950.

Nisbet, J. F. *The Insanity of Genius*, 1891.

Patton, Julia. *The English Village*, 1919.

Read, Herbert. *The True Voice of Feeling*, 1953.

Redding, Cyrus. *Fifty Years' Recollections*, 1858. *Past Celebrities Whom I have Known*, 1866.

Richmond, Kenneth. *Poetry and the People*, 1938.

Robinson, Henry Crabb. *Books and Their Writers*, 1950.

St. Andrew's Hospital Case-books.

Stephen, Leslie. *English Literature and Society in the Eighteenth Century*, 1904.

Sternberg, Thomas. *Dialect and Folk-lore of Northamptonshire*, 1851.

Strickland, Agnes. *Life of, by her Sister*, 1887.

Symons, Arthur. *The Romantic Movement in English Poetry*, 1908.

Taylor, John. *Bibliotheca Northantonensis*, 1869.

Theocritus. *Idylls* (Tr. by R. C. Trevelyan), 1949.

Thomas, Edward. *A Literary Pilgrim in England*, 1917.

Unwin, Rayner. *The Rural Muse*, 1954.

Walton, Robert. *Random Recollections of the Midland Circuit*, 1869.

Walker, Hugh. *The Literature of the Victorian Era*, 1913.

Wilson, John. *Recreations of Christopher North*, 1864.

ARTICLES AND REVIEWS
(A Selection)

1820. *London Magazine* (January, March).
,,   *Quarterly Review* (May).
1821. *London Magazine* (November).
1823. *London Magazine* (January, February).
1840. *Athenaeum* (June).
,,   *Times* (June).
,,   *London Saturday Journal* (July).
1841. *English Journal* (ed. by Cyrus Redding) (May).
1847–49. *Bedford Times*
1861. *Once a Week* (May).
1864. *Gentleman's Magazine* (July).
1873. *Manchester Guardian* (July).
1886. *Northamptonshire Notes and Queries.*
1902. *Gentleman's Magazine* (April).
1914. *Yale Review* (October).
1915. *Fortnightly Review* (May).
1918. *Fortnightly Review* (October).
1919. *Cornhill Magazine* (September).
1920. *Nation* (February).
,,   *Athenaeum* (March, April, October, November).
,,   *Peterborough Citizen* (March, September).
,,   *London Mercury* (July).
,,   *Poetry Review* (September, October).
1921. *Athenaeum* (January).
,,   *Sunday Times* (January).
,,   *Times Literary Supplement* (January, June, July).
,,   *Cornhill Magazine* (September).
,,   *Discovery* (August).
1922. *Nation.*
,,   *Bookman* (October).
1923. *London Mercury.*
1924. *Spectator* (August).
,,   *Times Literary Supplement* (August).
1925. *Spectator* (September, October).
,,   *London Mercury* (June, July).
1932. *Observer* (June).

1932. *Sunday Times* (June).
  ,,   *Spectator* (June).
  ,,   *Times* (June).
  ,,   *New Statesman* (July).
  ,,   *Peterborough Advertiser* (July).
1935. *Times Literary Supplement* (February).
  ,,   *Morning Post* (February).
  ,,   *Time and Tide* (February).
  ,,   *Spectator* (March).
  ,,   *Sunday Times* (March).
  ,,   *Life and Letters* (March).
  ,,   *Fortnightly Review* (April).
1941. *Hibbert Journal* (April).
  ,,   *Times Literary Supplement* (December).
1951. *Illustrated London News* (June).
1953. *Journal of Medical Science* (January).

INDEX

Abercrombie, John, 23; —'s *Gardener's Journal*, 33
Abercrombie, Lascelles, 187
Abington Abbey, 197
Æsculapius, 161
Æsop, Fables of, 34
Ailsworth (Emmonsales) Heath, 12
Akenside, Mark, 141
Albert, Prince, 175
Alfred, 151
Allen, Dr. Matthew, 161–164, 167, 168–169, 175, 183
Allen, Rev. W., 101
Alloway, 3
Amery the actor, 67
Analectic Magazine, 62
Anne, Queen, 174 *n.*
Antijacobin Review, 62
Aristotle, 187
Armours (Burns and), 52
Arnold Matthew, 172, 186
Arnold, Mr., M.D., 18, 107
Artis, Edmund Tyrell, 61, 80, 118
Ascham, John, 199
Ashton, 16, 37
Astley's Theatre, 114
Athenaeum, 151, 154
Aurelianus, Caelius, 161

Babes in the Wood, 18
Bachelors' Hall, 3, 49, 89
Bains, Granny, 10 *n.*
Baker, Anne Elizabeth, 142, 197
Baker, George, 142
Ball's *Astrology*, 34
Barbauld, Anna, 100
Barnack, 2
Beattie, James, 69, 84
Beddoes, Thomas Lovel, 120
Bedlam (Bethlehem Hospital), 162
Behnes Burlowe, Henry, 139, 140, 145, 146, 148, 151
Bell (bookseller), 63
Bellamy, Councillor, 19
Bellars, Mrs., 19, 200
Belvoir Castle, 58
Bennion, Thomas, 96, 114

Bewick, Thomas, 31, 35
Bible, 35, 125–127; Genesis, Book of, 126; Job, Book of, 15, 160, 175
Billings brothers, 3, 34, 35, 36
Birch Reynardson, General, 57
Blair's *Sermons*, 58
Blake, William, 32, 40, 84, 100, 113, 172, 182, 185, 188, 190, 194
Bloomfield, Robert, 28, 34, 50, 63, 68, 102, 154, 174
Blue Bell Inn, 3, 20, 200
Blunden, Edmund, IX, 5 *n.*, 93, 152 *n.*
Bodleian Mss., 123 *n.*
Bonnycastle's *Arithmetic*, 18; —'s *Mensuration*, 33
Borough, see Crabbe, George
Borrow, George, 112
Bostwick, 23 *n.*
Boston, 141
Boswells (gipsies), 31
Bowles, Dr., 2
Bowles, William Lisle, 86, 101, 112
Bowring, John, 111, 115, 154
Bridge Casterton, 42, 44, 51, 138, 178
British Museum, Clare Correspondence, 48, 70, 72, 74, 76, 77, 99, 101
Broome's *Poems*, 34
Brown, 'Capability,' 4
Browne, William, of Tavistock, 128
Burghley House, 22, 91, 175; — Park, 24; — gardens, 25
Burkhardt, 66
Burns, Robert, 3, 10, 29, 33, 40, 46, 52, 62, 64, 69, 125, 130, 182
Burton, Robert, 128
Byron, Lord, 63, 68, 85, 89, 90, 112, 114, 117, 128, 145, 164, 165, 176, 185, 196, 199; —'s *Childe Harold*, 163, 166, 170–172; —'s *Don Juan*, 124, 169, 186

Camden, 1
Campbell, Thomas, 63, 141
Canterbury, Archbishop of, 157
Carew, Bampfylde Moore, *Life of*, 34